Mahatma Gandhi

A Great Leader

Mahatma Gandhi
A Great Leader

Neeraj Gautam

Mahaveer & Sons
(Publishers & Distributors)
New Delhi–110002

Edition 2016

ISBN-978-81-8377-246-4

Published by
MAHAVEER & SONS
H-2/16, Ansari Road, Darya Ganj,
(Near Shiv Mandir) New Delhi-110002

Rs. 995/-

PRINTED IN INDIA

Published by Mahaveer & Sons, Publishers&Distributors, H-2/16 Ansari Road, Near Shiv Mandir, Daryaganj, New Delhi-110002, Printed at Himanshu Printers, Delhi.

Preface

Mohandas Gandhi was born on October 2, 1869, at Porbandar, on the western coast of India. His grandfather Uttamchand Gandhi and father Karamchand Gandhi occupied the high office of the diwan (Chief Minister) of Porbandar. To be Diwan of one of the princely states was on sinecure. Porbandar was one of some three hundred 'native' states in western India which were ruled by princes whom the accident of birth and the support of the British kept on the throne. To steer one's course safely between wayward Indian princes, the overbearing British 'Political Agent' of the suzerain power and the long-suffering subjects required a high degree of patience, diplomatic skill and commonsense. Both Uttamchand and Karamchand were good administrators. But they were also upright and honourable men. Loyal to their masters, they did not flinch from offering unpalatable advice. They paid the price for the courage of their convictions. Uttamchand Gandhi had his hose besieged and shelled by the ruler's troops and had to flee the State; his son Karamchand also preferred to leave Porbandar, rather than compromise with his principles.

In a time ravaged by large-scale violence and unending terror, nothing seems more promising and urgent than to be reminded of another possibility: the path of non-violent struggle for justice exemplified by Mahatma Gandhi. Gandhi continues to be the subject of enduring relevance and interest. 'Gandhigiri' is gradually entering into popular imagination and academic discourses. His writings, running into more than one hundred volumes, contain a wide range of views on different issues.

However, he was not destined to pick up the threads of his constructive Programme. He had a narrow escape on January 20, 1948, when a bomb exploded in Birla House in New Delhi where he was addressing his prayer meeting. He took no notice of the explosion. Next day he referred to the congratulations which he had received for remaining unruffled after the explosion. He would deserve them, he said, if he fell as a result of such an explosion and yet retained a smile on his face and no malice against the assailant. He described the bomb-thrower as a misguided youth and advised the police not to "molest" him but to convert him with persuasion and affection. "The misguided youth" was Madan Lal, a refugee from West Punjab, who was a member of a gang which had plotted Gandhi's death. These highly-strung Youngman saw Hinduism menaced by Islam from without and by Gandhi from within. Madan Lal having missed his aim, a fellow conspirator from Poona, Nathu Ram Godse, came to Gandhi's prayer meeting on the evening of January 30, whipped out his pistol and fired three shots. Gandhi fell instantly with the words 'He Rama' (Oh! God).

This book seeks to provide a new insight to the readers for understanding Gandhi and its relevance in the contemporary world. Special care has been taken to cater to the need of the newly introduced paper Mahatma Gandhi a Great Leader.

—Editor

Contents

Contents

1

Autobiography of Mahatma Gandhi

Gandhi's autobiography, which he had titled 'My experiments with Truth' can be rated as one of the most popular and the most influential books in the recent history. It was written at the instance of Swami Anand. It appeared in the Weekly 'Navjivan' during 1925-28. It covers Gandhi's life up to 1920. He did not cover the period after that as it was well known to the people and most of the concerned persons were alive. Besides he felt that his experiments in that period were yet to yield definite conclusions.

Gandhi's autobiography is very different from other autobiographies. The autobiographies normally contain self-praise by the authors. They want to criticize their opponents and boost their own image in the people's eyes. Gandhi's autobiography is completely free from all this. It is marked with humility and truthfulness. He had not hidden anything. In fact, he is rather too harsh on himself. He did not want to show to the world how good he was. He only wanted to tell the people the story of his experiments with Truth. Truth, for Gandhi, was the supreme principle, which includes many other principles. Realization of the Truth is the purpose of human life. Gandhi always strove to realize the Truth. He continuously tried to remove impurities in himself. He always tried to stick to the Truth as he knew and to apply the knowledge of the Truth to everyday life. He tried to apply the spiritual principles to the practical situations. He did it in the scientific spirit.

Sticking to the truth means Satyagraha. Gandhi therefore called his experiments as 'Experiments with Truth' or 'Experiments in the science of Satyagraha.' Gandhi also requested the readers to treat those experiments as illustrative and to carry out their own experiments in that light.

Gandhi: An Introduction

Mohandas Karamchand Gandhi was a man considered one of the great sages and prophets. He was held as another Buddha, another Jesus, Indians called him the 'Father of the Nation'. They showered their love, respect and devotion on him in an unprecedented measure. They thronged his way to have a glimpse of him, to hear one world from his lips. They applied on their foreheads the dust on the path he had trodden. For them, he was almost an incarnation of God, who had come to break the chains of their slavery. The whole world bowed to him in reverence. Even his opponents held him in great respect.

Mohandas Gandhi was, however, not a great scholar, nor was he a great warrior. He was not born with exceptional faculties. Neither was he a good orator, nor a great writer. He did not claim anything exclusively divine in him. He did not claim being a prophet or having superhuman powers. He considered himself an average man with average abilities. Born in a middle class Bania family in an obscure princely State in a corner of India, he was a mediocre student, shy and nervous. He could not muster courage to speak in public. His first attempt at legal practice miserably failed.

But he was a humble seeker of Truth. He was a man with exceptional sincerity, honesty and truthfulness. For him, understanding meant action. Once any principle appealed to him, he immediately began to translate that in practice. He did not flinch from taking risks and did not mind confessing mistakes. No opposition, scorn or ridicule could affect him. Truth was his sole guiding star. He was ever-growing; hence he was often found inconsistent. He was not concerned with appearing to be consistent. He preferred to be consistent only with the light within. He sacrificed his all and identified himself with the poorest of the poor. He dressed like them, lived like them. In the oppressed and the depressed people, he saw God.

For him, they too were sparks of the divine light. They might not have anything else, but they too had a soul. For Gandhi, soul-force was the source of the greatest power. He strove to awaken the soul-force within himself and within his fellowmen. He was convinced that the potentialities of the soul-force have no limit. He himself was a living example of this conviction. That is why this tiny and fragile man could mobilise the masses and defeat the mighty British empire. His eleven vows, his technique of Satyagraha, his constructive programme-all were meant to awaken and strengthen the soul-force. He awakened and aroused a nation from semi-consciousness. It was a Herculean task. For, India was not a united country, it was a sub-continent. It was a society divided in different classes, castes and races, in people with different languages, religions and cultures.

It was a society where almost half of the population *i.e.*, women, was behind purdah or confined to the four walls of houses, where one-fourth of the population-the depressed classes-was living marginalised life, where many did not have a single full meal every day. Gandhi made the oppressed sections wake up and break their chains. He mobilised the people and united them to work for the cause of Swaraj, which gave them a sense of belonging, a sense of purpose. Gandhi wanted to win Swaraj for the masses. For him, Swaraj did not mean replacement of White masters by brown masters. Swaraj meant self-rule by all. He said: "Real Swaraj will come, not by the acquisition of the authority by a few, but by the acquisition of the capacity by all to resist authority when it is abused." He worked to develop such a capacity. Development of such a capacity involved transformation of the individual.

Transformation of the individual and transformation of the society-they were not separate, unrelated things for Gandhi. Revolutionary social philosophies had concentrated on changing the society. On the other hand, spiritual seekers had concentrated on the inner change. Gandhi not only bridged the gap between these extremes, he fused them together. Gandhi was thus both a saint and a social revolutionary. For Gandhi, unity of life was great truth. His principle of nonviolence stemmed from this conviction. Nonviolence was not a matter of policy for him; it was a matter of faith. He applied the doctrine to all the departments of individual and social life and in so doing revolutionized the doctrine, made it dynamic and creative. He believed that a true civilization could be built on the basis of such nonviolence only.

He rejected the modern civilization. For him, it was a disease and a curse. This civilization leads to violence, conflicts, corruption, injustices, exploitation, oppression, mistrust and a process of dehumanisation. It has led the world to a deep crisis. The earth's resources are being cornered by a handful of people without any concern for others and for the coming generations. The conventional energy sources are getting depleted. Forests are being destroyed. Air, water, soil-everything has been polluted.

We are living under the shadow of nuclear war and environmental disasters. Thinking men the world over are looking to Gandhi to find a way out of this crisis and to build an alternative model of sustainable development. Gandhi knew that the earth has enough to satisfy everybody's need but not anybody's greed. He had called for the replacement of greed with love.

Gandhi is, therefore, now a source of inspiration and a reference book for all those fighting against racial discrimination, oppression, domination, wars, nuclear energy, environmental degradation, lack of freedom and human rights-for all those who are fighting for a better world, a better quality of life. Gandhi is, therefore, no longer an individual. He is a symbol of all that is the best and the most enduring in the human tradition. And he is also a symbol of the alternative in all areas of life-agriculture, industry, technology, education, health, economy, political organisations, etc. He is a man of the future-a future that has to be shaped if the human race has to survive and progress on the path of evolution.

Biography of Mahatma Gandhi

We hereby give a short version compiled from his Autobiography. We cover the period of his life from 1869 to 1922.

Birth and Parentage

Mohandas Karamchand Gandhi was born at Porbandar, a coastal city in Kathiawad (now a part of the Gujarat State) on the 2nd October 1869. He was the youngest child of his parents, Karamchand and Putlibai.

Gandhis belonged to the Modh Bania community. They were originally grocers. However, Uttamchand, Mohan's grandfather, rose to become Dewan of the Porbandar State. Mohan's father. Karamchand, also served as the Dewan of Porbandar, Rajkot and Vankaner States. Kathiawar then had about 300 small States. Court intrigues were the order of the day. At times, Gandhis became their victim. Uttamchand's house was once surrounded and shelled by the State troops. Karamchand was once arrested. However, their courage and wisdom earned them respect. Karamchand even became a member of the Rajashanik Court, a powerful agency to solve disputes among the States.

Karamchand had little education, but had shrewdness of judgment and practical knowledge acquired through experience. He had little inclination to amass wealth and left little for his children. He used to say that "My children are my wealth'. He married four times, had two daughters by the first two marriages and one daughter and three sons by his fourth marriage. Putlibai, his fourth wife, was younger to him by 25 years. She was not much educated but was well-informed about practical matters. Ladies at the palace used to value her advice. She was deeply religious and superstitious and had strong will-power. She used to visit the temple daily and regularly kept difficult vows. Mohan loved his mother. He used to accompany her to the Haveli (Vaishnav temple). Mohan had a great devotion for his father and he often used to be present at the discussions about the State problems. Gandhis had Parsi and Muslim friends and Jain monks used to make regular visit. Mohan thus had occasion to hear discussions about religious matters also. Being the youngest, he was the darling of the household.

Childhood

Mohan attended Primary School at Porbandar. When he

was seven, his family moved to Rajkot. He was a mediocre student, was shy and avoided any company. He read little besides the text books and had no love for outdoor games. He had no love for outdoor games. However, he was truthful, honest, sensitive and was alert about his character. Plays about Shravan and Harishchandra made a deep impression on him. They taught him to be truthful at any cost and to serve his parents with devotion.

He was married along with his brother and cousin for the sake of economy and convenience. He was only 13 then. He enjoyed the festivities of the marriage. Kasturbai, his wife, was of the same age. She was illiterate but strong-willed. His jealousy and immature efforts to make her an ideal wife led to many quarrels. He wanted to teach her but found no time. His experience later made him a strong critic of child-marriages.

Mohan joined High School at Rajkot. He was liked by the teachers and often received prizes. But he neglected physical training and hand-writing. Habit of taking long walks made up for the first neglect, but he had to repent later for the neglect of handwriting. He was devoted to his father and considered it his duty to nurse him during his illness. In the High-School, he made friends with one Sheikh Mehtab, a bad character. He stuck to the friendship despite warnings from family-members. He wanted to reform Mehtab but failed. Mehtab induced him to meat-eating, saying that it made one strong and that the British were ruling India because they were meat-eaters. Mohan was frail and used to be afraid even to go out alone in the dark. The argument appealed to him. Later, he realized that lying to his parents was worse than not eating meat, and abandoned the experiment.

Mehtab once sent him to a brothel, but God's grace saved him. He induced Mohan to smoking. This once led to stealing. But all this became unbearable for Mohan. He confessed his guilt to his father, who did not rebuke him but wept silently. Those tears cleaned Mohan's heart and taught him a lesson in nonviolence.

Mohan's father died when Mohan was 16. He had nursed him daily. But at the time of his death, Mohan was with his wife. He always felt ashamed for this lapse. Mohan passed the matriculation examination in 1887. He attended the College at Bhavnagar, but left after the first term. At that time, the idea of his going to England for studying law came up. Mohan was fascinated. He made up his mind and overcame resistance from the family-members. He took the vow not to touch wine, women and meat at the instance of his mother to remove her fears. He then sailed from Bombay in September 1888, leaving behind his wife and a son. The caste elders were against his going to England. They excommunicated him from the caste.

Gandhi in England

Gandhi reached England by the end of September 1888. Everything was strange to him. He was shy and diffident, could not speak English fluently and was ignorant of British manners. Naturally, loneliness and homesickness gripped him. Gandhi became a vegetarian for life. It was difficult to get vegetarian food. Friends persuaded him to break the vow of vegetarianism but he stuck to it. He began searching vegetarian restaurants and found one ultimately. He purchased Salt's book 'Plea for Vegetarianism', read it and became vegetarian out of conviction. He studied other literature and joined the Vegetarian Society.

He came in contact with the leaders of that radical cult, became a member of the Society's Executive Committee and contributed articles to the Society's paper. He even started a Vegetarian club in his locality and became its Secretary. This experience gave him some training in organising and conducting Institutions. Experiments about diet became a life-long passion for him.

Gandhi Tries to Play the 'English Gentleman'

For a brief period, Gandhi tried to become 'The English Gentleman' to overcome lack of confidence and to make up for the 'fad' of vegetarianism. He wanted to become fit for the British elite society. He got clothes stitched from an expensive and fashionable firm, purchased an expensive hat and an evening suit and learnt to wear the tie. He became very careful about his appearance. He even joined a dancing class, but could not go on for more than three weeks. He purchased a violin and started learning to play it. He engaged a tutor to give lessons in elocution. But all this was for a brief period of three months only. His conscience awakened him. He realised that he was not going to spend his whole life in England; he should rather concentrate on his studies and not waste his brother's money. He then became very careful about his expenses.

Study of Religions

Gandhi also started the study of religions. Before that, he had not even read the Gita. Now he read it in the English translation. He also read Edwin Arnold's 'The Light of Asia,' Blavatsky's 'Key to Theosophy' and the Bible. Gita and The New Testament made a deep impression on him. The principles of renunciation and nonviolence appealed to him greatly. He continued the study of religions throughout his life.

Gandhi becomes a Barrister

Bar examinations were easy. He therefore studied for and passed the London matriculation examination. Becoming a Barrister meant attending at least six dinners in each of the twelve terms and giving an easy examination. Gandhi, however, studied sincerely, read all the prescribed books, passed his examination and was called to the bar in June 1891. He then sailed for home.

A Period of Turmoil

Gandhi's three year's stay in England was a period of deep turmoil for him. Before that, he knew little of the world. Now he was exposed to the fast-changing world and to several radical movements like Socialism, Anarchism, Atheism etc. through the Vegetarian Society. He started taking part in public work. Many of his ideas germinated during this period.

Gandhi in South Africa

Gandhi returned to India as a Barrister, but he knew nothing about the Indian law. Lawyers used to pay commissions to touts to get cases. Gandhi did not like this. Besides, he was shy and an occasion to argue in the Court unnerved him. He became a disappointed and dejected 'Bridles Barrister'. At that time, a South African firm Dada Abdulla and Co. asked for his assistance in a case. Gandhi eagerly agreed and sailed for South Africa in April 1893.

Problems of Indians in South Africa

The small Indian community in South Africa was facing many problems at that time. It consisted mainly of indentured labourers and traders. The indentured labourers were taken there by the European landlords as there was acute labour shortage in South Africa. The condition of these labourers was like slaves. During 1860-1890 around 40,000 labourers were sent from India. Many of them settled there after their agreement periods were completed and started farming or business.

The Europeans did not like it. They did not want free Indians in South Africa. They also found it difficult to face competition from Indian traders. Therefore the White Rulers imposed many restrictions and heavy taxes on the Indians. They were not given citizenship rights, like right to vote. They were treated like dirt and constantly humiliated. All Indians were called 'coolies'. The newspapers carried out the propaganda that the Indians were dirty and uncivilized. The Indians could not travel in the railways and could not enter hotels meant for Europeans. They were hated and radically discriminated in all matters by the dominant White community.

Gandhi Fights Racial Discrimination

Right since his arrival, Gandhi began to feel the pinch of racial discrimination in South Africa. Indian community was ignorant and divided and therefore unable to fight it. In connection with his case, Gandhi had to travel to Pretoria. He was travelling in the first class, but a White passenger and railway officials asked him to leave the first class compartment. Gandhi refused, whereupon he was thrown out along with his luggage. On the platform of Maritzburg station. It was a severely cold night. Gandhi spent the night shivering and thinking furiously. He ultimately made up his mind to stay in South Africa, fight the racial discrimination and suffer hardships. It was a historic decision. It transformed Gandhi. He had also to travel some distance by a stage-coach. During this travel also, he was insulted and beaten. On reaching Pretoria, Gandhi called a meeting of the local Indians. There he learnt a lot about the condition of Indians. It was there that he made his first Public Speech and suggested formation of an association. He offered his services for the cause. Gandhi later settled the case, for which he had come, through arbitration. He then decided to return home. But at the farewell party, he came to know about a bill to restrict Indian franchise. Gandhi thought that it had grave implications. The people then pressed him to stay for some time. He agreed.

Gandhi's first major fight had started. He addressed meetings petitioned to the legislative assembly, conducted a signature campaign. He also started regular legal practice there and soon became a successful and leading Lawyer. For sustained agitations, a permanent organisation was needed and the Natal Indian Congress was born. Illiterate indentured labourers also joined the struggle. A proposed tax on them was fought and got abolished after a fierce battle.

In 1886, Gandhi visited India for a brief period. In India, he met renowned leaders and gave wide publicity to the South African struggle. Rumours reached South Africa that Gandhi had maligned the Whites there and that he was coming with a large number of Indians to swamp the Natal colony. It was wrong. But it made the Whites furious. Gandhi had to face the fury, when he returned with his wife and children, he had to enter the port town secretly, but he was found out and assaulted. The Whites wanted to hang him but he was saved by the Police Superintendent and his wife. He forgave his assailants.

The Boer War

Gandhi, however, remained a loyal citizen of the British Empire. In that spirit, he decided to help the British during the Boer War. The Boer were the Dutch colonizers who ruled some of the South African colonies. They were simple and sturdy people with strong racial prejudices. The British wanted to rule whole of the South Africa. The British-Boer broke out in 1899. Gandhi's sympathies were with the Boers. But being a British citizen, he considered it his duty to help the British. He also wanted to show that Indians were not cowards and were ready to make sacrifices for the empire while fighting for their rights. Gandhi raised an ambulance corps of 1100 persons. The work consisted of carrying the wounded on stretchers. At times, it required walking more than 20 miles. The corps had sometimes to cross the firing line. The Indians worked hard, their work was praised and the leaders of the corps were awarded medals. Indian community learnt a lot from this experience. Its stature increased. British won the war, although the Boers fought with determination, which made a deep impression on Gandhi.

The Fight Continues

In 1901, Gandhi returned to India. He travelled widely and worked closely with Gopal Krishna Gokhale, whom he considered his guru. He was about to settle down in Bombay, when he received an urgent telegram from South Africa to rush there. Gandhi again went to South Africa. He found that the condition of Indians had worsened. Gandhi had to devote himself to public work. In 1904, Gandhi started the journal 'Indian Opinion.'

The Phoenix Settlement

In 1904, Gandhi happened to read Ruskin's book 'Unto This Last.' He was deeply impressed by Ruskin's ideas and decided to put them in practice immediately. They were: (i) That the good of the individual is contained in the good of all. (ii) that all work has the same value and (iii) that the life of labour is the life worth-living.

Gandhi purchased some land near Phoenix station and established the Phoenix settlement in mid-1904. The settlers had to erect structures to accommodate themselves and the printing press. 'Indian Opinion' was transferred to Phoenix. The settlers had to go through many trials to print the issue in time. Everyone had to join in the work. The settlers were divided in two classes. The 'Schemers' made their living by manual labour. A few were paid labourers. To make a living by manual labour, land was divided in pieces of three acres each. Stress was on manual labour. Even the printing press was often worked with hand-power. Sanitary arrangements were primitive and everyone had to be his own scavenger. The colony was to be self-supporting and the material needs were to be kept to the minimum. A spirit of self-reliance pervaded the colony. Gandhi, however, could stay there only for brief periods. He had to be in Johannesburg in connection with his work.

The Zulu Rebellion

The Zulu 'rebellion' broke out in April 1906. It was not in fact a rebellion, but a man-hunt. The British wanted to crush the freedom-loving Zulu tribals. The operation to massacre them was, therefore, started under a flimsy pretext. Out of a sense of loyalty to the British empire, Gandhi offered the services of the Indian community, though his heart was with the Zulus. An ambulance corps of 24 persons was formed. Its duty was to carry the wounded Zulus and nurse them. The Zulus were flogged and tortured and left with festering wounds. Whites were not ready to nurse them. Gandhi was happy to nurse them. He had to work hard and walk miles through hills. It was a thought-provoking experience. He saw the cruelty of the British and the horrors of the war. While marching through Zululand, Gandhi thought deeply. Two ideas became fixed in his mind-Brahmacharya and the adoption of voluntary poverty.

Birth of Satyagraha

The White rulers were bent on keeping South Africa under their domination. They wanted as few Indians there as possible and that too as slave-labourers. In Transvaal, Indians were required to register themselves. The procedure was humiliating. The registration was proposed to be made stricter in 1906. Gandhi realised that it was a matter of life or death for the Indians. A mammoth meeting was held in September 1906 to oppose the bill. People took oath in the name of God not to submit to the bill at any cost. A new principle had come into being-the principle of Satyagraha. The bill about registration was however passed. Picketing against registration was organised. A wave of courage and enthusiasm swept the Indian community. The Indian community rose as one man for the sake of its survival and dignity.

The agitation was first called 'passive Resistance'. Gandhi, however, did not like that term. It did not convey the true nature of the struggle. It implied that it was the weapon of the weak and the disarmed. It did not denote complete faith in nonviolence. Moreover, Gandhi did not like that the Indian struggle should be known by an English name. The term 'Sadagrah' was suggested. Gandhi changed it to 'Satyagrah' to make it represent fully, the whole idea. Satyagraha means asserting truth through nonviolence. It aims at converting the opponents through self-suffering.

Gandhi was ordered to leave the colony. He disobeyed and was jailed for two months. Indians filled the jails. Repression failed to yield the results. General Smuts called Gandhi and promised that the law would be withdrawn if the Indians agreed to voluntary registration.

An Attempt of Gandhi's Life

Gandhi agreed. He and his co-workers were set free. Gandhi exhorted Indians to register voluntarily. He was criticized for this by some workers. A Pathan named Mir Alam was unconvinced by Gandhi's arguments and vowed to kill the first man who would register himself. Gandhi came forward to be the first man to register himself. When he was going to the registration office, Mir Alam and his friends assaulted him with lathis. Gandhi fainted with the words 'He Ram' on his lips. It was 10th February 1908. His colleagues tried to save him otherwise it would have been the last day for him. Mir Alam and his friends were caught and handed over to the police. When Gandhi regained consciousness, he inquired about Mir Alam. When told that he had been arrested, Gandhi told that he should be released. Gandhi was taken by his friend Rev. Doke to his house and was nursed there. Rev. Doke later became his first biographer.

Gandhi Betrayed

Smuts however, betrayed Gandhi. The agitation was again resumed. The voluntary registration certificates were publicly burnt. Meanwhile, Transvaal passed Immigration Restriction Act. This too was opposed by the Indians. They crossed

Transvaal border illegally and were jailed. Gandhi, too, was arrested and convicted. The fight continued in spite of the repression.

Tolstoy Farm

Gandhi realised that the fight would be a long one. He, therefore, desired to have a center where the Satyagrahis could lead a simple community life and get training for the struggle. Phoenix was at about 30 hours distance from Johannesburg. Gandhi's German friend Kallenbach therefore bought 1100 acres of land at a distance of about 20 miles from Johannesburg, where Tolstoy Farm was established. The community was named after Tolstoy to pay respect to the great Russian writer whose book 'The Kingdom of God is within You' had greatly influenced Gandhi and made him a firm believer in nonviolence.

The inmates numbered about 50-75. It was a heterogeneous group. It was a tribute to Gandhi's leadership that they remained together happily under hard conditions. The inmates erected sheds to accommodate themselves. They did all their work themselves. Drinking, smoking and meat-eating were prohibited. All ate in the community kitchen. Small Cottage Industries were started for self-sufficiency. Gandhi and his colleagues learnt shoe-making. A school was started. Gandhi himself undertook the responsibility of educating the children. The life was simple, hard, but joyful. Experiments at Tolstoy Farm proved to be a source of purification and penance for Gandhi and his co-workers.

The last Phase of Satyagraha

Satyagraha continued for four years. Gandhi discontinued his legal practice in 1910. After many ups and downs, the last phase of Satyagraha began in September 1913. A Black Law imposing three pounds tax on Indians provided occasion for it. Satyagrahis crossed Transvaal border defying the law. Even the women were invited to join. Indian workers in the Natal coal-mines struck work and joined the struggle. Gandhi led a large contingent of these workers. They were about 2200 in number. It was on epic march. It aroused sympathy for Satyagraha and indignation for the South African Government throughout England and India. Indian National Congress supported the Satyagraha. Gandhi was arrested. The Satyagrahis marched to Natal without their leader. There, they were arrested and jailed. Thousands of labourers struck work in sympathy. The public outcry in India forced the Indian Government to express sympathy for the Indian cause. The repression having failed, General Smuts had to bow ultimately. Indian demands were accepted. The fight was over. Gandhi now could return to India where a great work awaited him.

It was South Africa which made Gandhi. He had gone there as a young, shy, Briefless Barrister. He returned as an extraordinary leader who had mobilised masses to an unprecedented extent for a novel fight. In South Africa, Gandhi's ideas were shaped. He was influenced by Ruskin, Tolstoy and Thoreau. He made a deep study of religions there and became a staunch believer in nonviolence. The principle of Satyagraha was born in S. Africa.

Gandhi in India: Rise of Leadership

Gandhi returned to India in January 1915. He was welcomed and honoured as a hero. He spent a year touring the country at the instance of Gokhale, his guru. He travelled mostly in third class railway compartments. He saw the conditions in the country first-hand. He founded the Satyagraha Ashram in May 1915 and started getting involved in the social and political life of the country. The Champaran Satyagraha was his first major struggle.

Champaran Satyagraha

Champaran was a district in Northern Bihar. When Gandhi was called there, it was virtually under the rule of European indigo planters. They cruelly exploited and terrorised the tenants. Under the 'tinkathia' system, the tenants had to cultivate indigo in 3/20th part of the land. The tenants were oppressed and fear-stricken. The British administration supported the planters.

Gandhi was invited to visit Champaran by Rajkumar Shukla, a peasant from the area, in December 1916. Gandhi was first reluctant. But Shukla's persistent requests made him change his mind. He went to Champaran in April 1917 to know the conditions there and the grievances of the peasants. Before visiting the district, Gandhi visited Muzaffarpur and Patna. He discussed the matter with lawyers and social workers. Gandhi declined to seek legal remedies as he felt that law courts were useless when the people were fear-stricken. For him, removal of fear was most important. He made request to the lawyers for clerical assistance. Many of them gladly offered the same. Gandhi first met the planters and the District Commissioner. They were hostile. Gandhi was ordered to leave the area. He ignored the order. He was then summoned to the court. The news electrified the area. Crowds gathered at the court. Gandhi pleaded guilty, saying that he was obeying a higher law, the voice of conscience. The case against him was later dropped. Gandhi and his co-workers met thousands of the peasants. They recorded about 8000 statements. Efforts were made to ensure that they were true. Recording was done in the presence of police officials. Undue publicity and exaggeration were avoided. Planters' campaign of slander was ignored. The masses in Champaran overcame their fear. Public opinion in the country was aroused. The Government ultimately appointed an enquiry committee in June 1917, with Gandhi as a member. The committee recommended abolition of tinkathia system and partial refund of money taken illegal by the planters. The Satyagraha was thus successful. Champaran Satyagraha was the first Satyagraha on the Indian soil. It was Gandhi's first major political work in India. It was carried out strictly in accordance with the principles of Satyagraha. Attention was paid to constructive work like sanitation, education and primary health-care.

Ahmedabad Satyagraha

A dispute between the textile mill-owners and the labourers at Ahmedabad arose in 1918, about the grant of bonus and dearness allowance. The labourers wanted 50% increase allowance due to steep rise in prices. The mill-owners were ready to give only 20% increase. Gandhi was approached to find a solution. He persuaded both the parties to agree to arbitration. But after a few days, some misunderstanding led to a strike.

The mill-owners seized the opportunity and declared lock-out. Gandhi studied the case. He thought that 35% increase would be reasonable. He advised the labourers to demand the same. Regular strike began on the 26th February 1918. Thousands of labourers struck work. They took a pledge not to resume work till their demand was met or arbitration was agreed upon. They also decided to observe nonviolence and maintain peace. Gandhi had friends in both the camps. The mill-owners being led by Shri Ambalal Sarabhai. His sister Ansuyaben was leading the labourers. During the struggle, Gandhi's co-workers regularly visited the labourers' quarters to solve their problems and to keep high their morale. Daily meetings and prayers were held. Bulletins were issued. Gandhi did not like charity. Efforts were made to find alternative employments for the workers. However, after a fortnight, the workers started getting tired. It was difficult to face starvation. It was unbearable for Gandhi that they should break the vow. He then decided to undertake an indefinite fast. This strengthened the workers. It brought moral pressure on the mill-owners. They consented to arbitration after three days. Gandhi broke his fast. The Satyagraha was successful. The arbitrator studied the case for three months and recommended 35% increase in dearness allowance. The workers' demand was thus fully met. However, Gandhi's fast did involve in an element of coercion. But it was a spontaneous decision. The situation demanded some drastic action. The Satyagraha was significant in many respects. It was the first Satyagraha by industrial workers. It was wholly peaceful. It showed how workers could fight nonviolently. It also gave rise to a strong Gandhian Labour Union.

Kheda Satyagraha

Kheda was a district in Gujarat. In 1917, there was a crop failure due to famine. Peasants were unable to pay the land revenue. The rules permitted suspension of revenue collection when the crops were less than four annas. According to the peasants' estimate, the crops were less than four annas. Gandhi's inquiries, as well as inquiries by independent observers, showed that the peasants were right. The Government, however, thought otherwise. It even turned down a suggestion of an impartial enquiry. It started coercing the peasants to collect revenue. Petitions etc. were of no avail. Satyagraha was therefore started on the 22nd March 1918.

Gandhi advised the peasants to withhold payment to revenue. Satyagrahis took a pledge not to pay the same and resolved to be ready to face the consequences. Volunteers went to villages to keep up the morale of the peasants. As in Champaran, Gandhi's main concern was to remove the fear from the peasants' minds. The officials started attaching the property of the peasants including cattle and even standing crops. Notices were sent for attachment of the land. An occasion for civil disobedience arose when standing onion crop was attached at one place. Gandhi advised one Mohanlal Pandya and a few volunteers to remove the crop. This was done. The volunteers were arrested. Pandya earned the nickname 'Onion Thief.'

The struggle went on for about four months till July 1918. It tested the people's patience. The Government discontinued coercive measures. It advised that if the well-to-do peasants paid up, the poor ones would be granted suspension. In one sense, the Satyagraha was thus successful. The peasants' demand was not, however, fully met. Gandhi was not satisfied. He wanted people to come out stronger after Satyagraha. However, the Satyagraha resulted in awakening the peasants. It educated them politically. It was the first peasant struggle under Gandhi's leadership, the first nonviolent mass civil disobedience campaign organised by Gandhi in India. The peasants became aware of their rights and learnt to suffer for them.

Rowlatt Act

British Government appointed a Committee in 1917 under the chairmanship of Justice Rowlatt, (1) to enquire and report to the Government about the nature and extent of anti-government activities, and (2) to suggest legal remedies to enable the Government to suppress those activities. The Committee submitted its report in April 1918. Its work was carried out in secrecy. The Committee's recommendations were embodied in two bills.

The first bill sought to make a permanent change in the Criminal Law. The second bill intended to deal with the situation arising out of the expiry of Defence of India Rules. The first bill made punishable the possession of an antigovernment document with mere intention to circulate it. The second bill also gave sweeping powers to the officers. There were other harsh provisions also. The bills shocked the entire country. All the leaders considered the bills unjust, unwarranted and destructive of elementary human rights and dignity. The second bill was eventually dropped and the first one passed as a Law in March 1919.

Satyagraha against the Rowlatt Act

India had helped the British in the World War. She expected substantial political rights. Instead, she received the Black Rowlatt bills.

Gandhi had decided to help the British war efforts during the war. He undertook a recruiting campaign and worked hard which ruined his health. While he was recovering, he heard about Rowlatt bills. He was shocked. He took up the matter and started propaganda against the bill. Gandhi carried out propaganda against the bill. A separate body called Satyagraha Sabha was formed. A Satyagraha pledge was drafted and signed by selected leaders. The Government was, however, adamant. It then suddenly it occurred to Gandhi that a call for nationwide hartal should be given. Everybody in the country should suspend his business and spend the day in fasting and prayers. Public meetings should be held everywhere and resolutions passed for withdrawal of the Act.

The programme was taken up. 30 March was fixed as the day of the hartal, but it was later postponed to 6th April. The notice was very short. Still the masses rose to the occasion. The country rose like one man. Hartal was observed throughout India. Communal prejudices were forgotten. All fear disappeared. In Delhi, Swami Shraddhanand, the Hindu sanyasi was invited to Jama Masjid. It was also decided that civil disobedience should be offered to selected laws which could easily be disobeyed by the people. Gandhi suggested breaking of the Salt law and the sale of the banned literature. The civil disobedience was a great success. Throughout India, meetings were held and processions taken out.

The public awakening was unprecedented. It startled the British. Repression was let loose. Processions were broken up by mounted police and firing was done at several places. Many persons were killed. At some places, people lost balance in the face of repression. In such a situation, Gandhi thought it fit to suspend the Civil Disobedience Campaign. It was done on the 18th April. Satyagraha against the Rowlatt Act was historic. It was the first nationwide struggle, in which crores of people participated and showed exemplary courage. The Indian freedom movement was transformed into a truly people's movement. The period also witnessed Hindu-Muslim friendship to an extent that was never surpassed thereafter.

Jallianwala Bagh

Satyagraha in Punjab was also quite successful. Its leaders Dr. Satyapal and Dr. Kitchlew were arrested. People observed hartal and took out a procession in Amritsar to demand their release. It was fired upon, and many persons were killed. The crowd therefore became violent and killed 5-6 Englishmen. Some public buildings were burnt. Army troops were rushed in to stop the violence. This was on April 10th 1919. On April 11, a peaceful funeral procession was taken out.

General Dyer then took command of the troops. Meetings and gatherings were prohibited. Still a large meeting was held on April 12th at Jallianwala Bagh. General Dyer took no steps to prevent the meeting. But when the meeting was taking place, he surrounded the place and without any warning, gave orders of firing. The crowd of nearly 10,000 men and women was peaceful and unarmed. They had no idea that they would be fired upon. When the firing started the people became panicky. There was only one exit. Bullets were showered on the trapped people. 1650 rounds were fired. About 400 persons were killed and 1200 injured. General Dyer did this deliberately to teach the Indians a lesson. Jallianwala Bagh massacre shocked the country. It showed how brutal the British power could get. It was followed by many more atrocities. They turned Gandhi fully against the British Empire.

Amritsar Congress

The annual session of the Indian National Congress was held at Amritsar in Punjab in December 1919. Most of the leaders in jails were released before or during the session. The session was attended by 8000 delegates including 1500 peasants. It was the last Congress session attended by Lokmanya Tilak. The Moderates, however, did not attend it. Pandit Motilal Nehru was in the Chair. The Congress was now acquiring a mass character. The proceedings were conducted mainly in Hindustani.

The Congress passed a resolution for removal of General Dyer, the butcher of Jallianwala Bagh. Recall of the Punjab Governor and the Viceroy was also demanded. It was decided to erect a memorial for the Jallianwala Bagh martyrs. Gandhi moved a resolution condemning violence on the part of the people and got it passed. It was a very significant event. The resolution also urged the people to remain peaceful. The Congress also reiterated the demand for responsible Government. The Montague Reforms were considered inadequate, disappointing and unsatisfactory. But it was decided to work the reforms. Revival of hand-spinning and hand-weaving was recommended. The Congress appointed a subcommittee for reconsideration of the Congress Constitution with Gandhi as the Chairman. It was the first Congress session in which Gandhi took an active part. His leadership was strengthened in Amritsar Congress.

The Khilafat Question

During the First World Way, Turkey sided with Germany against the British. The Sultan of Turkey was the Khalifa, the religious head of the Muslim world. The future of Khalifa, therefore, became a matter of concern for Indian Muslims. The British Government promised them that the Khilafat would not be violated and favourable peace terms would be offered to Turkey. But when Turkey was defeated in the war, the promises were forgotten. Turkish Empire was broken. Indian Muslims felt agitated over this. Gandhi sympathised with the Khilafat cause. He felt that Hindus should help the Muslim in their need. For him, it was an excellent opportunity to forge communal unity, bring Muslims in the freedom movement and form a common front against the British. The Khilafat Committee was formed. It demanded that terms of treaty with Turkey should be changed to satisfy the Indian Muslims. Gandhi suggested the programme of Non-Cooperation with the British Government. This programme was adopted by the Committee in May 1920.

The Non Cooperation Movement

The redressal of injustice of Punjab and Khilafat and the attainment of Swaraj became the key issue. The masses were getting awakened. Gandhi announced the inauguration of Nonviolent Noncooperation Movement on the 1st August 1920. A special session of Congress in September accepted the programme. The Nagpur Congress in December 1920 endorsed it enthusiastically.

The programme consisted of the following points:

Surrender of titles and honours given by the British Government

Boycott of law-courts

Boycott of educational institutions

Boycott of councils and elections

Boycott of foreign cloth

Boycott of Government functions

Picketing of liquor shops

Refusal to get recruited in the army

The programme was not just negative. It included the building of new institutions. National Education was encouraged. Stress was laid on Khadi. Charkha became the symbol of freedom.

The Congress was completely reorganised and a new constitution drafted by Gandhi was adopted to make it a mass organisation and a useful tool for the struggle. The movement started with hartal, fasting and prayers. It soon spread like wildfire. The freedom movement had become a mass movement.

Gandhi declared the Swaraj could be won within one year if the programme was fully implemented. People showed great unity, determination and courage. Hundreds of National schools were established. Tilak Swaraj Fund was over-subscribed. About 20 lakh charkhas began to be plied in the country. The boycott shook the Government. 1921 was the year of the rise of Indian Nationalism Gandhi became a Mahatma, the most loved and revered figure in the country. Masses looked to him as a saint, as an incarnation of God who had come to free them from slavery and poverty.

The Government started repression. Arrests were made. Firing took place at some places. The country boycotted the visit of Prince of Wales, the British Prince in November 1921. Disturbances broke out at Bombay and Gandhi had to fast to control the situation. By the end of 1921, the number of prisoners had risen to 30,000. Processions and meetings were being broken up. The masses were getting impatient. Call was given for Civil Disobedience. Gandhi wanted to start the campaign step-by-step. He chose Bardoli in Gujarat for starting the campaign. Notice was given to Government on the 1st February 1922. However, the movement had to be called off within a few days. On the 5th February, a mob including Congressmen set fire to a police station at Chauri Chaura in U.P., killing about 22 policemen. Gandhi was shocked. He realised that people had not fully accepted nonviolence. He persuaded the Congress to suspend the agitation. Gandhi was arrested in March and was sentenced to 6 years' imprisonment. He was kept in the Yeravda jail near Pune.

The Life of Mahatma Gandhi (1922-1948)

Gandhi was freed from jail in 1924 on the ground of health. The country was witnessing a wave of communal riots. Gandhi fasted for 21 days in October 1924. He toured the entire country. He laid stress on the charkha and the removal of untouchability. Political atmosphere in the country began to change slowly. There was a wave of labour strikes in 1928-29. Armed revolutionaries stepped up their activities. There was widespread discontent among the peasants. The historic Satyagraha at Bardoli in Gujarat showed its intensity.

Bardoli Satyagraha

Bardoli was a tehsil in Gujarat. Government increased the land revenue assessment there by 30%. Protests brought it down to 22%. The peasants thought it unjust. Vallabhbhai Patel studied the case. He was convinced that the peasants were right. The peasants decided to withhold the payment until the enhancement was cancelled or an impartial tribunal appointed for setting the case. Gandhi blessed the Satyagraha. It started in February 1928.

Vallabhbhai Patel led the struggle. He organised sixteen camps under the charge of 250 volunteers. His organisation was superb. It earned him the title 'Sardar'. The government tried its best to terrorise the people and extract the payment. It tried flattery, bribery, fines, imprisonment and lathi-charge. Pathans were brought in to threaten the people. The cattle was taken away and lands auctioned at several places. Patel kept up the people's morale.

His volunteers were arrested. People imposed a social boycott on the Government officials and against those who bought auctioned property. Seven members of the Legislative Council resigned in protest against the Government repression. Several village officials, too, resigned their posts.

1) The Government issued an ultimatum for payment. Patel demanded that
2) The Satyagrahi prisoners should be released.
3) The lands sold and forfeited, should be returned.
4) The cost of seized movables should be refunded.

All the dismissals and punishments should be undone. Gandhi and Patel promised to call off the agitation if these demands were met and an inquiry ordered. The Government ultimately yielded. An Inquiry Committee was appointed. The Committee recommended an increase of 5.7% only. The Satyagraha was thus successful. The Bardoli struggle was very well organised one. The peasants remained united against all odds. Women took part in the struggle on a large scale. The struggle became a symbol of hope, strength and victory for the peasants in the country.

Rising Discontent

The discontent against the British Government was increasing. The Government appointed Simon Commission to decide about the grant of political rights of India. Indian leaders had not been consulted. There was no Indian Member in the Commission. The country boycotted Simon Commission.

Gandhi had regarded himself as a 'Prisoner' and refrained from political activities till 1928, when his jail term was to expire. He thereafter took the reins of Congress in his hands. Congress resolved in 1929 to fight for complete independence. Confrontation with the Government became imminent. Gandhi launched Civil Disobedience Campaign-the famous Salt Satyagraha.

The Salt Satyagraha

Gandhi wrote to the Viceroy, listing eleven demands which, according to him, formed the substance of self-government. They were rejected. Gandhi then decided to start Civil Disobedience by breaking the Salt Law, which heavily taxed the salt, an article of daily consumption for the poorest of the poor. He started his epic Dandi March on the 12 March 1930 from Ahmedabad. A carefully selected band of 78 Satyagrahis accompanied Gandhi in this March to Dandi, a deserted village on the sea-coat, at about 240 miles from Ahmedabad. As the March progressed, the atmosphere in the country was electrified. Several village officials resigned their posts. Gandhi declared that he would not return to Sabarmati Ashram till Independence was won. Congress Committee met on the 21st March to plan the strategy. Gandhi reached Dandi on the 6th April and broke the Salt law symbolically by picking up a pinch of salt. It was signal for the nation. Civil Disobedience campaign was started throughout the country. Salt Law broken at many places by illegal production of salt and its sale. Gandhi went to the surrounding places and started a campaign to cut toddy trees. Picketing of liquor and foreign cloth shops was started. Women were on the forefront in picketing the liquor shops. The whole country was stirred. Some other laws like Forest Laws were also taken up for disobedience at some places.

Government intensified the repression. Most of the important leaders including Gandhi were arrested. But the agitation grew in strength. People bravely faced police brutalities and even firing at many places. A wave of strikes and hartals swept the country. At Peshawar, soldiers of Garhwali regiment refused to fire on the unarmed people. They were court-martialled. Before his arrest, Gandhi hit upon a novel idea to raid salt depots. The Dharasana raid, in which several nonviolent Satyagrahis were mercilessly beaten, sent shock-waves throughout the world. It lowered the British prestige. The movement progressed till January 1931. The boycott of foreign cloth, liquor and British goods was almost complete. Gandhi and other leaders were subsequently released from jail. Government started negotiations. Gandhi-Irvin Pact was signed in March. The Satyagraha was discontinued. This was a major Satyagraha, during which 111 Satyagrahis died in firings and about one lakh persons went to jail.

A Phase of Repression

Gandhi took part in the Round Table Conference in England in 1931 as the representative of the Congress. It was a frustrating experience for him. The British were bent on prolonging their rule by following the policy of Divide and Rule'. Gandhi stayed in London in a poor locality. He even met the unemployed textile mill-workers who had lost the jobs due to Gandhi's movement of Swadeshi and Boycott. He explained to them the rationale behind Khadi. The workers showered love on him.

The Round Table Conference yielded nothing. Gandhi returned in December 1931. He was arrested and the Civil Disobedience Campaign was resumed. The Congress was declared illegal. The Government was determined to crush the movement. The leaders and a large number of workers were arrested. Ordinances were issued to arm the Government with wide powers. Gandhi was lodged in the Yervada jail.

Yeravda Pact

While Gandhi was in Yeravda jail the British Prime Minister Ramsay MacDonald announced the provisional scheme of minority representation, known as the Communal Award. The depressed classes (now known as Scheduled Castes) were recognised as a minority community and given separate electorates. Gandhi was shocked. It was an attempt to divide and destroy the Hindu Society and the Nation and in turn to perpetuate India's slavery. It was not good for the depressed also. Gandhi announced his decision to fast unto death from the 20th September 1932. He was fully for the representation to the depressed classes, but he was against their being considered as a minority community and given separate electorates. Gandhi's decision stirred the country. Indian leaders began hectic efforts to save Gandhi's life. But Dr. Ambedkar described the fast as a political Stunt. Gandhi's decision awakened the Hindu Society. It dealt a blow to the orthodoxy. Hindu leaders resolved to fight untouchability. Several temples were thrown open to the Harijans.

The fast began on 20th September. Attempts to evolve an alternative scheme were continuing. Gandhi's health started deteriorating. He had several rounds of discussions with Dr. Ambedkar. At last, an agreement was reached on the 24th September. The Government was urged to accept the same. The British Government ultimately gave its consent. Gandhi broke his fast on 26th September. The agreement is known as the Yeravda Pact or the Poona Pact. It provided for doubling the number of representatives of depressed classes. Separate electorates were however, done away with. It was decided that for every reserved seat, members of the depressed classes would elect four candidates and the representative would be elected from them by joint electorate. The system of primary election was to be for ten years.

Anti-untouchability Campaign

Yeravda Pact gave a great boost to the anti-untouchability work. Harijan Sevak Sangh was established. 'Harijan' Weekly was started. After his release, Gandhi put aside political activities and devoted himself to Harijan service and other constructive work. All-India Village Industries Association was also formed. Gandhi gave the Sabarmati Ashram to the Harijan Sevak Sangh and later settled at Wardha. He toured the entire country and collected Harijan Fund. The massive anti-untouchability propaganda launched by him had spectacular results. He had, of course, of face opposition. Even a bomb was once thrown at him. The campaign destroyed the legitimacy of untouchability. It cleared the way for legal ban. In 1936, Gandhi settled down at Sevagram, a village near Wardha. In 1937, he presided over the Educational Conference, which gave rise to the scheme of Basic Education.

India and the War

While Gandhi was busy in the constructive work, elections to the provincial assemblies were held in 1937. Congress Ministers were formed in several provinces. The Second World War began in 1939. The British Government dragged India into the War without consulting Indian leaders. Congress Ministries resigned in protest. The Congress expressed sympathy for the Allied powers' fight against Nazism and Fascism and offered cooperation provided responsible Self-Government was granted. Gandhi was however against any cooperation in war efforts on the ground of Nonviolence. When the Government turned down the Congress demand, Gandhi was requested to resume the leadership. Gandhi decided to launch Anti-War individual Satyagraha against curtailment of freedom. It was inaugurated by Vinoba in October 1940. Pandit Nehru was the Second Satyagrahi. The Satyagrahis were arrested. By May 1941, the number of Satyagrahi prisoners had crossed 25000.

Cripps Mission

The War was approaching India's borders with the advance of Japan. England was in difficulties. It could not afford any agitation in India. There were various other pressures on the British Government to make political concessions. As a result, Sir Stafford Cripps was sent to India in March 1942. Cripps discussed the matter with the Indian leaders. He proposed Dominion Status with power to the States and the provinces to secede and convening of a constitution-making body after the War. But the adherence to the constitution drafted by that body was not to be obligatory.

Indian leaders including Gandhi found the Cripps Proposals disappointing. They were aptly termed as post dated cheque on a crashing bank. The Muslim League wanted a definite pronouncement about Pakistan and therefore criticised the Cripps proposals. Congress rejected the Cripps scheme because it did not provide for the participation of the people of the states and the principles of non-accession was against Indian unity. The Cripps Mission failed.

'Quit India' Movement

The country wanted nothing but Complete Independence. The Congress passed the historic 'Quit India' resolution on 8th August 1942. Gandhi and other leaders were arrested. The country now rose in revolt. With most of the leaders in jail, it fought in the way it thought fit. Railway lines and telegraphic communications were interfered with. Government property was burnt or destroyed in several places. The people displayed unprecedented courage and heroism. Unarmed people faced police lathis and bullets. Young boys suffered flogging without flinching. Government machinery was paralysed and parallel Government was set up at some places. Many workers went underground. About 1000 people died in firings during the movement. About 1600 were injured and 60000 people were arrested. It was noteworthy that violence was done to Government property only. Englishmen were safe throughout the Movement. There was little personal violence. Thus, while the masses rose to great heights of heroism, they also displayed remarkable restraint. It was surely Gandhi's contribution. The rebellion was, however, gradually put down.

Gandhi was in Agakhan Palace jail. He was blamed by the British for the disturbances. He could not tolerate questioning of his faith and honesty and fasted for 21 days. Gandhi lost his wife Kasturba and his Secretary Mahadev Desai in the Agakhan Palace. It was a great blow to him. His health was not in a good condition. He was finally released in May 1944 on health grounds. He then started efforts to break the political stalemate.

Background of the Partition

The Hindu-Muslim unity, forged at the time of the Khilafat

agitation, collapsed thereafter. The country witnessed a wave of communal riots. The British encouraged Muslim communalism and used it to obstruct the path of the Freedom Movement. M. A. Jinnah, an erstwhile liberal leader, who had been sidelined when the Congress became a mass organisation, assumed the leadership of Muslim communalism.

The Muslim League under his leadership became more aggressive, unreasonable and violent. The two-nation theory-that Hindus and Muslims were two separate Muslim homeland called 'Pakistan,' consisting of the Muslim-majority provinces. Jinnah's shrewdness, ambition and ruthlessness, communalisation of large sections of society and the British support for Jinnah, brought about such a situation that the Muslim demands became an obstacle in the way of India's Independence. Jinnah kept the demands fluid and utilised every opportunity to frustrate the Nationalist Movement and further his end with the support of the British rulers.

The two-nation theory was an untruth. The Hindus and Muslims had lived together in India for centuries. Gandhi fought this untruth with all his might. He did everything possible, including meeting Jinnah several times. But he failed. Jinnah wanted recognition of the League as the sole representative of the Muslims. It was not acceptable to the Congress.

Cabinet Mission

The War ended in 1945. After an election, Labour Party's Government came to power in England. England had been extremely weakened financially and militarily. The Azad Hind Sena had shown that even the army was not untouched by nationalism. Mutiny of the naval ratings in February 1946 gave the same indication. The people were in an agitated mood. The British rule had lost legitimacy in the eyes of the people. The British, therefore, decided to withdraw from India.

Cabinet Mission was sent to India to help in the formation of Interim Government and to purpose a scheme regarding the transfer of power. The mission proposed that the provinces be divided in three groups, in one of which Hindus were in the majority while in the other two Muslims. Subjects like defence, foreign affairs, communications etc., were to be with the Central Authority and the groups were to be free to frame constitutions about other subjects. Gandhi found the proposals defective. Muslim League declared 'Direct Action' to get Pakistan. 'Direct Action' meant unleashing of violence. The Hindus retaliated. In Calcutta alone, over 6000 people were killed 4 days. The Hindu communalism too became stronger.

The Noakhali Massacre

In the Noakhali area of East Bengal, where Muslims formed 82% of the population, a reign of terror was let loose in a planned and systematic way in October 1946. The Hindus were killed and beaten, their property was burnt, thousands of Hindus were forcibly converted and thousands of Hindu women were abducted and raped. Temples were defiled and destroyed.

The League Government in Bengal aided the goondas. Even ex-serviceman joined in committing the atrocities. In Noakhali, about three-fourth of the land belonged to the Hindu landlords and the tenants were mostly Muslims. The peasant unrest was naturally there. It was now turned along communal channels. The Noakhali massacre had few parallels in the history. It showed to what level communal politics could stop to. It was meant to terrorise, kill, convert or drive away the Hindus from Muslim-majority areas so that Pakistan could become a reality.

Gandhi's Noakhali March

Gandhi was deeply shocked. He could not bear the defeat of his long-cherished principles. On 6th November 1946, he rushed to Noakhali. It was to be his final and perhaps the most glorious battle.

Gandhi reached Shrirampur and camped there for a few days. He sent his associates including Pyarelal and Sushila Nayyar to different villages which were mostly deserted by the Hindus. He did all his personal work himself. He worked like a possessed man. He walked barefooted, went from house to house, talked to Hindus and Muslims, heard their points of view, and reasoned with them and addressed meetings.

He wanted to instill fearlessness into the Hindus. He exhorted them to die nonviolently, if need be, but not to submit to terror. He did not appease the Muslim. He told the truth bluntly. He wanted to win their confidence and make them see reason and earn the confidence of the Hindus. He did not only preach, he served the village poor. He was testing his Nonviolence. It was very difficult to establish mutual trust. The League had made poisonous propaganda against him. But Gandhi's mission began to yield results. It boosted the morale of Hindus. Passions began to subside. Some evacuees started returning home. Some even returned to their original faith. Gandhi gradually succeeded in earning the love and confidence of even the Muslims.

India wins Independence

Noakhali had its reaction in Bihar, where Hindus resorted to violence. The country was seized by communal madness. Gandhi went to Bihar and brought the situation under control.

The situation in the country was explosive. Civil War was imminent. The Congress ultimately consented to the partition of India. Despite Gandhi's bitter opposition, he could not do anything to prevent the partition.

While the country was celebrating the Independence. Day on 15th August 1947, Gandhi was in Bengal to fight communal madness. Partition was followed by riots, a massacre of unparalleled dimensions. It witnessed movement of about one crore persons and killing of at least six lakh persons. Calcutta was once more on the verge of riots. Gandhi under-took a fast which had a magical effect. Lord Mountbatten described him as 'one-man peace army'. Gandhi continued to plead for sanity in those turbulent days.

Gandhi's Death

It was January 1948. Communal feelings were high due to the partition of the country. Hindu communalists thought that Gandhi was pro-Muslim. His fast for communal amity which resulted in the Government of India honouring its obligation of giving Rs. 50 Crores to Pakistan had further angered them. Gandhi was staying at the Birla house in New Delhi. He used to hold evening prayer meetings regularly. He used to speak on various issues. Once a bomb was thrown during his prayer meeting. Still, Gandhi did not permit security checks.

On 30th of January 1948, about 500 people had gathered for the prayer meeting on the lawns of the Birla House. Gandhi was a bit late as Sardar Patel had come to see him. At 5.10 p.m. he left the room and walked to the prayer ground. He was supporting himself on the shoulders of Abha and Manu, his grand daughter-in-law and granddaughter respectively. People rushed forward to get his darshan and to touch his feet.

Gandhi folded his hands to greet them. When he was a few yards away from the prayer platform, a young man came forward. He saluted Gandhi, suddenly took out a small pistol and fired three shots. The bullets hit Gandhi on and below the chest. He fell to the ground with the words. 'Hey Ram' on his lips. He died within minutes. The crowd was shocked. The assassin was Nathuram Godse,' a worker of Hindu Mahasabha. He was caught and handed over to the Police.

Gandhi's body was taken to Birla House. People thronged the place and wept bitterly. The whole world was plunged in sorrow. The next morning, Gandhi's body was placed on a gun-carriage and taken to Rajghat. Millions of people joined the procession to have the last darshan (glimpse) of the Mahatma. His son Ramdas lit the funeral pyre. The Mahatma had become a martyr for communal unity.

2

The Gandhian Approach to World Peace

The problem that faces the world today is not that of individual morality or social behaviour but of inter-group and international behaviour and morals. This problem today has reached such a critical and crucial stage, that either we solve it satisfactorily or we perish as the human race, along with the civilisation that we have created by painful effort and the travail of centuries. Every step in this advance has meant the devoted service of the pioneers, often enough carried through at the expense of their lives.

The problem has, I am afraid, largely been misconceived. It is not one concerned principally with organisation. It is not one of balance of power or of devising checks and balances. It is not one of inspection, complete or limited. It is not even one of organising a World Government, a highly desirable and useful proposal. The problem is primarily moral. Of course, political, social, economic, international issues do arise, and so also those of organisation. But these will not be difficult to tackle successfully if we can solve the fundamental moral problem involved. Let us for a moment examine the morality that guides groups and nations in their commerce with each other. In all its essentials it is diametrically opposite to the social morality, the observance of which among individuals has made our civilisation possible. What is good in individual and social conduct comes to be bad and undesirable in political and specially in international relations. In social intercourse we admire the man who is peaceful, truthful, modest, and helpful to others. We greatly-admire the man who at some personal inconvenience and loss serves his neighbour. However, in the international field we expect nations and their agents to be selfish, proud, overbearing and aggressive. A nation which sacrificed its real or fancied interests for that of a neighbouring nation would be considered foolish and even depraved.

In social life we denounce aggression and violence, but the successful use of these is not only not condemned but applauded in the relations between nations. In social life, a murderer pays with his life for his crime, but in international intercourse a politician or a general responsible for arson, loot, rape, mass murder is applauded as a great patriot and a hero. In his honour are erected arches and triumphant marches organised. In social life, individuals are enjoined generally to trust each other and keep their word. No nation ever keeps its word with another nation if it considers that its interests are involved. Nations betraying each other are not the exception but the rule. Even after a war fought to end war, nations who were allied betray each other when the war is over. After World War II, nations whose territories were invaded and occupied by the armies of Hitler and who organised inside and outside their country resistance movements and helped the Allies to win the war, were enslaved. If some of them have escaped this fate they have done so by the skin of their teeth. A nation which trusts another would be lost. India accepted Chinese professions of friendship and the result is wanton aggression, the end of which nobody can see today. Nations in their dealings with each other, however polite their mode of address, are proud and touchy and resent every real or fancied insult. In social life we are prepared to give and take, for the sake of compromise and for accommodating the other's point of view.

Unless, therefore, the collective mind of groups and nations is civilised there can be no peace in the world. Rather, the very social advance that man has made so far will be destroyed. This is so with every armed conflict. Instruments of destruction get ever sharper until now they have arrived at the nuclear stage. Even then the tests must continue. One wonders what more is possibly wanted, when several nations already have with them the instruments which can destroy the whole of humanity over and over again.

It was not an international problem of the present intensity that confronted Gandhi. However, the moral quality of the problem, though not to the present degree, was the same. How did he try to tackle it? He saw that human life is one and cannot be divided into different compartments, social, economic, political and international. Therefore he sought the solution of its troubles on a moral and ideological plane. He held that the same rules of morality that guide individuals in their social conduct must also guide groups and nations in their mutual intercourse. It should be as immoral and sinful for nations to cheat, deceive and injure each other as it is for individuals to do so in their civil life. Murder does not cease to be a crime and a sin if it is committed in the interest of the self, the family or the nation. It must be remembered that the nation is only a big family. If an administrator cannot take bribes to support his family, he cannot also engage in acts of doubtful morality to serve what he considers would be in the best interests of the nation. Evil is evil, whatever the apparent interest served. Means, as in civil life, must not be subordinated to the ends, which should be pure, whether for individuals, groups or nations. There must be only one conscience, the same for the group and the nation as for the individual. The dichotomy between individual and collective morality results in creating split personalities. Collective immorality is bound to poison the moral springs of the individual. Moral man cannot live in an immoral or non-moral international order, without impairing his higher nature. Gandhi believed that every action, whether performed for self, family, group or nation, must produce its own appropriate result, karma. Evil actions create evil karma. In the international field this evil karma seems to have overtaken the world today. Every previous war has been the cause of a subsequent conflict. World War I was the cause of World War II. It was caused by the unbalance produced by World War I. The Cold War of today is the result of the cruelties and injustices practised during the Second World War. If it flares up into a hot World War III, it would be due to the karma created by the two previous world wars. There is no escape from the law of karma. As an individual sows, so must he reap. As a nation sows so must it reap. It cannot sow thistles and reap mangoes. The vicious circle that has been created by ever recurring wars in human society can only be broken when nations refuse to play the international game with the same loaded dice of war and violence. Gandhi has said: "You cannot successfully fight them with their weapon. After all you cannot go beyond the atom bomb. Unless we have a new way of fighting imperialism of all brands in place of the outworn one of violent resistance there is no hope for the oppressed races of the earth."

In consonance with the spirit of the sages, prophets, reformers and pioneers of old, Gandhi prescribed moral means for the settlement of international disputes. It is true that his canvas was limited. It was confined to two nations, India and Britain. But he held that the independence of India could be achieved through truth and nonviolence and when so achieved it would be real independence. In such a struggle no residue of evil karma, of violence and deceit will be left behind, to be paid for afterwards, as is the case with war. Though in India it was fundamentally a dispute between one nation and another, there was no question of any bilateral restraints. Indians could not return violence for violence. They had to do the right thing because it was right, because in the words of the Gita it was kartavya-karma, because it was one's duty. However, Gandhi had also the faith that when there is right action right results must follow, right not as the individual in his partial knowledge sees but right in the total scheme of things. "The doer of good can never come to evil", as the Gita says.

There is another aspect of Gandhi's thought about international intercourse which we must note. His idea of Indian independence was different from the usual historical idea of it. Like every fighter for national independence he loved freedom. It was something good in itself, something that every nation should have. But Gandhi's conception of a nation's freedom was different from the usual one. He wanted the freedom of India not only for the sake of his country, but for the good of humanity and for its service. As an individual must sacrifice himself for the nation when necessary so also must a nation be prepared to sacrifice itself for humanity. As I have already said, organised nations came to develop a personality. This personality, as in the case of the individual, must be subject to the moral law. Moral law often involves martyrdom. The nation as a person, if it must follow the moral law, must also be prepared for martyrdom for the sake of humanity. Martyrdom, as in the case of the individual pioneer and renovator, may or may not come but a nation, if it is to be moral, must be prepared for it. Gandhi said: "I want the freedom of my country so that other countries may learn something from my free country, so that the resources of my country might be utilized for the benefit of mankind. Just as the call of patriotism teaches us today that the individual has to die for the family, the family has to die for the village, the village for the district, the district for the province, the province for the country, even so a country has to be free in order that it may die if necessary for the benefit of the world. My love, therefore, of nationalism or my idea of nationalism, is that my country may become free, that if need be the whole country may die, so that the human race may live."

During the last World War Gandhi advised England not to fight Hitler with arms. He said that the result would be that Hitler's armies would march into England. He would allow them to march in but there should be perfect noncooperation with them from every Englishman. No Englishman should have dealings with the occupying forces. He believed that when a whole population non-cooperates it will be impossible for a conquering force to occupy the conquered territory for long. For this he wanted people to train themselves in individual civil resistance.

I need not go into the details of the training he prescribed for individual nonviolent resisters, satyagrahis. But Gandhi did contemplate such contingencies as when conquering armies would be on the march. As things are today, his strategy will be the best even for violent fighters. An army marching into a foreign territory which it wants to occupy cannot be resisted today if it is backed with nuclear weapons. The only possibility of resistance in such cases is guerrilla warfare. Resisting armies can be demoralised by a single nuclear bomb. But separate individuals, working from innumerable centres, cannot be so demoralised. If this today is the only strategy left for violent national freedom fighters against a Hitlerian marching army supported by nuclear war-heads then surely such an individual nonviolent guerrilla warfare is not quite such a fanciful idea as it would at first sight appear.

If humanity, then, is serious about avoiding the possibility of nuclear destruction, nations must be prepared first to regulate their mutual intercourse, as individuals do in civil life, by observing the rules of the moral law. As many pioneering reformers and prophets had to suffer in the cause of establishing the moral law in civil life, so some nation or nations must be prepared to suffer for the establishment of the moral law among nations. If Gandhi would have been alive today, he would have wanted and advised the Indian nation to dispense with its fighting forces whatever the consequences. He would have advised that this question of India's disarmament should be irrespective of what others did or did not. If it was good, it must be done irrespective of consequences. He had the faith to believe that India making such a sacrifice could never die. But even if physical extinction was the result it would be welcome in the service of humanity. In this mortal world everything, every individual, every institution, is subject to time, kala, death. The only thing that one can aspire for is a glorious death in a good cause. More than this nobody can expect or wish for. It is therefore that I said at the beginning that the question before us as national entities is a moral one and not merely external or organisational.

It may be said, But who is to bell the cat? Has any government the right to require such a stupendous national sacrifice? Martyrdom for a whole people? This question is asked as if the same kind of sacrifice is not asked for by governments from their people when they call them to arms! The political leaders of all countries have always compelled people to take the risks of war. But when it comes to the question of taking risks in the cause of peace, which after all are fewer as evidenced by India's struggle, they take refuge behind the people's will. The leaders have never, even in democracies, taken the people into their confidence when declaring war. It is governments that decide the questions of peace and war.

But it may be asked, Can a nation be educated in nonviolence? The education of a nation into a new ideology or morality does not consist in each member of the nation being educated separately. There are no schools and colleges where national ideologies and moralities can be learnt. Even in physical warfare most of the fighting is learnt during the war or there would be no universal military service. The very acceptance of a new idea by the leadership makes for rapid public education. For his new weapon of nonviolent resistance Gandhi did not open educational institutions. He took great pains in educating the leaders. The conversion of the public then was easy. Also knowledge of a new technique improves with its practice. Even when soldiers are educated in military colleges their military education takes place on the battlefield. Every war uses new and untried instruments and strategy. Nor is every soldier in the army a brave and courageous man. He may be a veritable coward but under proper leadership and discipline he too can give a good account of himself. He would disdain to desert his colours, because this is a thing not done in the army. This is the rule. Exceptions to this rule are few and far between.

It is plain today that if the leaders of countries carrying on nuclear tests abandoned them, the common people will not rebel. If the leaders of the countries which possess nuclear stockpiles decide to destroy them, the people will not resist. Even if some nation took, in this respect, unilateral action there will be no revolt. Rather people may take pride in such a step being taken by their nation.

In this connection Gandhi says: "If the recognised leaders of mankind, who have control over the engines of destruction, were wholly to renounce their use, with full knowledge of its implications, permanent peace can be obtained. This is clearly impossible without the Great Powers of the earth renouncing their imperialistic designs. This again seems impossible without great nations ceasing to believe in soul-destroying competition and to desire to multiply wants and, therefore, increase their material possessions."

However, the condition is that the leaders should have a burning faith in nonviolent resistance. It must be nothing put-on or dramatic. It must be the genuine stuff. It must be a belief that will stand all pressure. If need be, the leaders must be prepared to give up power and office in the pursuit of their ideal. Such a belief, Gandhi held, can come only from a belief in God. But for Gandhi God and the moral law were synonymous. He said that Truth is God. He held that there is no difference between the law and the Lawgiver. A person who observed the moral law, whether he believed in a God as popularly conceived or not, according to Gandhi had a spiritual belief. This is necessary because without faith nothing great can be done. It is faith which makes people believe that ultimately victory will be with them. Even if there is defeat it will be good with them.

When the battle for nonviolence in international relations is won, it will not be difficult to devise institutional measures to check anti-social nations. But first the victory must be won on the moral and spiritual plane. Why did the League of Nations fail? It failed because the leaders of the member nations had not reformed their minds and purified their hearts. They believed in aggression, conquest and exploitation of weaker peoples. So long as this is the case any organisational devices will break down at critical moments.

THE GRASS-ROOTS OF WORLD PEACE

It is impossible to believe in the sanctity or in the ultimate validity of nationalism. I think nationalism and what are called Nation States have become largely menaces to the human spirit and to human society. Perhaps in Europe and America there are more mature countries which are willing to go beyond the frontiers of Nation States. But here in Asia, with the newly awakened nationhood of many of its peoples, we are in the grip of nationalism and we are proud of our new Nation States. The European and American peoples are at a great advantage in comparison with the people of India because they can think a little more quickly than we can of the world as a whole; we are much more concerned with the problems inside our own country.

But we need not go all the way of the European and American countries to learn the lessons that they have learnt. We should be able to learn from history. I do not believe that these powerful Nation States and their governments will ever make the peace of the world. By their very structure and composition, by the very inner law of their being, I think they are incapable of making the peace of the world. The collapse of Summit Meetings in recent years is no accident. It is inevitable in the history of today. I do not think any Summit will make the peace of the world. It is the base, the common people, that will have to make the peace. I simply cannot understand how anyone can imagine that half a dozen people meeting somewhere in the name of countless millions of people can make the peace of the world.

THE WAR AND PEACE MAKERS

Some day little groups, meeting in tens of thousands of places in the world, standing for peace, federating together and creating a people's movement might make the peace of the world. So I am, so far as I can think about it today, a sceptic and I cannot bring myself to believe that big and powerful Nation States are going to make the peace of the world. I think they will not. What then can we do? I foresee that the next great step in peace-making in the world would be for the peoples to turn their faces towards their own governments. No government is standing for peace as we understand peace, not even the Indian Government. The Indian Government is as much armed as any other government, consistent with its resources. If it had more resources, there will be more and bigger arms. Each one of us in our own country must create a people's movement against the attitudes of governments which consider that war is still a method for settling any problem in the world. This is treading on dangerous ground; this cuts across what is called patriotism and nationalism. I think the peace-makers of the world must get beyond patriotism and nationalism. Man is one. Humanity is one and we are citizens of one world. This is a very difficult concept. But unless we reach up to that level some day, peacemaking will remain a pious dream. If we let our own governments commit our people to war, then where are we? One remembers with gratitude the work that is being done by the peace workers, by those who want to abolish nuclear warfare totally, in England, the United States, and other countries. I wonder if in India we have done even that much to turn our faces towards our own government and to say that we give them no moral right to commit our people to war, for any purpose whatsoever, because we are convinced that war is a total evil. If there is any shadow of a doubt anywhere in our minds, that after all war can do some good, then we destroy our creed. We then commit moral and spiritual suicide within ourselves in regard to this basic problem of world peace. So maybe, if we are treading this path, which is sharp as a razor's edge, we shall some day have to come in conflict with our own national governments everywhere, refusing them the moral right to commit our peoples to war for any reason or purpose.

But we must remember that the war-makers of the world are a powerful community. They have tremendous material resources at their command, and even the psychological resources for awakening the passions of patriotism and nationalism and working people into a kind of fury against some enemy State. Against that, what have we but our conviction and our faith and our dedication"? On the other hand, it is unfortunate that the peacemakers of the world are themselves divided. There has come about a kind of broad division in peace-making, two camps of peace-making. One suspects the other. I think this is not morally right, nor is it good peace strategy. Peace-making is the monopoly of no party, no country, no group in the world. Peace has become today such a terrific and emergent need for bare survival that whoever asks for peace is a friend and an ally. We must not divide the forces of peace-making in the world. We may be as cautious as you like, as circumspect about it as you like, refusing to be taken in by every kind of pretension, but let us not cut the peace-forces of the world into sharp and hostile divisions, glaring at each other, so that peace-makers themselves create a new kind of conflict in the world over the issue of peace. If we do that, we shall weaken ourselves. With open eyes, with open minds, and certainly with clear convictions, we should be able to close our ranks all over the world. All parties, groups and peoples deliberately standing for peace, whatever be the reason, must unite.

Dr. Radhakrishnan, the great Indian philosopher-statesman, has said that the cold war is in some ways even more dangerous than the hot war. The cold war corrodes men's souls and prepares for the destruction of their bodies. We now see signs of it in our own country, in this country of Gandhi and Vinoba cold war between Pakistan and India, and between China and India. Maybe, if somebody works up our passions, we in India are as much prone to cold war and hot war as any other people in the world. Maybe the heritage which has come from Gandhi and the inspiration which today comes from Vinoba may help us a little to stand on firm ground. But one has yet to see how far and how long these influences can succeed with the same kind of human material in this country as exists in every other country. We must nevertheless not become parties in any sense to the cold war.

There has been some criticism that Indian peace-workers look at European and American peace-workers and say they are not doing enough constructive work. I think we have outlived such a view note. We have realised that European and American and other peace-workers do a lot of constructive work along their own lines. Having said that, I do not hesitate to say that all of us peace-workers all over the world are not doing sufficient day-to-day work which alone can lead to the peace of the world. Peace-making begins from the roots of life, it is not something that merely flowers at the top. How we order our economic life together is part of peace-making. You cannot have an exploiting society building for peace. You cannot evade the issue of injustice and then talk of peace. I think peace without justice will be a complete fraud. Gandhi used prophetic words. He said he did not want "the peace of the grave-yard". It is easy to have the peace of the grave-yard. If Ave are thinking of the peace of human beings living together, on terms of equal rights and privileges and sharing everything justly together, then our present society has to be completely transformed before it can become the crucible which can hold the fiery lava of the peace which lives and throbs in the hearts of men and women. We want a radical change of social conditions effected peacefully. Here again is a challenge to each one of us peace-workers in our own countries. As we go back to our work, let us look at the society in which we live, discover the roots of injustice and apply non violent pressure to pluck them out. Every little nonviolent struggle to turn injustice into justice is a token for peace. If we do that we gather more strength, more unity, and we grow towards a just and lasting world peace.

IS THERE A NONVIOLENT ROAD TO A PEACEFUL WORLD?

In facing this problem it is necessary to get down to its roots, and the first fact to emphasise is that war is an expression of bad human relationships, whereas peace expresses the tranquillity of harmonious human relationships. Hence the difference between war and peace is the difference between a knowledge and a lack of knowledge of the art of living and the conditions of personal and social wholeness, of physical, moral and spiritual health. The art of living includes stern discipline in obeying the commands of Truth.

Failures in human conduct there will always be in the very nature of things, but what is important is that such aberrations be prevented from spreading by means of social vigilance and a powerful social awareness of vital social values and standards of behaviour. There should be ample institutional means of insuring these in every society. Eternal vigilance is still and always will be the fundamental law of moral and spiritual health and of social progress.

Today, however, we are confronted with a wave of materialism that is sweeping across the world like a hurricane, in spite of professed religions and politics. In every country spiritual values are declining and moral standards weakening under the pressure of growing appetites and demands for all manner of excitements and self-indulgences.

Throughout the West the prevailing aim of governments, political parties, and the public generally is maximum incomes and maximum production and consumption of goods and services. The outcome is a persistent demand for higher incomes, more markets for bigger exports of goods in order to import large quantities of food, raw materials and luxuries, increasing social tensions at home, and dangerous international tensions arising from the intensive competition of an ever-increasing number of "devouring" nations for markets and supplies.

In this situation it is idle to think in terms of a short cut to world peace. No conceivable peace conference could now take one firm, fundamental step towards that goal. The whole world lives in fear of a nuclear war, while a vast network of vicious international relationships holds the nations in the grip of mutual fear under the burden of mounting armaments. These are the realities behind the issue of peace and war today, and from them governments flinch as before a plague.

The two primary forces that are determining the course of events within and between the nations today are fear and greed, and to a large extent the fear is the product of greed.

The main cause of the changes that have led to the extension of the greed principle to its present dimensions, was the Industrial Revolution which took root some two centuries ago, in Britain. The building of factories fitted out with mechanisms where people were called upon to work various stipulated hours, for wages dictated by the owners, later called capitalists, was an innovation in production. It enabled an employer to live on the labour of his fellows, even sumptuously, and to give his family a good education and privileges which to the factory workers seemed fabulous.

From these simple beginnings sprang the powerful industrial: states of today. In their wake came endless problems and all manner of proposed solutions. Among the latter were trade unions and political parties, Labour, Socialist, Anarchist and Communist, all of which were fighting instruments aimed at freeing the workers from the injustices and exploitations of capitalism. As already stated, the greed principle expressed itself in competition for world markets and supplies and also for the capture and exploitation of Colonial territories, which together ultimately led to the first world war, which also gave birth to Communist Russia. There followed the Treaty of Versailles which hurled Germany into complete bankruptcy, whence came Hitler and Nazism and ultimately the second world war.

But, as always when power becomes tyranny, there comes a day of reckoning. The logic of these shattering events penetrated into the millions of working-class minds in every Western country. Why, they asked, should all these evil things happen in a "Christian" country? The churches supported the two world wars, and have always supported capitalism with all its class divisions and antagonisms. What, then, is the church's defence? Is religion played out? The answer came in empty churches. Orthodox Christianity lost its power and its leadership. The worker turned away, devoid of all spiritual guides, since no other religion, culture or philosophy was at hand. Thus deserted the common people gradually accepted the materialistic values of capitalism. The consequences are before us. Today the workers of all classes, also the professions, including teachers, doctors, lawyers, scientists and at last civil servants are waging a gigantic social conflict for bigger shares of the national cake, to some extent against one another, and all against the Government.

One result has been a catastrophic lowering of moral standards. What wins money is justified. Gambling and all games of chance formerly under the condemnation of an almost universal conscience are now almost as universally accepted, openly and without shame or compunction, while the clamour for money as] profit or wages or what, is breaking down the barricades of probity and honesty at an appalling rate.

In consequence, politics are becoming increasingly suspect. Even the labour and socialist movement has largely lost its soul, most of it having become middle class.

So far as the West is concerned, we have thus reached the era of a triumphant materialism. Today that materialism and the economic and social trends out of which it sprang, are extending their tentacles to the ends of the earth. They have gripped Japan, are penetrating into India and are now entering Africa.

Thus the time has come for the whole world to face the bleak realities of our time, especially the fact that over the last few decades the condition of man has markedly deteriorated. His future is threatened by two major evils: a war of extermination and the persistent and growing tendency towards the centralisation of industrial, financial and political power in the hands of tycoons and small coteries of politicians and others well entrench-in social and titled power.

There is no time to lose. The latest targets of armaments expansion indicated by the two Dinosaurs, register the supremacy and the impasse of economic and military power in the modern world. The high percentage of their total wealth which this expenditure consumes, indicates the magnitude of their fear, which is a demoralising and spiritually destructive force. Yet neither Dinosaur acknowledges a limit to such power or the necessity of setting a limit to its accumulation, although there exists a law which cannot be transgressed with impunity-the law of human limitation, or frailty. Once the concept of human wholeness vanishes the time soon comes when living ceases to be worth the candle.

That point is now being reached in the West, despite the e heightening glamour and frenzy of perpetual excitement, indulgence and riotous living. Already behind the facade of a commercialised, vulgarised way of life one may feel the throb of a deep depression, perceive the shadows of harassing doubt and even a longing for the sweet Fresh air of a simple, wholesome 'life.

The megatons multiply, but depressed imaginations refuse to face the magnitude of their menace, whence wide sections of the public barely move a muscle when informed that megatons are now assembled that could wipe out entire continents in the space of a few minutes. The grim fact is that the fear of living is becoming as frightening as was once the fear of death. Life has become so cheap that the gulf between it and death has almost vanished. Death having lost its sting, the grave spells freedom to an ever-increasing extent.

All this was bound to happen when the cash values of capitalism began to descend to the bottom of the social ladder. Today at every social level the paramount passion is to raise its allocation of the national income, whence politics have degenerated into a dog-fight for better shares of it. Thus the idealism of fifty years ago-Christian, socialist, or what-has vanished, as has the concept of an equal society, leaving behind the dead weight of a rabid materialism that is obliterating the last vestiges of once highly esteemed spiritual values.

In this very serious situation I would make three submissions: First, that the foregoing material provides the background against which every effective instrument in the fight for world peace must be tested. Second, that no peace policy can succeed in the midst of the prevailing and growing materialism and all the antisocial activities and institutions to which it has given rise. Third, that the emergence of a peaceful world must follow a two-sided revolution in which both sides operate simultaneously, namely, a widespread personal resistance to war and all nuclear armaments, unilaterally, and a social and industrial decentralisation and fulfilling the right of every person to responsibility, creative self-expression and the spiritual values of cooperative participation in the running of industry.

War and violence are obviously played out and must be totally abandoned if civilisation is to survive. The only civilisation that can survive the storms and conflicts that are inseparable from the aggressive societies of today must rest on whole persons, and thus on a culture and way of life which can produce them. Peace is not a sacred symbol which sits on top of a civilisation like a gilded God, but a way of life which must be supported by society's major institutions-cultural, industrial, religious. Gandhi was one of the first to see the full significance of that truth, and to recognise the importance of developing India, both industrially and culturally, on very different lines from those now operating in the West.

During his later years Gandhi gave much thought to the problem of human wholeness and its achievement. He concentrated on two integral institutions, industry and education. His inquiries in England during his student days had convinced him that India would make a tragic mistake if she copied Western industrial methods. He deplored the very thought of India transforming men into machines as was happening in the West. He preferred a slower, more wholesome growth. Let there be mechanisms, so long as they assist the craftsman by taking out donkey work, but they must not be allowed to rob the craftsman of the right to responsibility in industry, to self-expression, and to the human values of cooperative working for common ends. He saw in India, with its 500,000 villages, a great opportunity of erecting a quite new kind of village democracy. In every village there would be agriculture, and a number of small industries. These would start with hand tools, but the workers would use their brains, study Western tools and methods and then select their own tools and mechanism with a view to high quality production and its satisfactions. The entire village economy would be developed stage by stage as meditation and experience determined. To meet the needs of this industrial and social pattern he evolved his system of Basic Education, which seeks to balance book learning and theoretical instruction with creative hand labour. In India I myself have witnessed small girls of six, spinning cotton in school while joyfully singing their spinning song. The system expresses the harmony of knowing, doing and being. It was first adopted in small village schools but it now runs right through to the university. This concept that education, industry and community self-government are all aspects of a process of producing whole persons reveals Gandhi's means of building a peaceful society in India, and throughout the world.

Obviously the highly industrialised and centralised West cannot copy Gandhi's pattern. It must therefore find another way of reaching the same goal. The basic principles involved in the Gandhian vision are unassailable. They include the universal right to responsibility, to creative self-expression and to the human values of cooperation, in one's daily labour. These rights demand the culture of small communities as the necessary basis of a valid democracy. Just how fast we can move towards industrial decentralisation cannot now be said. Obviously the start must be made with the small industries.

It is thus imperative that we of the West begin to think in terms of inaugurating a new creative era in which quantity yields to quality, abundance to sufficiency, complexity to simplicity, haste to meditation, fashion to individuality, limitation to character, mental fragmentation to spiritual wholeness, satiation to satisfaction and cash to culture.

Traditionally in most of Western Europe education meant the culture of the whole person, not only in private schools and universities, but in apprenticeship. Practically all the old craft Guilds stipulated in their list of principles that a master craftsman must prepare his apprentices for whole living, including his habits and morals generally. In some cases he had to teach them a foreign language, usually French, in order that when they had completed their apprenticeship as builder, wood craftsman, painter, etc. they might travel across Europe to study the works of the great masters in France, Belgium, Holland, Italy, etc., and as the Guilds had close relationships with the Church, their members were given free hospitality in the monasteries, of which there were many thousands enroute from London to Rome.

Happily there are many signs of the disquiet on the part of lone thinkers and small groups concerning present trends, in most countries, and numerous outspoken protests against some of the more sinister trends are being made. Indeed I could fill several pages with a brief account of them. Many community business enterprises are functioning in many European countries, while not a few private business concerns are endeavouring to cultivate a team spirit by various means which involve some degree of sacrifice of profits. An organisation has appeared in Britain under the name of "Demintry" which preaches and practises the decentralisation of at least a percentage of the capital of a business. One of these concerns describes itself as a "Commonwealth", another as an "industrial community". The verdict of these experiments is "Satisfaction all round". They have definitely proved that co-ownership is a valid business principle both financially and spiritually, having revolutionised human relationships and developed a sense of unity of purpose. One of these firms allocates, by general agreement, 20 per cent of its profits to its workers, and a like sum, again with common consent, to a wide variety of public causes, local, national and international, thus establishing vital connections with its own locality, with the nation and with the wider world.

The case for co-ownership is strong. Labour is a vital factor in production, but it could be infinitely more vital and fruitful under co-ownership. Money is invested in machines, then why not in human beings who possess power which if appealed to in a just and human way could improve output enormously both in quantity and quality. The greatest crime of capitalism has been its rejection of the vast reservoir of creative power and enthusiasm by regarding its workers as machines rather than as persons whose natural instincts and impulses crave for self-expression. The means must be found of reawakening and using their long ignored finer powers.

Moreover current financial operations strongly vindicate the demand for co-ownership. During the last few decades enormous profits from most of our productive and distribution business have been handed out to shareholders for which they did nothing more than sign receipts, whereas in strict justice a considerable percentage of it should have been returned to the public in lower prices and to the workers in higher wages or as co-ownership capital.

The important fact is that the industrial revolution on behalf of human wholeness has begun. The task note is to extend it in every possible way. It is for the workers in the smaller industries to take the lead in agitating for co-ownership, and as far as possible with the backing of their trades unions. Only a little success is needed to open the way to what might become a general awakening and a powerful swing towards a creative democracy. Advancement in the main industries will help to point the way to the decentralisation of the giant industries.

In the West the public protests against the production and use of nuclear arms have had spectacular results, yet they have only touched the fringe of public opinion. It is my conviction that in a period of social decay like the present they will not succeed in their ultimate purpose without the inspiration of a constructive social revolution. It is in simultaneous direct action on both these fronts that I see the only hope of moving towards a free humanity and a peaceful world.

NUCLEAR EXPLOSIONS AND WORLD PEACE

The present age is faced with a dilemma in the world of power politics which it may fairly be claimed is new: either the great nations of the world must honestly agree to renounce the use of the newest type of weapon, or the world will speedily be brought to an end. Hitherto, however drunk with power some world conqueror might become, he could only scourge half a continent at the most; and normally, after the armies had passed, the peasants who remained alive would soon begin to rebuild their huts, replough their fields, and rebuild the foundations of civilized life. Indeed, as Gandhi long ago pointed out, if the history of man had really consisted, as the history books too often suggest, of the deeds of emperors and war lords only, mankind would long ago have perished. Happily, the truth has always been that the vast majority of human beings have lived peaceably with their neighbours, and have gone on quietly producing food and other necessities for life with little regard to the misdeeds of their rulers.

Today this is no longer the situation. Unless the rulers of the world learn to restrain their use of power, unless the poison of power can somehow be eradicated from the texture of the great Nation State of our time, mankind is almost certainly doomed to perish, and to destroy this beautiful earth, with its inhabitants, trees and flowers, animals, birds and fishes, and all.

The philosopher, duly instructed in modern astronomical knowledge, may say: What does it matter, from the angle of eternity, whether life on one tiny satellite of one little star disappears into oblivion? Will there not still be millions of stars and planets left? But such an attitude will hardly appeal to the ordinary man. This earth, and this earth alone, is the home of the human species as we know him. Apparently millions of years have been spent in bringing the earth to its present state of development. The cultural achievements of man even in the past few centuries of that vast story are such that every decent-minded human being must wish to pass them on, enriched if possible, to unborn generations for centuries to come. Perhaps the most horrible blasphemy of all is to suggest that perhaps it is now "God's will" that the world should come to an end. Whatever else may be said about human folly, let not man accuse God of making him a fool. In this whole discussion, perhaps it is better to leave theology out.

Of course this does not mean that the issue facing the human race can be decided without some ultimate sense of values. Indeed, it is just here that we are in the greatest difficulty. Gandhi's life-task consisted in the effort to apply the moral law to politics. He refused to believe in the ordinary laws of political expediency. In particular, it was his conviction that the Nation State should rely no longer on military force for its defence, but that it should have the courage to disarm, even if necessary in the face of threats of armed invasion from its neighbours. But at the same time he was a realist. He knew that in fact neither the people of India nor the people of any other modern State had today the immense moral courage to follow this bold line. The vast majority of thinking citizens of every State believes that it is a vital necessity to keep up armed forces adequate for "defence". And as it is futile to rely on armament that is out of date, this today comes very near to saying: "We (Indians, Pakistanis, French, Germans, Japanese, whom you will) must have the latest nuclear bombs at our disposal; otherwise, the 'enemy' will suddenly overwhelm us". So we are back at our dilemma. Either we all agree to renounce these weapons, or we all go on making them, till someone starts the shooting, and the world ends in a mass of deadness.

Is there any way out? It must be confessed that the outlook is extremely gloomy. Deep mutual distrust still separates the nations of the world. The Americans do not believe that the Russians can ever be trusted to keep their promises, nor the Russians the Americans. The same, I think, is generally true as between Indians and Pakistanis; perhaps as between French and Germans, and so on. So what hope is there?

Some of our statesmen assure us that the chief hope comes from fear. All the statesmen today know that once the nuclear explosions begin, ruin is almost inevitable for every country, including even the one that begins the bombing. Therefore, no statesman really wants war. This is perhaps an advance from only twenty-five years ago when Hitler, for example, almost certainly wanted to wage a war of revenge, and would have felt himself cheated if he had got what he wanted without war. Of course, he calculated that he was bound to win. He was wrong, but only just wrong.

Today, it would be rasher than ever for a powerful statesman to assume that his country would win. So, up to a point, fear is doubtless a deterrent on reckless policies. But as I write, the great powers still seem to be following their policies of "brinkmanship" that is, of pressing their opponent as hard as possible, under threat of letting loose the bombers if he does not give way, so that one wonders how long human endurance, on the part of innumerable young airmen poised for instant action, to say nothing of their exhausted chiefs, endlessly negotiating for ends that are for ever as far away as the carrot suspended in front of the donkey's nose, can continue. Within another few years, surely there will be a catastrophe unless this unbearable tension is somehow relaxed. But how?

Philip Noel-Baker, in his remarkable book The Arms Race, has demonstrated that the powers have, within recent years, come near to a general agreement on disarmament, in spite of all the technical details. The failure has been due, not to technical difficulties, but to political considerations. His conclusion is that if, in every land, hundreds of dedicated men and women will devote themselves to the task of pressing for an agreed disarmament, the governments will be obliged to make the agreements that have been so near and yet so far. At least, one may urge that citizens of the world who care for world peace should try to instruct themselves on what has happened, and continue to press their Government to show greater courage.

Another type of action that is at least getting some attention from press and public is typified by the so-called Aldermaston marches in England. Those who take part in these marches are all dedicated to the conviction that it would be right for Britain to renounce the nuclear bombings absolutely, and to stop the manufacture of bombs without waiting for any international agreement, and to face the possible consequences, however disastrous from the point of view of national survival, without fear. This is, in fact, an appeal to the very opposite of fear, an appeal to what Gandhi called the matchless power of truth.

I have not been able to participate in these marches; but those who have done so, including some middle-aged men and women who are not, I am sure, carried away by easy heady enthusiasm, have found them profoundly stimulating and hopeful; and the response of the public has been more and more positive. It may well be that less than one per cent of the population of England is directly affected by such action. But the spiritual forces of mankind hate little relation to numbers or democratic majorities. If a mighty force is being engendered it will begin to influence the whole national mind, spreading hope and confidence and courage in the place of apathy, indifference, fear and despair.

I do not expect that these actions of a small minority, however dedicated, will suddenly lead the British Government to announce its determination to stop all nuclear preparations. Its effect is likely to be much less spectacular; but perhaps, in the end, even more profound.

So long as it is tacitly assumed on every-side that the only things that finally count in human affairs, even in world politics, are military-and economic might, there is little hope for mankind. Gandhi believed, and tried to demonstrate in his whole life, that the power of the human spirit is mightier than the power of any bomb. The right use of both reason and conviction can turn the world from suicide to a new era of fruitful cooperation. If we have faith that in the hearts of all peoples everywhere, whether they are Russians or Chinese or Pakistanis or Americans, whether they are statesmen or financiers or ordinary men and women, there is an essential element of goodness, which can be released if they see that their neighbours have faith in them, then there is still hope that mankind can find the way to paths of peace and goodwill.

3

Political Significance of Gandhi

On 30 January 1948 on his way to prayers Gandhi was assassinated, killed by three bullets in his abdomen and chest. The young assassin was a fanatical Hindu who among others had been inflamed by Gandhi's efforts to bring reconciliation between Hindus and Muslims in riot-torn independent India. After a year of bloody strife, Gandhi's fast had brought peace to Calcutta and all Bengal. Later, sensing an incendiary situation under the surface, he fasted the last time in Delhi and restored an atmosphere of peace. For these and similar acts, he was not loved by all. In Calcutta a mob attacked his residence, a brick was thrown at him, and someone swung a heavy bamboo rod (lathi) at his head, Both narrowly missed. During his Delhi fast some shouted outside his quarters, "Let Gandhi die!" A week before his death, a small home-made bomb was thrown at him from a nearby garden during afternoon prayers.

With those three bullets came the bitter fruit of the murder of an important political leader. India and the world were saddened. Political leaders and ordinary people alike felt a personal loss.

In the years which have passed since that January day, many important events have taken place which have altered the world significantly: the death of Stalin, the Communist victory in China, the development of the hydrogen bomb and intercontinental missiles, the Hungarian Revolution, the trial of Eichmann, the end of the British and French colonial empires,

President Kennedy's assassination, and the "Negro Revolution" in the United States, to list only a few.

After such events in a world in which history now moves so quickly, does Gandhi still have any political significance? Now, with the passing of years and the opportunity for a more distant perspective, how is Gandhi to be evaluated? Are there points at which our earlier judgment must be revised?

Evaluating Gandhi

For a Westerner-and perhaps particularly for an American-Gandhi poses special problems in such an evaluation. Often his eccentricities get in the way so that it is difficult to get beyond them, or to take other aspects of his life seriously. Even for religious people in the West, his constant use of religious terminology and theological language in explanation or justification of a social or political act or policy more often confuses than clarifies. The homage which most pay to him by calling him "Mahatma"-the great-souled one-usually becomes a kind of vaccination against taking him seriously. If he was such a saint and holy man, it is thought, this is a full explanation of his accomplishments; we need investigate no further. As a Mahatma, he can be revered while being placed in that special category of saints, prophets and holy men whose lives and actions are believed to be largely irrelevant to ordinary men.

It is sometimes the case that Gandhi's own candid evaluations of himself and his work now appear to be more accurate than the opinions of some of his followers and the homage-bearers. "I claim", he once wrote, "to be no more than an average man with less than average ability". Indeed, in important respects this was probably true. He only went to South Africa after having failed in his attempt to be a lawyer in India.

Nor was he pleased at the homage given him, although he cherished the affection of people where it was genuine. "My Mahatmaship is worthless", he once wrote "I have become literally sick of the adoration of the unthinking multitude." "I lay no claim to superhuman powers. I want none. I wear the same corruptible flesh that the weakest of my fellow-beings wears, and am, therefore, as liable to err as any." There are further difficulties in evaluating Gandhi. These include widespread misrepresentations of Gandhi and his political opinions. These misrepresentations are not usually deliberate, but often are made by people who have just not made a detailed study of Gandhi's views on the point in question. It is, for example, widely claimed that Gandhi approved of Indian military action in Kashmir, that he would have approved of the Indian invasion of Goa, and even that he would have supported the present nuclear weapons program.

Such misrepresentations are not only made by Westerners, but commonly by educated Indians who often assume, because they are Indians, have read newspaper reports and repeatedly discussed Gandhi, that they know what they are talking about. Gandhi's own scepticism about the degree of understanding of his nonviolence and views among Western-educated Indians continues to be verified.

Part of the difficulties in understanding Gandhi's views on such questions as these has its roots in the attempt to fit Gandhi into our usual categories. It is, for example, assumed often that he must fit the traditional view of a pacifist or that he is a supporter of military action. When he asserts the existence of political evil which must be resisted, many people assume that he thereby "of necessity" has supported violence.

Gandhi's thinking, as constantly developing, and early in his career he did give certain qualified support to war. But at the end of his life this had altered. But this did not mean he favoured passivity. Thus, while believing the Allies to be the better side in the Second World War, he did not support the war. Similarly in Kashmir, while believing the Pakistanis to be the aggressors, and while believing that India must act, he did not favour military action.

Instead he placed his confidence in the application of an alternative nonviolent means of struggle against political evil. Here he as constantly experimenting, and his advocacy of the efficacy of nonviolent action in crises was not always convincing to the hard-headed realists. This sometimes meant-as at the time of Kashmir-that he was not politically "effective". But that is quite different from claiming that he had rejected his own nonviolent means.

As we shall note later in more detail, it was Gandhi's primary contribution, not only to argue for, but to develop practically nonviolent means of struggle in politics for those situations in which war and other types of political violence were usually used. His work here was pioneering, and sometimes inadequate, but it was sufficient to put him outside the traditional categories. Gandhi was neither a conscientious objector nor a supporter of violence in politics. He was an experimenter in the development of "war without violence".

A final confusion handicaps our attempt to evaluate Gandhi. His politics are sometimes assumed to be identical with those of the independent Indian Government under Nehru. Although Nehru has long had a very deep regard for Gandhi, and although Gandhi cooperated with the Indian National Congress in the long struggle for independence, the policies which Gandhi favoured are not necessarily those of the Congress government today.

Indeed, saddened by the riots between Hindus and Muslims and busy in Calcutta seeking to restore peace, Gandhi refused to attend the Independence ceremony and celebrations on 15 August 1947. The riots saddened him both for their own sake and because he believed they reflected a weakness in Indian society which could bring India again under foreign domination by one of the Big Three (which included China).

Gandhi had opposed partition into Pakistan and India. Congress leaders had accepted it. His plea for nonviolent resistance in Kashmir with nonviolent assistance from India was ignored. Gandhi had dreamt that a free India would be able to defend her freedom without military means. Yet in the provisional government before independence, and in the fully independent government, military expenditure and influence increased, while Gandhi warned of the danger of military rule and of India's possible future threat to world peace. Her freedom could be defended non-violently, Gandhi insisted, just as by nonviolent means the great British Empire had been forced to withdraw.

Political independence had not brought real relief to the peasants, who Gandhi had said ought non-violently to seize and occupy the land, and even to exercise political power. Gandhi's picture and name are widely used by the Congress Party in election campaigns. Yet Gandhi had written: "We must recognize the fact that the social order of our dreams cannot come through the Congress Party of today......" The day before his assassination he drafted a proposal for abolishing the Congress as it had existed and suggested a constitution for converting it into an association for voluntary work to build a nonviolent society and guide India's development from outside the government.

Gandhi must be evaluated on the basis of his own outlook and his own policies, not those of others. And it is also important that we re-examine some of the views about Gandhi and the nonviolent struggle which he led which are widespread in the West. In large degree these are views which have masqueraded as "realistic" assessments. I suggest, however, that as we shall see these views are often contrary to the facts and may be more akin to rationalization which help one to avoid considering Gandhi and the Indian experiments seriously. Let us look at six of these a bit more closely.

Outside of India, during and for some years after the Indian nonviolent liberation struggle, it was widely said that such nonviolence was simply a characteristic of Indians who were presumed to be, for various reasons, incapable of violence. The implication of this was that the Indian experiments with nonviolent action deserved very little further analysis. For fairly obvious reasons this assumption that Indians were incapable of violence for political ends is almost never heard any longer. But the implications of this altered view are likewise almost never explored. It is forgotten (except in India) that the 1857-59 Indian War of Independence-which the English called the "Mutiny"-ever occurred, and this included not only guerrilla campaigns but full scale battles. In the late 19th and early 20th centuries a terrorist movement developed among Indian nationalists (especially in Maharashtra, Bengal and the Punjab) which was responsible for a number of assassinations by bombings and shootings. Even after Gandhi was as actively on the scene, the terrorists continued their actions. For example, as late as 1929 bombs were thrown. and shots were fired in the Legislative Assembly in New Delhi. At the end of that year a bomb exploded under the train carrying the Viceroy, Lord Irwin (later known as Lord Halifax when he was British Foreign Secretary and Ambassador to the United States). And that was not the end of the terrorist movement.

Subhash Chandra Bose by 1928 had achieved an impressive following with his cry of "Give me blood and I promise you freedom". That year both he and Jawaharlal Nehru (later a supporter of Gandhi's methods) favoured an immediate declaration of independence to be followed by a war of independence.

Bose was President of the Indian National Congress in 1938 and was elected at the 1939 convention though he then resigned under pressure from Gandhi. During World War II, Bose headed the "Indian National Army" and fought on the side of the Japanese capturing the imagination of a significant section of the Indian public.

The religious riots prior to and after Independence are well known. Thousands were killed. Five millions migrated across the new borders of India and Pakistan. There were well-grounded fears of war-first civil war, and later between the newly independent countries. Troops faced each other in Kashmir.

During the Sino-Indian border conflict, it became unmistakably clear that when faced with a crisis affecting its frontiers the Indian Government was prepared to involve itself in large-scale military preparations. By and large the Indian people shared this reaction. Indeed, the most vocal critics of the government felt that it was not being sufficiently ready to go to war. The indications of the Indian invasion of Goa and the war in Nagaland, that the Indian government was ready to use military force, were emphatically confirmed. This was as Gandhi had expected. The Indian Government had demonstrated that when it came to military defence, it differed little in its basic approach from other governments.

Indeed, it can be expected that when China gets nuclear weapons, India will not be far behind, despite her non-alignment policy and Nehru's aversion to such means.

All these facts should make it quite clear that the Indians have all along been quite capable of using violent means, and that there must have been something special which led them to rely on nonviolent struggle as the main strategy for achieving independence.

It is of course true that there were elements in Indian religions and traditions which were conducive to Gandhi's approach, and that as Gandhi drew upon these and spoke in their language, the religious peasants understood him. The most important of these was probably the principle of ahimsa, which roughly meant non injury to living things in thought, word, and deed. These elements were doubtless important, but, as we shall note later, when Gandhi drew upon them, he always gave them new and vital interpretations.

But just as there are in Western civilization traditions and principles counteracting the Christian principle of love for one's enemies, so in Indian religions and traditions there were also counteracting principles. Sikhs and Muslims, for example, believed in military prowess. And the Hindu caste system itself provided for a warrior caste. The Bhagavad-Gita-which Gandhi so revered and which he re-interpreted symbolically-related the story of physical warfare and dwelt upon the justification for fighting.

In the light of these various evidences of the Indians being willing to use violence in political struggles, the view that the Indian independence struggle was predominantly nonviolent because Indians were incapable of approving of violence collapses. While for strategic reasons a full-scale war with traditional front-lines might not have been possible, a major guerrilla war certainly would have been feasible. (Assuming that the percentage of casualties in proportion to the total population would have been about the same in such a struggle in India as later proved to be the case in Algeria, that would have meant between 3,000,000 and 3,500,000 Indian dead. The estimate of Indians killed or who died from injuries incurred while participating in the nonviolent struggle given by Richard Greg, is about 8,000. One cannot claim that the French are by nature so much more cruel than the English!)

Thus, rather than Indian nonviolence being entirely natural and inevitable, it is clear that Gandhi deserves considerable credit in getting nonviolent action accepted as the technique of struggle in the grand strategy for the liberation movement. It is clear that this acceptance by the Indian National Congress was not a moral or religious act. It was a political act which was possible because Gandhi offered a course of action which was nonviolent but which above all was seen to be practical and effective.

It is widely believed that Gandhi was simply a personification of Indian traditions. As we have pointed out, however, and as has been amply demonstrated by Dr. Joan Bondurant of the University of California, wherever Gandhi drew upon traditional Indian concepts, he gave them a fresh and vital interpretation which differed significantly from the original. At the same time, it is usually forgotten how un-Indian Gandhi was in many ways. He openly in words and actions defied widely accepted traditions and orthodoxies. His fight against untouchability which he undertook several decades ago when it was many times more entrenched than today is simply an example. His whole experimental approach to life and to politics (he called his autobiography, "The Story of My Experiments with Truth") has overtones of influence by Western science.

Gandhi's basic assumption that one must not "accept" or "understand" evil but fight it, although supported by some, also was in diametrical opposition to other schools of Hindu philosophy which held that one must not fight evil, but transcend it, seeing the conflict between good and evil as something which ultimately contributes to a higher development, and hence about which one ought not to be particularly concerned.

Gandhi's activity and sense of struggle not only challenged (or ignored) those schools of Hindu thought. They went contrary to widely established patterns of actual behaviour. Passivity and submission were such common traits among Indians of his day that Gandhi found frequently that these qualities, not the British, were the main enemy blocking the way to independence. Gandhi is widely credited with a major influence in their reduction and replacement by action, determination and courageous self-reliance. "Nonviolence", wrote Gandhi in 1920, "does not mean meek submission to the will of the evildoer, but it means the pitting of one's whole soul against the will of the tyrant.... And so I am not pleading for India to practise nonviolence because she is weak. I want her to practise nonviolence being conscious of her strength and power."

A third popular view of Gandhi and the Indian struggle has been especially expounded by Marxists. They have frequently argued that Gandhi's nonviolent action had little or nothing to do with the British leaving India, but that they did so because it was no longer profitable for them to hold on to the subcontinent. These Marxists often demonstrate their ignorance of Gandhi and his nonviolent action by their assumption that these had nothing to do with reduced economic benefits to the British rulers. This assumed separation is manifestly untrue. The new spirit of resistance and independence among the Indians to which Gandhi contributed, in turn increased the difficulties and expense of maintaining the British Raj, especially during the major noncooperation and civil disobedience campaigns.

But even in purely economic terms of trade with India, Gandhi's program had a significant impact. This is particularly demonstrated by the impact of the boycott during the 1930-31 civil disobedience campaign. This coincided with the world depression, but as will be demonstrated, the drop in purchases of British goods by India was not solely the result of that depression but significantly also attributable to the boycott programme.

The British Secretary of State for India, in the House of Commons in late 1930 (according to J. C. Kumarappa) credited the general depression with a 25 per cent fall in the export trade to India, and credited the balance of 18 per cent in the fall directly to the boycott programme carried on by the Indian National Congress. Total British exports to India according to statistical abstracts declined (in millions of pounds sterling) from 90.6 in 1924, to 85.0 by 1927, then to 78.2 in 1929 and in the boycott year, 1930, to 52.9.

The total import of cotton piece-goods by India from all countries rose from 1.82 billion yards in 1924 to 1.94 billion yards in 1929 and declined only to 1.92 billion yards in 1930. However, the British export of the same commodity to India fell from 1.25 billion yards in 1924 to 1.08 billion yards in 1929-a decline of 14 per cent.

Then it fell to 0.72 billion yards in 1930-a decline of 42.4 per cent. Between October 1930 and April 1931, when the boycott was at its height, there was a decline of 84 per cent.

This is, of course, no attempt to evaluate the variety of specific factors influencing the achievement of political independence by India. But this should make it clear that the Marxist view that economic factors were completely separate from Gandhi's nonviolent action is not based on facts.

A fourth view, often expressed by political "realists", is that Gandhi's nonviolent action is incapable of wielding effective political power, and is hence irrelevant for practical politicians. This view frequently presumes both naiveté on Gandhi's part and that the kind of action he proposed was impotent and no real threat to a political opponent. Neither of these presumptions is borne out by the facts.

Some of Gandhi's statements at the beginning of the 1930-31 civil disobedience campaign are enlightening. "The British people must realize that the Empire is to come to an end. This they will not realize unless we in India have generated power within to enforce our will." "It is not a matter of carrying conviction by argument. The matter resolves itself into one of matching forces. Conviction or no conviction, Great Britain would defend her Indian commerce and interests by all the forces at her command. India must consequently evolve force enough to free herself from that embrace of death." "The English nation responds only to force." "I was a believer in the politics of petitions, deputations and friendly negotiations. But all these have gone to dogs. I know that these are not the ways to bring this Government round. Sedition has become my religion. Ours is a nonviolent battle." Rather than being ignorant of the need to wield political power, Gandhi sought to exercise it in ways which maximized the Indian strength and weakened that of the British. By withdrawing the cooperation and obedience of the subjects, Gandhi sought to cut off important sources of the ruler's power. At the same time the noncooperation and disobedience created severe enforcement problems. And in this situation, severe repression against nonviolent people would be likely, not to strengthen the government, but to alienate still more Indians from the British Raj and at the same time create-not unity in face of an enemy but dissent and opposition at home.

This was thus a kind of political jiu jitsu which generated the maximum Indian strength while using British strength to their own disadvantage. "I believe, and everybody must grant", wrote Gandhi, "that no Government can exist for a single moment with out the cooperation of the people, willing or forced, and if people suddenly withdraw their cooperation in every detail, the Government will come to a standstill."

The view that Gandhi was ignorant of the realities of political power and that his technique of action was impotent would have been vigorously denied by every British Government and Viceroy that had to deal with him and his movement.

In a most revealing address to both Houses of the Indian Legislative Assembly in July 1930, the Viceroy, Lord Irwin declared: "In my judgment and in that of my Government it [the civil disobedience movement] is a deliberate attempt to coerce established authority by mass action, and... it must be regarded as unconstitutional and dangerously subversive. Mass action, even if it is intended by its promoters to be nonviolent, is nothing but the application of force under another form, and when it has as its avowed object the making of Government impossible, a Government is bound either to resist or abdicate." "So long as the Civil Disobedience Movement persists, we must fight it with all our strength." Apparently the political "realist" who has dismissed Gandhi and his technique has some re-thinking to do. A fifth very common view, especially in Britain and among some Indians, is that Gandhi's nonviolent campaigns were only possible because the opponent was a British Government who were, of course, only very gentlemanly. While this has an element of truth in it, the degree of validity is almost always exceeded so that rather than this being a useful contribution to an analysis of the events, it becomes a means of dismissing those events without thought.

Admittedly, the British were not nearly so ruthless as Hitler or Stalin would have been, but they were far more brutal in repression than is today remembered. People not only suffered seriously in foul prisons and prison camps, but literally had their skulls cracked in beatings with steel-shod bamboo rods (lathis) and were shot while demonstrating. In a more famous and grave case, the shooting at Jallianwala Bagh in Amritsar, unarmed Indians holding a peaceful meeting were without warning fired upon. According to the Hunter Commission 379 were killed and 1,137 wounded.

If the British exercised some restraint in dealing with the nonviolent rebellion, this may be more related to the peculiar problems posed by a nonviolent resistance movement and to the kind of forces which the nonviolence set in motion, than to the opponent being "British". The same people showed little restraint in dealing with the Mau Mau in Kenya, or in the saturation bombings of Germans cities.

It is interesting that Hitler saw no chance of a successful nonviolent or violent revolt in India against British rule. "We Germans have learned well enough how hard it is to force England", he wrote in Mein Kampf.

The view that nonviolent action could only be effective against the British was more credible in the days when the Indian experiments were the main example of nonviolent action for political objectives. Now that this is no longer true and the technique has spread to other parts of the world under a variety of political circumstances-as we shall shortly note-including Nazi and Communist rule, more careful examination of the circumstances for effectiveness is required.

The last popular view which we shall examine is this: Nonviolent action for political ends is only practical under the particular set of circumstances which prevailed in India during

Gandhi's time. People outside India interpret this to mean that nonviolent action is impractical for them, and Indians mean that whereas it once was practical for them, it no longer is. Sometimes, the view is even more specific: that such nonviolent action is only possible for people who share the peculiar Hindu religious outlook.

This last view is repudiated by the Indian experience itself. Among the most courageous and consistent of the nonviolent Indian freedom fighters were the Muslim Pathans of the rebellious and never fully conquered North-West Frontier Province. These men, with a long tradition of military prowess and skill in war, quickly became under the leadership of Khan Abdul Ghaffar Khan expert and brave practitioners of nonviolent struggle.

Although this is not our main concern, it should be noted that there are Indians who believe that nonviolent action is still possible in India. There has been a considerable use of the technique domestically since independence, and there are exponents of its use in place of military resistance in dealing with any possible invasion, as by China or Pakistan, although it is true that detailed preparations have not been completed for meeting such an eventuality.

Nonviolence in the 20th Century

One of the most remarkable developments of the twentieth century has been the development and spread of the technique of nonviolent action. Nonviolent action includes the types of behaviour known as nonviolent resistance, Satyagraha, nonviolent direct action, and the large variety of specific methods of action, such as strikes, boycotts, political noncooperation, civil disobedience, nonviolent obstruction, etc. This technique has a long history, but because historians have been more concerned with violent conflicts and wars than with nonviolent struggles, much information has been lost.

In modern times the technique initially received impetus from three main groups: (1) social radicals, such as trade unionists, anarchists, syndicalists and socialists, who sought a means of struggle-largely strikes, general strikes and boycotts-for use against what they regarded as an unjust social system; (2) nationalists who found the technique useful in resisting a foreign enemy (such as the Hungarian resistance versus Austria, 1850-1867, and the Chinese anti Japanese boycotts), and (3) individuals, both pacifist and non-pacifist, who were pointing a way by which a new society might be achieved (such as Leo Tolstoy in Russia, Henry David Thoreau in America, Gustav Landauer in Germany, etc.)

Little serious attention was given, however, to refining and improving the technique, to the development of its strategy, tactics and methods of action. Neither was it linked with a general programme of social change. The technique remained essentially passive, the Action being in most cases a reaction to the initiative of the opponent.

While religious groups, such as the early Quakers, had practised nonviolent action as a reaction to persecution, the link between the moral qualities of nonviolence and the technique of action in social and political struggles was rarely made, except by individuals such as Tolstoy, and even then remained on the level of ideas.

It remained for Gandhi to make the most significant political experiments to that time in the use of noncooperation, disobedience and defiance to control rulers, alter policies and undermine political systems.

With Gandhi's experiments with the technique, its character was broadened and refinements made. Conscious efforts were now made in developing the strategy and tactics. The number of specific forms or methods of action was enlarged. He linked it with a programme of social change, and the building of new institutions.

Nonviolent action became not passive resistance, but a technique capable of taking the initiative in active struggle. A link was forged between a means of mass struggle and a moral preference for nonviolent means, although for participants this preference was not necessarily absolutist in character.

This technique Gandhi called Satyagraha, which is best translated as the firmness which comes from reliance on truth, and truth here has connotations of essence of being. A rather philosophical term, perhaps, but this technique was in Gandhi's view based on firm political reality and one of the most fundamental of all insights into the nature of government-that all rulers in fact are dependent for their power on the submission, cooperation and obedience of their subjects. "In politics, its use is based upon the immutable maxim that government of the people is possible only so long as they consent either consciously or unconsciously to be governed."

Following the widespread experiments under Gandhi, this technique of nonviolent action spread throughout the world at a rate previously unequalled. In some cases this was directly and indirectly stimulated by the Gandhian experiments. Where this was so,it was often modified in new cultural and political settings. In these cases, the technique has already moved beyond Gandhi.

One of the most important instances of this development is of course the adoption of nonviolent action in the American Negro struggle against racial segregation and discrimination. This was a possibility envisaged by Gandhi, as he revealed in conversations with visiting American Negroes. In 1937 Dr. Charming Tobias and Dr. Benjamin Mays visited Gandhi, and asked him what advice they might relay from him to the American Negroes, and what he saw as the outlook for the future of their struggle.

Gandhi called nonviolent action the way "of the strong and wise", and added: "With right which is on their side and the choice of nonviolence as their only weapon, if they will make it such, a bright future is assured."

Earlier, in 1936, Gandhi told Dr. and Mrs Howard Thurman that "it may be through the Negroes that the unadulterated message of nonviolence will be delivered to the world".

Contemporaneously with the spread of Gandhi-inspired nonviolent action in other parts of the world, there emerged in Communist countries and Nazi-occupied countries independent demonstrations of the technique under exceedingly difficult circumstances.

While no totalitarian system has been overthrown by nonviolent action, there has been more such resistance than is generally recognised. In these cases the fact that the resistance was nonviolent often seemed almost an accident, often without any conscious choice and certainly not the result of moral or religious qualms about violence. Often the nonviolent action even accompanied violence or was tinged with violence, but nevertheless remained basically dependent upon the nonviolent solidarity in noncooperation and defiance of men and women acting without external arms.

The Norwegian resistance during the Nazi occupation is perhaps the most significant case. It was largely through such resistance that Quisling's plans for establishing the Corporate State in Norway were thwarted. The heroism of the Norwegian teachers in refusing to indoctrinate school children with the National Socialist ideology or to become part of the fascist teachers' "corporation" is perhaps the best known part of this resistance. But it is by no means the only one. Clergymen, sportsmen, trade unionists and others played their part too.

Other important cases include: major aspects of the Danish Resistance, 1940-45, including the successful general strike in Copenhagen in 1944; major aspects of the Dutch Resistance, 1940-45, including large-scale strikes in 1941, 1943 and 1944; the East German Rising of June 1953, in which there was massive nonviolent defiance including women in Jena sitting down in front of Russian tanks; strikes in the political prisoners' camps (especially at Vorkma) in the Soviet Union in 1953, which are credited with being a major influence for improving the lot of the prisoners; and major aspects of the Hungarian Revolution, 1956-57 in which in addition to the military battles there was demonstrated the power of the general strike, and large-scale popular nonviolent defiance. Also, the impact of popular pressure in Poland for liberalising the regime was considerable despite the difficulties.

The degree of "success" and "failure" varies in such cases. These instances have occurred without advance preparations, with neither serious thought nor training nor preparation for such action. These cases are nevertheless significant, for they prove something that is often denied: that nonviolent action is possible under at least certain circumstances against a totalitarian system and that in certain conditions such action can force concessions and win at least partial victories.

In some circumstances such action may lead-and has led in Denmark, East Germany and Hungary, for example-to increasing unreliability of the regime's own troops, administration and other agents. Mutiny is simply the extreme form of this.

Other significant developments of nonviolent action have taken place in various parts of Africa, Japan, South Vietnam and elsewhere. The process is continuing.

Already this technique has moved very far from its role in politics when Gandhi first began his experiments with it in South Africa, and later in India. Contrary to the former situation, now for the first time people and some social scientists operating as yet with the most meagre resources are attempting to study this technique, and to learn of its nature, its dynamics, the requirements for success with it against various types of opponents, and to examine its future potentialities.

The view that this technique can only be used in the peculiar Indian circumstances at the time of Gandhi is thus seen also to be one which has little basis in fact. Indeed, it was argued a long time ago by an Indian sociologist, Krishnalal Shridharani, in his doctoral thesis at Columbia University (and later in his book, War Without Violence) that the West was more suitable than India for the technique: "My contact with the Western world has led me to think that, contrary to popular belief, Satyagraha, once consciously and deliberately adopted, has more fertile fields in which to grow and flourish in the West than in the Orient. Like war, Satyagraha demands public spirit, self-sacrifice, organization, endurance and discipline for its successful operation, and I have found these qualities displayed in Western communities more than my own. Perhaps the best craftsmen in the art of violence may still be the most effective wielders of nonviolent direct action."

This view has in the intervening years become not only more credible but one for which there is increasing supporting evidence. This is supported by an elementary examination of a large number of cases of nonviolent action which reveals that, contrary to popular belief and the rather conceited assumption of pacifists, in an overwhelming number of such cases leaders and followers have both been non-pacifists who have followed the nonviolent means for some limited social, economic or political objective. This has profound implications.

Thus Gandhi emerges, along with the technique of action, to the development of which he contributed so significantly, as being important for the world as a whole. Gandhi and nonviolent action clearly can no longer be pigeon-holed and dismissed without serious consideration by informed people.

Gandhi's role in politics was rather peculiar. He was not a student of politics, as we would think of one. He was not a political theoretician or analyst. Nor was he inclined to write, and perhaps was not capable of writing, a systematic treatise on his approach to politics. These were serious weaknesses and have continued to have important consequences. Indeed, he admitted that he could not lay claim to "much book knowledge".

Yet, despite this Gandhi was an innovator in politics. He often demonstrated that despite his lack of political "book knowledge" he had a very considerable understanding of political realities. He relied upon this and his intuition, as well as his constant "experiments". He had a capacity to sense the feelings and capacities of ordinary people about political issues, clearly understanding the peasants better than his more intellectual fellow nationalists.

His capacity to inspire people to act bravely and to gain a new sense of their capacities was combined with great organizational ability and attention to details. The combination of these various factors resulted in his important contributions to the development of "the politics of nonviolent action". Dr. S. Radhakrishnan, now President of India, wrote in his introduction to the Unesco edition of Gandhi's writings that "Gandhi was the first in human history to extend the principle of nonviolence from the individual to the social and political plane". This development which has taken place side by side with the most extreme forms of political violence-typified by the Hitler and Stalin regimes and by nuclear weapons-has led some people to ask whether the solution to such violence is developing while the problem is becoming more acute.

After the achievement of political independence, the new Indian Government did not-as Gandhi had hoped-assert its confidence in nonviolent means to defend the newly won freedom. The assumption of some pacifists that after experience with nonviolent action people would rather easily adopt the whole "gospel" was not borne out. Although Gandhi had hoped to the contrary he had expected independent India to have its army.

The Indian nationalists were willing to adopt the nonviolent course of action which Gandhi proposed to achieve political freedom, but when the struggle was won, they did not automatically continue their adherence to nonviolent means. This was a somewhat natural and predictable development.

This is because the adoption by India of the nonviolent struggle to deal with British imperialism was not a doctrinal or a moralistic act. It was a political act in response to a political programme of action proposed to deal with a particular kind of situation and crisis. A distinguished Muslim President of the Indian National Congress, Maulana Azad, once said: "The Indian National Congress is not a moral organization to achieve world peace but a political body to acquire freedom from the foreign yoke." Thus, for most Indian nationalists, it happened, almost parenthetically, that this nonviolent programme offered by Gandhi was morally preferable to violent revolutionary war.

In addition to strategic and tactical advantages, this choice of nonviolent means in some ways increased the strength of the movement by giving it an aura of moral superiority. It was also probably psychologically and morally more uplifting to the society as a whole and to individual participants. But these were certainly not the prime factors determining its acceptance.

In this new situation in which independent India no longer followed his nonviolence, Gandhi was unsure about the best way to proceed, except that he was convinced of the importance of having people who believed in "the nonviolence of the brave and the strong" out of moral convictions. He was so busy with the riots and other problems that he did not work out a satisfactory solution to the new problem before his assassination.

In the years after, the Gandhians were for some time uncertain as to how to proceed. When they gained a strong sense of direction it was to follow the initiatives of Vinoba Bhave and the land-gift and associated movements for social and economic reform which he launched. Vinoba, however, is a very different person from Gandhi and is often content with broad generalizations where detailed policies are needed.

When he launched the Shanti Sena, or Peace Army, of a core of volunteers committed to the development of alternative nonviolent ways of dealing with the tasks normally assigned to the police and soldiers, the programme was not worked out in such a way (as Gandhi had done) to appeal to the hard-headed realist and the political leaders. There are now-with the shock of the Indian Government's actions in Goa and the Chinese border-signs of new life within it, but the Shanti Sena still is far from adequately developed.

Meanwhile, the Indian Government sought to pursue a "neutralist" foreign policy while continuing a conventional military defence policy. Inevitably this meant that if confronted with international dangers the Indian Government would demonstrate in action the same faith in military defence as other countries.

If this was not to be, someone would have had to formulate at least the framework for a consciously adopted, carefully prepared, systematically trained programme for the nonviolent defence of India's newly gained freedom. No one did this.

In this situation it is significant that now Jayaprakash Narayan-who left politics to work in the nonviolent movement, although many expected him to be the next Prime Minister after Nehru-has come to a new awareness of the importance of this task.

In a speech in May 1963, Jayaprakash declared that he rejected both "meek submission to the Chinese injustice to us" and "compromise with cowardice". "There is no failure in a nonviolent war and we cannot forget all that Gandhi taught us. The alternative to violent war is total disarmament and nonviolent rearmament. If we actually demobilize the army, what would this mean? It would mean that we had shed all our fear of the Chinese, Russians and others and were determined not to bow our head before any aggressor; we will offer nonviolent resistance to them."

This was probably the first time such words had been heard from the lips of so prominent an Indian since that fateful afternoon of 30 January 1948. Obviously, however, the extraordinarily vast and difficult problems which are involved in the preparations for and execution of such an undertaking require the most serious programme of research and planning. There are not yet signs that this is being undertaken. The financial requirements of such a programme of investigation are large: £ 1,000,000 a year could be spent very usefully, given the right projects and personnel. Is the Indian Government likely to help? It is doubtful, although it is widely recognised that the present military programme is going to increase seriously India's economic problems, and hence may help indirectly to increase the strength of the Communists within India. Yet Nehru recognised the importance of further investigation of the nonviolent technique. He told Joan Bondurant: "I do not pretend to understand fully the significance of that technique of action, in which I myself took part. But I feel more and more convinced that it offers us some key to understanding and to the proper resolution of conflict." Gandhi's way showed achievement, Nehru said. "That surely should at least make us try to understand what this new way was and how far it is possible for us to shape our thoughts and actions in accordance with it."

However, the problem of tyranny and the problem of war are the problems not only of India, but of the whole world. Even if one thinks the chances of nonviolent action turning out to be an effective substitute for war are very small, the desperate nature of our situation is such that even such a small chance deserves full investigation.

This is the kind of tribute and remembrance which Gandhi would have appreciated. He was never one to claim he had all the answers or the final truth. He did not want people to be thinking always of him, but of the task which he had undertaken.

"I am fully aware that my mission cannot be fulfilled in India alone", Gandhi once wrote to an American correspondent. "I am pining for the assistance of the whole world..... But I know that we shall have to deserve it before it comes."

The quest for an alternative to war is now our common task in which Gandhi pioneered so significantly. Is it not now time that a full investigation into the potentialities of nonviolent action is both deserved and required?

THE IDEAL AND THE ACTUAL IN GANDHI'S PHILOSOPHY

The question: "How is the ideal related to and distinct from the actual?" is crucial to the understanding of Gandhi's philosophy. The failure to appreciate this has led his critics either to misrepresent him or to call him inconsistent and full of contradictions. Gandhi has often been quoted against himself. Dr. Bondurant writes: "Gandhi's political philosophy is, indeed, elusive.

To the scholar who seeks internally consistent, systematised bodies of thought, the study of Gandhi is unrewarding." She attributes this to the "result of his thinking in public." Another recent writer, Dr. Paul F. Power, writes: "Divergent and sometimes conflicting positions can be traced throughout most of his public life, although one may dominate the others during particular phases."

He tries to classify Gandhi's idea into different categories at different times and concludes that they "cut across." At the same time, later on he observes: "And if one of Gandhi's characteristics was rigid adherence to principle, another, equally notable, was his capacity of adaptation to people and circumstances." But how he made this "adaptation to people and circumstances" is not explained. To Mr. Hiren Mukherjee, an Indian communist, Gandhi was a Utopian "running what he imagined were model settlements". 5 There are, however, others who think differently. Professor Morris Jones observes: "The wonder begins to be that over a half century of social change, over a number of diverse situations, so much consistency should remain." Professor Tinker writes: "Few political leaders have been so fundamentally consistent as Gandhi, with a consistency impossible of achievement."

Understanding Gandhian Philosophy

Gandhi, it is true, was not concerned with constructing a system of philosophy, but mainly with applying the ideals and principles that had become a part of his life. Therefore, we do not find the distinction between the ideal and the actual explicitly stated. One discovers this only when studying his ideas in the context of his background, which was essentially that of Hindu philosophy. Cut off from this source, his ideas sometimes produce the impression of inconsistency; read in the context, they form a coherent whole. He may, therefore, not appear to be consistent with his previous statements, but be is, in his own words, consistent with truth as it may present itself at a given moment. He explains it further: "Whenever I have been obliged to compare my writing even fifty years ago with the latest, I have discovered no inconsistency between the two. But friends who observe inconsistency... should try to see if there is not an underlying and abiding consistency between the two seeming inconsistencies."

Although for understanding Gandhi's philosophy it is necessary that the concepts be understood in the context of Hindu philosophy, it is equally important to bear in mind that Gandhi's connotations of terms are different from the prevalent ones. Quite often they sound national or geographical, when in fact they are universal. He never seems to have realised that this could sometimes have the effect of damaging his own purpose.

The ultimate ideal for Gandhi, as he repeated several times, is unrealised and unrealisable; its value consists in pointing out the direction. According to him, there must always be an unbridgeable gulf between the ideal and its practice. The ideal will cease to be one if it becomes possible to realise it. He argues: "Where would there be room for that constant striving, that ceaseless quest after the ideal that is the basis of all spiritual progress, if mortals could reach the perfect state while still in the body?" Striving after the ideal is the very essence of practising Gandhi's philosophy. To the extent we make this effort, to that extent we realise the ideal.

Truth and Nonviolence

Two basic principles, Truth and nonviolence, are the foundations of Gandhi's philosophy. At the highest level of experience they merge and become one with God. The ideal of reality is also the ideal of value-a distinctive mark of Hindu philosophy. God, therefore, has been referred to by Gandhi as Truth or Love (nonviolence in its perfection). His ideal of life, self-realisation, therefore, is couched in ideal terms, when the Unity of Man and God has also been achieved. Gandhi, however, is fully aware that in actual fact, at the present level of human experience, there is a gulf between man and God; indeed, this gulf will never be completely bridged as long as we are in this body. "Being necessarily limited by the bonds of flesh we can achieve perfection only after the dissolution of the body." But while in this body, the gulf can certainly be narrowed. Thus recognising the imperfect nature of man, Gandhi's prescription would be to follow the relative truth persistently which he called "Satyagraha". This shows the dynamic character of his ideas.

In order to achieve this ideal, he prescribed an ethical discipline-the observance of vows which he defined as "doing at any cost something that one ought to do". But taking of a vow does not mean that we are able to observe it completely from the very beginning, but it does mean "constant and honest effort in thought, word and deed, with a view to its fulfilment". It is no doubt true that in this way the practice of the ideal becomes very slippery indeed-anything could be justified as following the ideal. But this is unavoidable as is the fate of all ethical ideals whose observance can hardly be a matter of strict objective scrutiny; it would ultimately depend on the spirit of the person who observes it and which no outsider can determine fully. At the same time, it does not condone the moral lapses of the individual; rather, this consciousness should make one strive to overcome the imperfections. Gandhi's adoption of nonviolence as a method of pursuing truth is due to the fact that man, imperfect as he is, can only strive, he cannot command the result. Perfect nonviolence, being the attribute of God alone, cannot be practised by human beings.

Being a part of society, man cannot but participate in "himsa" that the very existence of society involves. Gandhi, therefore, would consider a person true to his faith if "there is an effort to avoid the violence that is inevitable in life". That is how Gandhi's ideal of nonviolence is translated into actual practice. In essence, it consists "in allowing others the maximum of convenience at the maximum inconvenience to us, even at the risk of life. Everyone has to determine for himself the amount of inconvenience he is capable of putting up with. No third party can determine it for him." Gandhi believed that one should rather be conscious of one's imperfections than that one should lower one's ideal; this would spur the individual to perfect himself.

The application of nonviolence and Satyagraha to social and political fields has been a subject of great controversy. So complete was Gandhi's faith that he considered it a remedy against all social evils. What makes it a unique method of bringing about change is the transformation of the whole atmosphere, satyagrahi and the opponent included. Its success or failure is not to be judged in terms of victory or defeat of one party but in terms of a change of heart of both. It is not merely a form of persuasion which is aimed in one direction only. If, in spite of the best efforts of the satyagrahi, some moral coercion is felt by the opponent, then such coercion is unavoidable because of the imperfect nature of the satyagrahi. However, he is obliged to try his best to reduce this unavoidable coercion to the minimum. That alone would make it different from passive resistance.

Ideally not even a group organisation is necessary. "A man or woman who is saturated with ahimsa has only to will a thing and it happens." This is because a perfect satyagrahi would be nearer to God; and what is beyond His power! Since such a perfect satyagrahi is not available, Gandhi realised the necessity of group action. Also Satyagraha has its educative purpose, which is to bring about confidence in the community. Gandhi's method strongly emphasizes the need of ethical discipline, whose essential ingredient is courage-the courage of dying without killing. Having decided upon the rightness of a situation, Gandhi would not like one to be a passive spectator to evil. That would be participation in the evil itself. If one does not have sufficient nonviolence to die without killing one should not shamefully flee from the danger in the name of nonviolence. Rather, Gandhi would advise killing and being killed. While for himself he did not believe in the use of arms at all, he would not hesitate to advise their use by those who had no faith in nonviolence. "If there was a national government, whilst I should not take any direct part in any war, I can conceive occasions when it would be my duty to vote for the military training of those who wish to take it.

For I know that all its members do not believe in nonviolence to the extent I do. It is not possible to make a person or a society nonviolent by compulsion." Under certain circum stances, nonviolence may be only a matter of policy, as it was with the Indian National Congress. But this cannot be identified with the level of nonviolence which Gandhi personally was capable of. There is not a uniform pattern of application of nonviolence for all individuals and societies. Gandhi is some times talking in terms of the ideal, sometimes from his personal level; and sometimes from the point of view of what he considered the Indian masses were capable of doing. It is this distinction, which is not always made explicit, that gives the impression of inconsistency.

Sometimes a confusion is made between the acts of the individual and those of the State, and it is expected that Gandhi's State is to be nonviolent. But how is the State to act nonviolently, when for Gandhi it "represents violence in a concentrated and organised form"? Indeed a nonviolent State is a contradiction in terms. Ultimately, when nonviolence is the governing principle of society, we could not call it a State-it could only be called a nonviolent stateless society. And that is the ideal for Gandhi. In such a society people would simply grow accustomed spontaneously to observe their social obligations without the operation of the state. The necessity of legal enforcement arises because of human imperfections. The more the individuals have imbibed the spirit of nonviolence, the less the necessity of the state. This is the implication of Gandhi's concept of Swaraj. "The attempt to win Swaraj is Swaraj itself." It is a developing ideal and is "better than the best". Gandhi calls it "indefinable". In the context of the Indian National Movement, he said that Swaraj did not mean merely political independence but "many other things". A Western style of parliamentary government lie would accept as Swaraj for the time being only. While in the ideal society there is no room for the military and the police, yet in the actual State there is provision for it according to the moral level of its citizens. That is to say, a predominantly nonviolent State is the practical possibility and is the second best ideal of Gandhi. Failure to recognise the levels in Gandhi's thought results in such confused statements as this: "It is indeed clear that Gandhi held essential ideals in common with anarchists, that lie was willing, as they are not, to accept a degree of state organisation and control. He believed that government to be best which governs least, and yet he held that 'there are certain things which cannot be done without political power', even though there are 'numerous other things which do not at all depend upon political power'.... It would, of course, be incorrect to suppose that Gandhi thought of retaining the state as some intermediate step in a determined progress towards anarchical society."

Gandhi's actual State does concede the desirability of using the military and the police to deal with anti-social elements and defend the country. What, however, distinguishes his approach is the admission of weakness not of the doctrine of nonviolence or of Satyagraha, but of the individuals who practise it. Whatever political institutions Gandhi accepted, he did so only as a transitional device, to be transcended by better ones. No institutional device is final. They must evolve with the evolution of individuals. In actual practice, it would be a mixture: "A government cannot succeed in becoming entirely nonviolent because it represents all the people." He expected that the national policy would incline towards militarism of a modified character.

While fighting for the independence of India, Gandhi was conscious all the time of the necessity of moral uplift of the individuals who are to work the institutions after independence. In directing his energies towards political reform his method was equally directed "to educating the individuals to rise to a moral stature". He says : "Responsible government, which is a gift without the will and power of the people behind it, will be a mere paper responsibility hardly worth the paper on which it may be printed. If it is a fact that the atmosphere for immediate self government among the states is not propitious, and the people are not ready to pay the price, it follows that they should have the proper training."

When, therefore, Gandhi is criticised as a politician, such criticism is mainly based on his having one end in view, *viz.* the national independence of India; it ignores the other important principle of Gandhi, namely the moral training of the individual.

In the economic field, Gandhi holds to the ideal of Trusteeship. Ultimately he subscribes to "non-possession". But in actual life he admits that some possession is unavoidable for the maintenance of the body and its needs so that it may be used for performing its duties. But property must always be held as a trust for the people and must satisfy this instrumental character. While absolute trusteeship is no doubt an abstraction and is unattainable, like Euclid's point, an effort in this direction will remove the hardships of inequality. In the actual world, Gandhi would not even mind State regulation, but with the minimum use of power-by which he means constitutional machinery. He goes to the length of saying: "Every vested interest must be subjected to scrutiny and confiscation ordered where necessary-with or without compensation, as the case may be." This is what he said in 1932 at the Round Table Conference in London. As a part of a civil disobedience movement in 1942 he could expect "the peasants to stop taxes" and even "to seize the land". But this was not a matter of "advance", as Mr. Mukherji terms it; nor "a. signal change in Gandhi's ideology" as "dictated by politics"; it was indeed the application of his philosophy of property when trusteeship had failed. Gandhi never failed to emphasise the need for his ideals which sometimes even seem to blur the distinction between the ideal and the actual. He talked of independent India adopting,-with qualifications-the Satyagraha technique against aggression if India could acquire enough nonviolence. He knew very well that the people of India did not have nonviolence of his standard even to expel the British government: why then did he continue to talk of repelling armed aggression nonviolently? For Gandhi, nonviolence was not merely a weapon to achieve self-government: for once independence was achieved, a constant effort was to be made to reach the ideal when it would, of course, be possible to defend the country non-violently. Such an ideal, it is true, was not to be realised immediately after the British government withdrew, but was to be striven for.

To conclude: Gandhi's philosophy lays down moral ideals for individuals and groups to strive for-their value consists in pointing out the direction, not in their realisation. They cannot be enforced from above but depend upon their voluntary acceptance. Unavoidable use of force he considers to be a necessary evil-but an evil all the same. The extent to which these ideals can be practised depends on the ethical capacity of individuals or groups. Accordingly, the actual practice of these ideals cannot be uniform. As a social and political reformer, Gandhi spoke from different levels at different times. But three levels mainly dominate his writings: first, that of the perfect ideal (unrealisable); second, that of his own personal point of view (admitting himself to be far from perfect, yet sufficiently advanced to practise his ideals); third, that of the point of view of the Indian masses. Yet what is implied throughout is this: that even though the ideal may be impossible of attainment, the very act of pursuing it generates the goodwill essential for the well-being of the corporate life.

4

Basic Principles of Gandhism

Mahatma Gandhi was an intensely active personality. He was interested in everything that concerns the individual or society. He is best known as the matchless political leader who evolved the new technique of "Satyagraha". His fight against untouchability and the notions of superiority and inferiority by birth are also fairly well known. For India, his greatest service was, perhaps, the emancipation of Indian women.

It is generally known that he lived an austere life, practised strict vegetarianism and abstained from alcoholic drinks, tobacco and even the milder stimulants like coffee and tea. His attachment to simple natural remedies against illness and disease and his radical ideas on education are not so well known to the outside world and, even in India, they have not made much impact. Gandhi deliberately refrained from making these public issues and thereby confusing the people. The only exception was prohibition of intoxicating drinks which became a tool in the armoury of Satyagraha. Therefore it became a plank in the Congress program but it was well known that many an important supporter of Gandhi was privately addicted to drink and the great leader did not take undue notice of it. Even though it got into the Constitution in the form of a Directive Principle, there has been no honesty about prohibition among the Congress Governments and Congressmen in general. Gandhi's views on language, government and economics played a considerable part in his political movements; and in the program of Khadi and Village Industries included in the Five

Year Plans and in the Panchayat Raj which has recently been established, they have been accepted and implemented to some extent.

If all these ideas and activities are viewed in isolation, they constitute a miscellaneous and rather archaic collection, the importance of which will dwindle and fade away with time. It is only when it is realised that Gandhi was fundamentally a moral and social philosopher and that, through these items, he sought to experiment with certain far-reaching fundamental principles, of whose absolute truth he was convinced beyond all doubt, that their true significance becomes clear.

The Gandhian Principles

1. The first principle which guided all his thoughts and activities is the complete unity and integrity of body, mind and soul in the individual human being. He was never tired of saying that the body should be controlled by the mind and the mind by the soul. But this control is not to be achieved by despising or neglecting either the body or the mind or in the mystic exaltation of the soul by itself. He attached to physical health and well-being as much importance as to plain and logical thinking or moral responsibility. He was one of the most logical and powerful writers-yet, he was never tired of decrying all idle and purposeless playing with words and ideas or deification of thought as such. He was convinced that real thought must be organically connected to moral purposes on the one side and useful and right action on the other. It has been claimed that the greatest achievement of Gandhi was the spiritualization of politics. This is undoubtedly true; but he had no faith in spirituality by itself as an abstract virtue. He conceived it as a kind of illumination or fragrance which should accompany every thought and action. It is difficult to define it, except, perhaps, through the verses of the Bhagavad Gita which constituted his daily prayer.
2. The second principle of Gandhian philosophy may be stated as follows: All social action should be governed by the same simple set of moral values, of which the

main elements are selflessness, non-attachment, nonviolence and active service. It will take me too long to define and elaborate his ideas in respect of each of these; but he believed that the growth of a mans personality is proportionate to his faith in and practice of these virtues. This is possible only when he identifies himself more and more with an ever-increasing circle till it embraces all humanity and even all living beings. He judged the value and vitality of social institutions by their capacity to foster such growth.

3. His third conviction was that no society, state or any other institution has any worth or importance apart from its part in contributing to the growth of the individuals of which it is composed. The State, the Nation, the community and other traditional groupings had no intrinsic value for him. In the pages of Young India in the earlier years, he defended the caste system as a great scheme of social and sexual discipline; but in the light of actual experience he abandoned it as an impractical system, though to the end he believed in some kind of voluntary and ideal social groups based on qualifications and capacity for service.
4. It was Gandhi's firm conviction that means are at least as important as, and often even more important than, ends. It is, of course, desirable that ends should be good and reasonable. But they merely give a direction to life while the means adopted constitute life itself. Therefore, if the means are right, that is, if they conform to the tests of truth and nonviolence, even mistakes, errors and failures aid the growth of the individual. On the other hand, wrong means corrupt the soul and no good can ever come out of them. Gandhi repudiated categorically the idea that ends justify the means. This implies the rejection of war, espionage and crooked diplomacy, even when they are adopted for the so-called noble ends of defending the country, religion or humanity.
5. Faith in God is, according to Gandhi, the foundation of

all moral values. He never defined God and was prepared to allow every person to have his own idea of God. For himself, he was inclined to think of Him as the Upanishadic Brahman. But, so long as a person believes in some source of spiritual life and holds it superior to the material universe, he is a believer in God. Gandhi had no objection even to a formal profession of agnosticism, so long as a person demonstrated by his attachment to moral values that this outlook was essentially spiritual in essence.

I believe that the influence of Gandhi in the future will depend more and more on the realisation that these fundamental principles constitute the core of his teachings and that all his actions were merely illustrations of their application. He considered his life as a series of experiments with truth. Therefore, it is his conception of truth that is central to his life and work. I do not claim that the principles I have indicated exhaust his conception; but I believe that they constitute its basic elements.

MEANS AND ENDS IN POLITICS

Most political and social thinkers have been concerned with the desirable (and even necessary) goals of a political system or with the common and competing ends that men actually desire, and then pragmatically considered the means that are available to rulers and citizens. Even those who have sought a single, general, and decisive criterion of decision-making have stated the ends and then been more concerned with the consequences of social and political acts than with consistently applying standards of intrinsic value. It has become almost a sacred dogma in our age of apathy that politics, centred on power and conflict and the quest for legitimacy and consensus, is essentially a study in expediency, a tortuous discovery of practical expedients that could reconcile contrary claims and secure a common if minimal goal or, at least, create the conditions in which different ends could be freely or collectively pursued. Liberal thinkers have sought to show that it is possible for each individual to be used as a means for another to achieve his ends without undue coercion and to his own distinct advantage. This occurs not by conscious cooperation or deliberately pursuing a common end but by each man pursuing diverse ends in accordance with the "law" of the natural identity of interests, a "law" that is justified if not guaranteed in terms of metaphysical or economic or biological "truths". Authoritarian thinkers, on the other hand, justified coercion in the name of a pre-determined common end, the attainment of which cannot be left to the chaotic interplay of innumerable wills. The end may simply be the preservation of a traditional order, or the recovery of a bygone age of glory, or the ruthless reconstruction of society from the top to secure some spectacular consummation in the future.

It appears to be common to most schools of thought to accept a sharp dichotomy between ends and means, a distinction that is deeply embedded in our ethical and political and psychological vocabulary, rooted in rigid European presuppositions regarding the very nature of human action. Distinctions have been repeatedly made between immediate and ultimate, short-term and long-term, diverse and common, individual and social, essential and desirable ends, as also between attainable and utopian goals. Discussion about means has not ignored questions about their moral implications and propriety or about the extent of their theoretical and contingent compatibility with desired ends or widely shared values. But despite all these reservations, the dangerous dogma that the end entirely justifies the means is merely an extreme version of the commonly uncriticised belief that moral considerations cannot apply to the means except in relation to ends, or that the latter have a moral priority.

Gandhi seems to stand almost alone among social and political thinkers in his firm rejection of the rigid dichotomy between ends and means and in his extreme moral preoccupation with the means to the extent that they rather than the ends provide the standard of reference. He was led to this position by his early acceptance of satya and ahimsa, truth and nonviolence, as twin moral absolutes and his consistent view of their relationship. In Hind Swaraj he wrote that even great men who have been considered religious have committed grievous crimes through the mistaken belief that there is no moral connection or interdependence between the means and the end. We cannot get a rose through planting a noxious weed. "The means may be likened to a seed, the end to a tree; and there is just the same inviolable connection between the means and the end as there is between the seed and the tree."

It is not as though violence and nonviolence are merely different means to secure the same end. As they are morally different in quality and essence, they must necessarily achieve different results. The customary dichotomy between means and ends originates in, and reinforces, the view that they are two entirely different categories of action and that their relationship is mainly a technical matter to be settled by considering what will be effective and what is possible in a given situation, that the ethical problem of choice requires an initial decision regarding the desired end and the obligatory acceptance of whatever steps seem necessary to secure it or are most likely to do so. Gandhi, however, was led by his metaphysical belief in the "law" of karma-the "law" of ethical causation or moral retribution that links all the acts of interdependent individuals-to the view that the relationship between means and ends is organic, the moral quality of the latter being causally dependent upon that of the former. The psychology of human action in a morally indivisible community of apparently isolated units demands that the means-end relationship must be seen in terms of the consistent growth in moral awareness of individuals and communities and not in relation to the mechanical division of time into arbitrary and discrete intervals. If for Gandhi there was no "wall of separation" between means and end, this was because of his basic belief that in politics as in all spheres of human action we reap exactly what we sow.

Gandhi's view of the means-end relationship may be put in the form of the following statements, which overlap and yet express several distinct ideas: "For me it is enough to know the means. Means and end are convertible terms in my philosophy of life." "We have always control over the means but not over the end." "I feel that our progress towards the goal will be in exact proportion to the purity of our means." "They say 'means are after all means'. I would say 'means are after all everything'. As the means so the end."

The first statement rejects the notion that in our actual conduct we can make a firm and decisive distinction between means and ends. Gandhi's conception of the psychology of human action requires this rejection of a conventional conceptual habit which makes us ascribe to ourselves greater knowledge, and greater assurance, than we actually possess.

The second statement asserts a contingent truth about the extent and the limit of our free will, that the individual's capacity to determine what he can do in any specific situation at any given time is much greater than his power of anticipation, prediction and control over the consequences of his actions. The third statement expresses the metaphysical belief in the moral law of karma, under which there is an exact causal connection between the extent of the moral "purity" (detachment and disinterestedness or the degree of moral awareness) of an act and the measure of individual effectiveness in promoting or pursuing and securing a morally worthy end, over a period of time. Clearly, this metaphysical belief cannot be conclusively verified or falsified by evidence. The fourth statement is a practical recommendation that we must be primarily or even wholly concerned with the immediate adoption of what we regard as a morally worthy (*i.e.* intrinsically justifiable) means. This recommendation may be accepted by those who subscribe to the second statement and it is mandatory for those who share the metaphysical belief implicit in the third statement.

The closest approximation to Gandhi's view of the means-end relationship is that of Jacques Maritain, who regards the problem of End and Means as the basic problem in political philosophy. There are two opposite ways of understanding the "rationalization of political life". There is the easier nay of "technical rationalization" through means external to man, versus the more exacting way of "moral rationalization" through means which are man himself, his freedom and virtue. It is a universal and inviolable axiom for Maritain, an obvious primary principle, that "means must be proportioned and appropriate to the end, since they are ways to the end and, so to speak, the end itself in its very process of coming into existence. So that applying intrinsically evil means to attain an intrinsically good end is simply nonsense and a blunder."

If Maritain and Gandhi have no use for the "easier way of technical rationalization" or for piecemeal "social engineering", this is not merely because of their rejection of an utilitarian in favour of an absolutist (or non-naturalistic) ethic, but also because of their daringly unorthodox repudiation of the so-called pragmatist view of politics and the dominant doctrine of "double standards" which requires a sharp separation between the moral consideration applicable to individual conduct and those (if any) regarded as relevant to political action.

Gandhi's view of the morally legitimate means to be exclusively employed in furthering political ends was deeply affected by the doctrine of dispassionate action in the Gita. He was convinced that an intense concentration upon the task at hand can and must be combined with a degree of detachment, a freedom from anxiety about the future consequences. If we are sure of the "purity" of the means we employ, we shall be led on by faith, before which "all fear and trembling melt away". Unconcern with results does not mean that we need not have a clear conception of the end in view. But while the cause has to be just and clear as well as the means, it is even more important to recognise that "impure" means must result in an "impure" end, that we cannot attain to any truth through untruthful means, that we cannot secure justice through unjust means, or freedom through tyrannical acts, or socialism through enmity and coercion, or enduring peace through war. The man who wields force does not scruple about the means and yet foolishly imagines that this will make no difference to the end he seeks. Gandhi explicitly rejected the doctrine that the end justifies the means," and went so far as to assert that a moral means is almost an end in itself because virtue is its own reward.

The doctrine that the end justifies the means goes back to Kautilya in India and to Machiavelli in the West, and is connected with the notions of self-preservation at all costs and of raison d'etre and in more recent times with the attainment of a secular millennium through revolutionary action. The doctrine was implicit in Killing No Murder, Colonel Sexby's incitement to political assassination published in 1657. This once famous pamphlet argued that tyrants accomplish their end much more by fraud than by force and that if they are not eliminated by force the citizens would be degraded into deceitful, perfidious flatterers. It is not only "lawful" and even glorious to kill a tyrant, but indeed "everything is lawful against him that is lawful against an open enemy, whom every private man hath a right to kill". It is no doubt possible to justify tyrannicide without going so far as to say that a worthy end legitimizes any and every means. The difficulty, however, is that few practitioners would admit to holding to this maxim in an unqualified and unconditional form.

It has been argued repeatedly that any means is legitimate that is indispensable at least for internal security or to defend society against its external enemies. The sole reason for restricting the choice of means is expediency rather than principle, prudence rather than (non-utilitarian) morality. It is taken for granted that cunning and force must unite in the exercise of power. Power may he justified as a means to a higher end but in the attempt to employ any and every means to secure and maintain power it becomes an end itself. The idea that one is serving some higher entity which rises far above individual life and that one is no longer serving oneself makes one no less indifferent to the morality of the means employed than the open pursuit of naked self-interest. Alternatively, we have the straightforward Machiavellian notion that the individual agent cannot escape the nature he is born with, that as fortuna is malicious so virtu must also be malicious when there is no other way open. If virtu is the vital power in men which creates and maintains States, necessita is the causal pressure required to bring the sluggish masses into line with virtu. If there is a moral law, it must be flouted in the practice of politics and this infringement can be justified by the plea of unavoidable necessity. This line of reasoning is commoner than we like to think and is sometimes couched in such specious or emotive language that in moments of crisis many people are hardly aware of the wider implications of a doctrine that they invoke for their special pleading in what seem to be exceptional situations. Hume thought that this doctrine was so widely practised that it is safer in politics to assume that men are scoundrels even if we do not believe that all men are knaves.

It is true that thinkers like Machiavelli and Bentham have been rather unfairly accused of actually holding that there is an end justifying all means to it. Bentham said only that happiness is the end justifying all means, which is more an empty than a pernicious doctrine. Again, Machiavelli never said that power justifies all means to it, but merely that the gaining of power often involves committing some very nasty crimes. A similar defence could also be made on behalf of Kautilya. The important point, however, is not the precise standpoints of Bentham, Machiavelli or Kautilya, but the dangerous uses to which their doctrines could be put. Just as Benthamites, Machiavellians and followers of Kautilya could be charged with ruthlessness (even more than their teachers), so too Gandhians also could be accused of coercive tactics ("nonviolent" only in a very restricted sense) in the pursuit of worthy ends. But it would be much easier to challenge such Gandhians in terms of Gandhi's fundamental tenets than to appeal to the writings of Machiavelli or Bentham against diehard Machiavellians or Benthamite planners.

The doctrine that the end justifies the means does not even require any special justification for the Marxist who accepted no supra-historic morality, no categorical imperative, religious or secular. Engels declared in his letter to Herson Trier in 1889 that "any means that leads to the aim suits me as a revolutionary, whether it is the most violent or that which appears to be most peaceable". In his pamphlet on Socialism and War Lenin said that Marxists differed both from pacifists and anarchists in their belief that the justification of each war must be seen individually in relation to its historical role and its consequences. "There have been many wars in history which, notwithstanding all the horrors, cruelties, miseries and tortures inevitably connected with every war, have a progressive character, *i.e.* they served in the development of mankind, aiding in the destruction of extremely pernicious and reactionary institutions.... or helping to remove the most barbarous despotism in Europe." Whether an action is justifiable or not simply depends on what historical end it serves.

Unlike Engels and Lenin, Trotsky stressed what he called the dialectical interdependence of means and ends. He argued that the means chosen must be shown to be really likely to lead to the liberation of mankind. "Precisely from this it follows that not all means are permissible. When we say that the end justifies the means then for us the conclusion follows that the great revolutionary end spurns those base means and ways which set one part of the working class against other parts, or attempt to make the masses happy without their participation; or lower the faith of the masses in themselves and their organisation, replacing it by worship of the leaders" (Their Morals and Ours). This is clearly an improvement on Lenin, for it at least provides a criterion by which a collectivist regime or revolutionary leaders could be criticised for pushing an exclusively utilitarian creed to extremes of practical ruthlessness in perpetuating a monopoly of power and privilege.

Although Trotsky denied that the end justifies any and every means, he still insisted that a means can be justified only by its end, which for him is the increase of the power of man over nature and the abolition of the power of man over man. For Gandhi, on the other hand; the end is satya or truth, which requires no justification, and the means (ahimsa or non-coercion) must be justified not merely with reference to the end but also in itself; every act must be independently justified in terms of the twin absolutes, satya and ahimsa. It is, therefore, not permissible or possible to justify a single act of untruth or violence by appealing to the past or future possession of satya and ahimsa, though no man can wholly avoid a measure of himsa or asatya or claim to possess in their fullness absolute truth and absolute, universal love. Weakness and error are ubiquitous and inescapable, but their justification and rationalization make all the difference to our personal and political integrity. We cannot condone our untruthfulness in the present on the ground that we shall be truthful tomorrow when we are stronger or conditions are more favourable. A violent revolution cannot lead (and, in any case, cannot be justified on the ground that it is expected to lead) to a nonviolent society in the fullness of time. Further, in Gandhi's view it is not sometimes, as Trotsky suggested, but always (under the moral law of karma) that the end changes in character as a result of the means adopted in its attainment.

If the doctrine that the end justifies the means is invoked in the attainment of the good society through a single, violent revolution, it could also be made to justify repression in the aftermath of revolution.

In Abram Tertz's The Trial Begins we have the following dialogue between Rabinovich and Globov. Rabinovich holds that "every decent End consumes itself. You kill yourself trying to reach it and by the time you get there, it's been turned inside out. These Jesuits of yours made a miscalculation, they slipped up." Globov answers: "They were right. Every educated person knows that the end justifies the means. You can either believe it openly or secretly but you can't get anywhere without it. If the enemy does not surrender, lie must be destroyed. Isn't that so? And since all means are good, you must choose the most effective. Don't spare God himself in the name of God..... And as soon as one end is done with, another bobs up on the stage of history."

Similarly, when Rubashov in Darkness at Noon points out that violence starts a chain of cumulative consequences, Ivanov replies that no battalion commander can stick to the principle that the individual is sacrosanct, that the world has permanently been in an abnormal state since the invention of the steam engine and that the principle that the end justifies the means remains the only rule of practical ethics. It is ironical that while this doctrine is increasingly taken for granted by some Benthamite planners and Kautilyan diplomats in Gandhi's India, it has been openly questioned even in the most powerful society that has adopted Marxism as a State religion. Tile Russian poet, Yevgenv Yevtushenko, has stated, in a remarkable article, that Stalin was forgiven much in his lifetime because Soviet citizens were led to think that his acts were necessary for some higher purpose. "They steadily impressed upon us that the end justified the means. A great pain gives birth to a great 'flow of energy', as Stalin once declared. But even as we lamented him, many of us recalled our kin and our friends who had perished in the prisons. Naturally, to lock up such an enormous number of people required a truly prodigious amount of 'energy'. But people did not ponder on the fact that the aim itself may cease to be great, if one strives after it only with great energy and without paying much attention to the means. We realised that the means must be worthy of the end. This is an axiom, but an axiom that has been proved through much suffering."

Gandhi's way of combating the doctrine that the end justifies the means was by asserting not merely that unworthy means could belittle a great end but also that evil means can never, as a matter of fact, lead to good ends. Like the majority of Russian Populists, Gandhi was horrified by the advocacy of Machiavellian tactics and he thought that no end, however good, could fail to be destroyed by the adoption of monstrous means. His reason for believing this to be wholly and always true was his metaphysical conviction that the whole world is governed by the law of karma, that there is a moral order (rita) at the heart of the cosmos. Those who do not share this conviction, which is common to all the great religions and is especially prevalent in peasant societies, may well think that a lesser evil could lead to a greater good. This latter belief, which is no less non-empirical than the former, is taken for granted by many contemporary intellectuals, power holders, leaders of organizations and evangelists (whether theological teleologists or secular historicists). It is hardly surprising that Gandhi who even earlier than Benda recognised the betrayal of and alienation from the masses of narrowly based classes of intellectuals and power-seekers, appealed over their heads to the toiling masses to find recruits willing to dedicate themselves to the Constructive Programme and the development of a new social and political ethic. Gandhi did more than base his view of ends and means on a metaphysical faith in the moral law or his account of the necessary as well as contingent connection between satya and ahimsa. Truth and nonviolence, tolerance and civility. He also rejected the moral model underlying the sharp dichotomy between ends and means.

Moral life was not for Gandhi mainly a matter of achieving specific objectives, nor was politics like a field game in which a concrete objective is given in advance and known to all. No doubt, he regarded satya as the supreme common end for all men but its content cannot be known in advance. For Gandhi, as for the ancient Greeks, satya refers to the highest human activity rather than an imposed and pre-determined target. He evolved his political and social ethic in terms of a theory of action under which all our thinking and activity can be corrected and justified only by reference to satya and ahimsa, which are good in themselves and not merely the means to a higher good. It is only for the sake of these goods-in order that as much of them as possible may at some time exist-that anyone can be justified in undertaking any social or political activity. They are the raison d'etre of virtue and excellence; the ultimate test of human endeavour, the sole criterion of social progress.

In stating that Gandhi rejected the sharp dichotomy between ends and means, it is obviously not suggested that the distinction is entirely false and useless. Surely, everyone (including Gandhi) would agree that it is often possible to distinguish between ends and means, and also useful to do so. The distinction is most easily made when we are considering some particular purpose that a man might have in mind before embarking on a specific action. But if, like Bentham, we say that what a man wants is to get or to maximise "happiness" then it becomes much more difficult to make a clear distinction between the end (the greatest happiness) and all the various things said to be means to it.

For a man's conception of happiness depends largely upon his desiring the things said to be means to it. It happens to be true that the things usually held up as supreme ends of human endeavour (happiness, freedom, welfare, etc.) are empty notions, apart from the things said to be means to them. We must distinguish between men's goals and their principles, the rules they accept. Sometimes, of course, their goal is to inculcate a principle or to observe it themselves or get others to do so, but they have many other goals. But it seems to be more realistic to think of men as having a variety of goals, some of which matter more than others, than to think of them as having a supreme goal to which all others are subordinate, either as means to it or being willingly sacrificed whenever they conflict with it. The distinction between ends and means becomes misleading and dangerous when we dogmatize that there is a single supreme good or even a fixed hierarchy of goodness.

Gandhi did not lay down the law for all men or impose on nature a rigid, teleological pattern of his own. He merely argued from the proposition that all men have some idea of truth (satya) but no adequate conception of Absolute Truth (sat) to the prescription that society should regard the pursuit of satya as a common end. He further pointed out that in seeking the truth, we cannot help being true to our "real" natures (identical with that of all others) and this means exemplifying a measure of nonviolence in our attitudes and relations towards others.

It is possible (though questionable) for people to argue that the un happiness of some is required to maximize collective happiness, that individual citizens have to be coerced for the sake of general freedom, that the maintenance of public virtue sometimes requires subjects to choose (or support) privately corrupt but efficient and outwardly respectable rulers. It would, however, be difficult to contend that the collective pursuit of truth is compatible with the adoption of dishonest devices or the condoning of untruth. This could be advanced if a pre-ordained, collectivist conception of truth is imposed on the members of a society. A dogmatic ideology may be propagated by dishonest and ruthless methods.

Gandhi explicitly believed that no person or group could speak in the name of sat or Absolute Truth for the very reason that all are entitled to their relative truths, to satya as it appears to different people. As truth in this conception is identical with integrity (fidelity to one's own conscience), Gandhi could claim that no man can pursue greater integrity as an end by adopting means involving a sacrifice of the integrity he already has. The test of one's immediate moral integrity is nonviolence, it is a test of one's genuineness in the pursuit of, truth (*i.e.* of intellectual integrity) through one's actions in the midst of society.

If we understand the concept of satya and accept its pursuit as a common end, we cannot make a hard-and-fast distinction between this end and the means towards it that we employ. On the other hand, it is particularly if we regard the promotion of happiness as the whole duty of man that one become careless about the means and violate the "laws of morality". "The consequences of this line of thinking are writ large on the history of Europe", said Gandhi in his introduction to his paraphrase of Ruskin's Unto This Last. For Gandhi the polis is nothing more or less than the domain in which all men are free to gain skill in the art of action and learn how to exemplify satya and ahimsa; the arena in which both the individual quest could be furthered and the social virtues displaced among the masses of citizens in a climate of tolerance and civility; a morally progressive society in which neither the State nor any social organization is allowed to flout with impunity the sacred principle that every man is entitled to his relative truth and no one can claim the right to coerce another, to treat him as a means to his own end.

5

Brief Outline of Gandhi's Philosophy

This summary will attempt to describe Gandhi's philosophy in as simple a way as possible. Inevitably this must be a personal interpretation, but I hope it has some merit.

What is Gandhian philosophy? It is the religious and social ideas adopted and developed by Gandhi, first during his period in South Africa from 1893 to 1914, and later of course in India. These ideas have been further developed by later "Gandhians", most notably, in India, Vinoba Bhave and Jayaprakash Narayan. Outside of India some of the work of, for example, Martin Luther King Jr. can also be viewed in this light. Understanding the universe to be an organic whole, the philosophy exists on several planes-the spiritual or religious, moral, political, economic, social, individual and collective. The spiritual or religious element, and God, is at its core. Human nature is regarded as fundamentally virtuous. All individuals are believed to be capable of high moral development, and of reform.

The twin cardinal principles of Gandhi's thought are truth and nonviolence. It should be remembered that the English word "truth" is an imperfect translation of the Sanskrit, "satya", and "nonviolence", an even more imperfect translation of "ahimsa". Derived from "sat"-"that which exists"-"satya"contains a dimension of meaning not usually associated by English speakers with the word "truth". There are other variations, too, which we need not go into here. For Gandhi, truth is the relative truth of truthfulness in word and deed, and the absolute truth-the Ultimate Reality. This ultimate truth is God (as God is also Truth) and morality-the moral laws and code-its basis. Ahimsa, far from meaning mere peacefulness or the absence of overt violence, is understood by Gandhi to denote active love-the pole opposite of violence, or "himsa", in every sense. The ultimate station Gandhi assigns nonviolence stems from two main points. First, if according to the Divine Reality all life is one, then all violence committed towards another is violence towards oneself, towards the collective, whole self, and thus "self"-destructive and counter to the universal law of life, which is love. Second, Gandhi believed that ahimsa is the most powerful force in existence. Had himsabeen superior to ahimsa, humankind would long ago have succeeded in destroying itself. The human race certainly could not have progressed as far as it has, even if universal justice remains far off the horizon. From both viewpoints, nonviolence or love is regarded as the highest law of humankind.

Although there are elements of unity in Gandhi's thought, they are not reduced to a system. It is not a rigid, inflexible doctrine, but a set of beliefs and principles which are applied differently according to the historical and social setting. Therefore there can be no dogmatism, and inconsistency is not a sin. Interpretation of the principles underwent much evolution during Gandhi's lifetime, and as a result many inconsistencies can be found in his writings, to which he readily admitted. The reader of Gandhi's works published by Navajivan Trust will notice that many are prefaced with the following quotation from an April 1933 edition of "Harijan", one of Gandhi's journals. He states straightforwardly: "I would like to say to the diligent reader of my writings and to others who are interested in them that I am not at all concerned with appearing to be consistent. In my search after Truth I have discarded many ideas and learnt many news things.... What I am concerned with is my readiness to obey the call of Truth, my God, from moment to moment, and therefore, when anybody finds any inconsistency between any two writings of mine, if he still has any faith in my sanity, he would do well to choose the later of the two on the same subject."

That there are inconsistencies in Gandhi's writings accords with the fact that the ideas are not a system. In coming to grips with Gandhi's way of thinking it is most important to understand that the perception of truth undergoes an ongoing process of refinement which is evolutionary in nature.

In Gandhi's thought the emphasis is on idealism, but on practical idealism. It is rooted in the highest religious idealism, but is thoroughly practical. One label (and almost the only one) Gandhi was happy to have pinned on him was that of "practical idealist". The important principle of compromise is relevant here, as is the acknowledgement that perfect truth and perfect nonviolence can never be attained while the spirit is embodied.

As alluded to above, Gandhian philosophy is certainly considered by Gandhians as a universal and timeless philosophy, despite the fact that on the more superficial level it is set in the Indian social context. They hold that the ideals of truth and nonviolence, which underpin the whole philosophy, are relevant to all humankind. (Recently some have been suggesting that a distinction can be made between the core elements of Gandhi's thought and peripheral elements which, depending on the particular element under consideration, may or may not have timeless relevance.)

Also, it can be universal despite being fundamentally religious, as its religious position stresses not so much the Hindu interpretation of reality as the beliefs which are common to all major religions, and that commonality itself. It holds all religions to be worthy of equal respect and in one sense to be equal. As all are creations of mortal and imperfect human beings, no single religion can embody or reveal the whole or absolute truth.

Gandhian philosophy is also compatible with the view that humankind is undergoing gradual moral evolution. While conflict is seen as inevitable, in fact not always undesirable, violence as the result of conflict is not regarded as inevitable. Simply put, human beings do have the capacity to resolve conflict nonviolently. This might be difficult, but it is not impossible. Liberation from a violent society is seen as requiring many decades or longer-but it is not an imposible ideal.

Importantly also, it is not an intellectual doctrine. Gandhi was not an intellectual. Rather, Gandhi's thought was conceived, to a great extent, out of action and as a guide to action, by a man of action. He hesitated to write about anything of which he did not have personal, first-hand experience. In the sense of it being a call to action, Gandhi's thought can also be seen as an ideology.

As a guide to action, Gandhian philosophy is a double-edged weapon. Its objective is to transform the individual and society simultaneously (rather than in sequence, as Marxism describes), in accordance with the principles of truth and nonviolence. The historic task before humankind is to progress towards the creation of a nonviolent political, economic and social order by nonviolent struggle. The social goal was described by Gandhi as Sarvodaya, a term he coined in paraphrasing John Ruskin's book Unto This Last, meaning the welfare of all without exception. Its political aspect was expressed by the late eminent Gandhian Dr. R.R. Diwakar in the following words: "The good of each individual in society consists in his efforts to achieve the good of all." As the foundation of the Gandhian or nonviolent social order is religious or spiritual, economic and political questions are seen from the moral or humanistic perspective. The welfare of human beings, not of systems or institutions, is the ultimate consideration. Materially, it centres on the following concepts and ideals:

- Political decentralisation, to prevent massive concentrations of political power in the hands of too few; rather, to distribute it in the hands of many. The Gandhian political order takes the form of a direct, participatory democracy, operating in a tier structure from the base village-level tier upward through the district and state levels to the national (and international) level.
- Economic decentralisation, to prevent massive concentrations of economic power in the hands of too few, and again, to distribute it in the hands of many. Therefore villages, which are anyway geographically decentralised, become the basic economic units.

However, where unavoidable, certain industries may be organised on a more centralised basis, and their ownership and control come under the umbrella of the State.

- The minimisation of competition and exploitation in the economic sphere, and instead, the encouragement of cooperation.
- Production on the basis of need rather than greed, concentrating where India is concerned first on the eradication of poverty (and on the worst extreme of poverty).
- Recognition of the dignity of labour and the greater purity of rural life.
- The practice of extensive self-reliance by individuals, villages, regions and the nation.
- Absence of oppression on the basis of race, caste, class, language, gender or religion.
- A deep respect for mother nature, necessitating an economic system based upon the preservation rather than destruction of the natural environment.

Such concepts clearly represent pillars for a new social order.

A theory closely linked to the concept of Sarvodaya, also developed by Gandhi, is that of Trusteeship. Its fundamental objective is to create nonviolent and non-exploitative property relationships. Gandhi believed that the concepts of possession and private property were sources of violence, and in contradiction with the Divine reality that all wealth belongs to all people. However, he recognised that the concept of ownership would not wither easily, nor would the wealthy be easily persuaded to share their wealth. Therefore a compromise was to encourage the wealthy to hold their wealth in trust, to use themselves only what was necessary and to allow the remainder to be utilised for the benefit of the whole society.

It is apparent that Gandhi's philosophy has much in common with several Western philosophies which uphold the ideal of a more just and equitable society. For example, the Gandhian social order has been described as "communism minus violence". (However, Marxists have traditionally rejected Gandhi because of what they regard as his "bourgeois" outlook. Gandhi rejected violent class conflict and the centralisation of political and economic power in the hands of the State as counterproductive to the development of a nonviolent society.) Nevertheless, Gandhian philosophy, particularly in the Sarvodaya ideal, does contain many socialist sentiments. In fact, such an entity as Gandhian Socialism emerged in theoretical literature during the 1970s and 1980s. Gandhi's thought has been likened also to Utopian Socialism and Philosophical Anarchism, and can be compared with strands of Maoist thought (though not a Western philosophy), and even Western liberal thought. However, Gandhi is incompatible with many aspects of Liberalism and is virtually entirely incompatible with the modern, intensely competitive, ecologically destructive and materialistic capitalism of the West.

As already observed, Gandhi's thought is equally a philosophy of self-transformation. The individual's task is to make a sincere attempt to live according to the principles of truth and nonviolence. Its fundamental tenets are therefore moral. They include-resisting injustice, developing a spirit of service, selflessness and sacrifice, emphasising one's responsibilities rather than rights, self-discipline, simplicity of lifestyle, and attempting to maintain truthful and nonviolent relations with others. It should be understood that by simplicity is meant voluntary simplicity, not poverty, which has no element of voluntarism in it. If there is one thing Gandhi does not stand for, it is poverty. A Gandhian should also avoid political office. He or she should remain aloof from formal party politics and equi-distant from all political groupings. But this is not to say, and in my view Gandhi does not require, that the individual should remain aloof from all politics. For often injustice cannot be resisted unless the political power holders and structures are engaged, nonviolently. What was the freedom struggle itself if not a political struggle, against the greatest concentration of political power the world had ever known, the British Empire? In my eyes, there is no particular virtue in attempting to avoid contact with politics. What must be avoided, however, is assumption of political power by a Gandhian (at least this is necessary in the short and medium terms in India), and cooperation with unvirtuous holders of political power on their terms. The ultimate responsibility of a Gandhian is to resist clear injustice, untruth, in conjunction with others or alone. Resistance should be nonviolent if at all possible. But Gandhi did condone use of violent means in certain circumstances, in preference to submission which he regarded as cowardice and equivalent to cooperation with evil. In relation to the use of violence he stated categorically: "Where there is only a choice between cowardice and violence I would advise violence..." As surprising as it no doubt sounds, Gandhi disliked most not violence, but cowardice and apathy. The eminent peace researcher Johan Galtung has correctly observed that Gandhi preferred first, nonviolent resistance, second, violence in a just cause, and third, meaning least of all, apathy. In general, however, it is held that immoral means, such as violence, cannot produce moral ends, as means are themselves ends or ends in the making.

For the individual self-transformation is attempted with deliberateness rather than with haste. One should not seek to become a Mahatma overnight, because such attempts will surely fail, but to reform oneself over the whole of one's life, as far as one is capable. (Nor should there be any question of superficial imitation of Gandhi.) Gandhi viewed his own life as a process of development undertaken "one step at a time". He saw the need to continually "experiment with truth" (from which he derived the title of his autobiography) in whatever field, in order to come to see the truthful path. Though they were rooted in the highest idealism, the experiments were carried out on a very down-to-earth plane-India's moral, political and social needs as he saw them. Such an approach is available to all at all times. Gandhi believed his own moral and spiritual development to be far from complete at the time of his death. Despite the great heights he had attained, this was indeed true. He had not achieved perfection, as some of those who were close to him have testified.

The perception of what is the truthful path is largely a matter for the individual's reason and conscience, which therefore play key roles. The individual should subject each idea to the test of his or her own conscience and reason. Reason and rationality have enormous roles to play in the Gandhian way of thinking. This, I feel, is one of the major Western influences in Gandhi. If there is genuine, sincere disagreement, an idea can be discarded. However, once a principle is accepted a sincere attempt must be made to adhere to it. Ideally there should be harmony between thought, word and action. In this way the outer life becomes a true reflection of the inner, and a mental harmony is also achieved.

The remaining central concept in Gandhi's philosophy is Satyagraha. Defined most broadly (as Gandhi defined it), Satyagraha is itself a whole philosophy of nonviolence. Defined most narrowly, it is a technique or tool of nonviolent action. Because of the intention here to keep this discussion as simple as possible, Satyagraha will be described here in its latter guise. As a technique, Satyagraha was developed by Gandhi in South Africa to give the Indian population there a weapon with which to resist the injustices being perpetrated upon it by the colonial government. But Satyagraha can be practised in any cultural environment-provided the necessary ingredients are present, not least Satyagrahis (those capable of Satyagraha).

A Satyagraha campaign is undertaken only after all other peaceful means have proven ineffective. At its heart is nonviolence. An attempt is made to convert, persuade or win over the opponent. It involves applying the forces of both reason and conscience simultaneously. While holding aloft the indisputable truth of his or her position, the Satyagrahi also engages in acts of voluntary self-suffering. Any violence inflicted by the opponent is accepted without retaliation. But precisely because there is no retaliation (which can make the opponent feel his violence is justified), the opponent can only become morally bankrupt if violence continues to be inflicted indefinitely.

Several methods can be applied in a Satyagraha campaign, primarily noncooperation and fasting. The action is undertaken in the belief in the underlying goodness of the opponent, and in his or her ability to acknowledge the injustice of the action and to cease the injustice, or at least to compromise.

Satyagrahain this sense is highly creative. It creates no enemies, hatred or lasting bitterness, but ultimately only mutual regard.

After a successful campaign there is not the least hint of gloating, nor is there any desire to embarrass the opponent. The former opponent becomes a friend. There are no losers, only winners. A truthful Satyagraha campaign, though it demands courage, self-discipline and humility on the part of the Satyagrahi, brings to bear tremendous moral pressure on the opponent and can bring about remarkable transformations.

Two factors are absolutely crucial to understand. There can be no Satyagraha in a cause which is not indisputably just and truthful. Nor can there be any element of violence or bitterness in a Satyagraha campaign-it must be conducted in a spirit of genuine nonviolence. Any campaign which is insincere in its spirit of nonviolence, or is not undertaken in a clearly just cause is not Satyagraha as Gandhi meant it.

To sum up, Gandhian philosophy is not only simultaneously political, moral and religious, it is also traditional and modern, simple and complex. It embodies numerous Western influences to which Gandhi was exposed, but being rooted in ancient Indian culture and harnessing eternal and universal moral and religious principles, there is much in it that is not at all new. This is why Gandhi could say: "I have nothing new to teach the world. Truth and nonviolence are as old as the hills." Gandhi is concerned even more with the spirit than with the form. If the spirit is consistent with truth and nonviolence, the truthful and nonviolent form will automatically re sult. Despite its anti-Westernism, many hold its outlook to be ultra-modern, in fact ahead of its time-even far ahead. Perhaps the philosophy is best seen as a harmonious blend of the traditional and modern. The multifaceted nature of Gandhi's thought also can easily lead to the view that it is extremely complex. Perhaps in one sense it is. One could easily write volumes in describing it! Yet Gandhi described much of his thought as mere commonsense. Dr. Diwakar sums up Gandhi's thought in a few words: "The four words, truth, nonviolence, Sarvodaya and Satyagraha and their significance constitute Gandhi and his teaching." These are indeed the four pillars of Gandhian thought.

6

Mahatma and the Masses

It was the Rowlatt Bill with its denial of civil liberties which finally brought Gandhi into active Indian politics. From 1919 to his death in 1948, he occupied the centre of the Indian stage and was the hero of the great historical drama which culminated in the independence of his country. He changed the entire character of the political scene in India. He only grew. In the thick of the battle he remained a man of God.

Since the Rowlatt Bill was not a local issue and the struggle was to be launched on an all-India scale, Gandhi pondered deeply what shape it should take. He had to rouse the people's enthusiasm and yet keep their passions from breaking into violence. Finally, he hit upon the idea of hartal or a national observance of mourning or protest by the closing of shops and places of business.

The hartal was observed all over India, by Hindus and Muslims alike, with an enthusiasm which surprised every one. Even Gandhi had not realized how great was his hold on the imagination of the Indian masses. The Government's complacency received a rude shock to see the war-time "recruiting sergeant" of the Empire turn a rebel. When Gandhi who was now in demand everywhere left for Delhi and Amritsar, he was served with a notice at Palwal station forbidding him to cross into the Punjab. On his refusal to obey the order, he was arrested and brought back to Bombay.

The news of his arrest spread like wild fire and created great excitement among the people. Crowds gathered in cities and some violence took place. When Gandhi came to Ahmedabad and found that a police officer had been killed by the mob, he was horrified and felt that "a rapier run through my body could hardly have pained me more". He suspended the Satyagraha movement and undertook a fast for three days as penance for the violence committed by people.

On the very day, April 13, 1919, when Gandhi announced his three-day fast in Ahmedabad, the British General Dyer ordered the massacre of unarmed and peaceful citizens attending a meeting in Jallianwala Bagh at Amritsar. Later, even the official report admitted that 400 people had been killed and between 1,000 and 2,000 wounded, though the unofficial inquiry conducted by the Gandhi himself estimated 1,200 dead and 3,600 wounded. This cowardly massacre of the innocent was followed by the declaration of martial law in the Punjab, with wholesale arrests, floggings and the inhuman order by which no Indian could pass a certain street except by crawling on his belly. The events of that day which has been called by Sir Valentine Chirol as "that black day in the annals of British India" mark a turning point in the history of the Indian struggle. The moral prestige of Britain received a fatal blow. Henceforth, Gandhi could not keep away from the battlefield of Indian politics.

It was typical of Gandhi that great as was his concern over the happenings in the Punjab, he shared with equal zeal the Indian Muslim's concern at the rate of the defeated Turkish Sultan who was also the Caliph or the religious head of Islam. In fact, it was at a Muslim Conference held in Delhi in November 1919 that he first advocated noncooperation with the British Government.

It is interesting to recall that four years earlier, when he attended the Lucknow session of the Congress, he was more an observer than a participant and had seemed to Jawaharlal Nehru "very distant and different and unpolitical". In 1920, he dominated the political scene. In fact, he recreated the Congress and turned talking politicians into active revolutions and anglicized leaders of society into servants of the people who henceforth wore white homespun. He bridged the gulf between the intelligentsia and the masses and widened the concept of Swaraj to include almost every aspect of social and moral regeneration. From now on, the story of life is the story of how Congress fought for and won India's freedom.

Like a magician, Gandhi roused a storm of enthusiasm in the country with his call to non-cooperate. He began the campaign by returning to the Viceroy the medals and decorations he had received from the Government for his war-services and humanitarian work. "I can retain", he wrote to wrong to defend its immorality." Many Indians renounced their titles and honours, lawyers gave up their practice, students left colleges and schools, and thousand of the city-bred went into the villages to spread the message of nonviolent noncooperation with the "satanic" government and to prepare the masses of defy the law. The somnolent people woke up in a frenzy of courage and self-sacrifice. Bonfires of foreign cloth lit the sky everywhere and the hum of the spinning wheel rose like a sacrificial chant in thousands of homes. Women, secluded for centuries, marched in the streets with men and incidentally freed themselves from age-old shackles. In speech after speech, article after article in his two weeklies, Young India and Navjivan, Gandhi poured forth his passionate utterances which electrified the people. Thousands of people were put in prison and many more thousands were preparing to court arrest.

The anticlimax came suddenly in February 1922. An outbreak of mob violence in Chauri Chaura so shocked and pained Gandhi that he refused to continue the campaign and undertook a fast for five days to atone for a crime committed by others in a state of mob hysteria. Many of his colleagues protested and though Gandhi admitted that "the drastic reversal of practically the whole of the aggressive programme may be politically unsound and unwise", he maintained that "there is no doubt that it is religiously sound". He felt that "it is a million times better to appear untrue before the world than to be untrue to ourselves". Where Gandhi's conscience was concerned he was always ready to stand alone.

However, the immediate result was that the British Government found this anticlimax a convenient opportunity to arrest him. He told the English judge at the trial : " I have no personal ill-will against any single administrator, much less can I have any disaffection towards the King's person. But I hold it a virtue to be disaffected towards a government which in its totality has done more harm to Indian than any previous system. India is less manly under British rule than ever before. Holding such a belief I consider it a sin to have any affection for the system.......... The only course open to you, the judge is either to resign your post and thus dissociate yourself from evil, if you feel that the law you are called upon to administer is an evil and that in reality I am innocent; or to inflict on me the severest penalty if you believe that the system and the law you are assisting to administer are good for the people of this country, and that my activity is therefore, injurious to the public weal."

The judge sentenced him to six years' simple imprisonment and expressed the hope that "if the course of events in India should make it possible for the Government to reduce the period and release you, no one will be better pleased than I."

Prison was for Gandhi more a luxury than a punishment. He could devote more time to prayer, study and spinning than he could outside. But in January 1924 he fell seriously ill with acute appendicitis. He was removed to a hospital in Poona where a British surgeon performed the operation. While he was convalescing he was released by the Government.

What he saw of India as a free man greatly pained him. At the time of his arrest he had left his people on the wave of a great moral upsurge which had united Hindus and Muslims as never before. But in the meanwhile the Khilafat issue had been killed by Kamal Ataturk. The Muslims no longer needed Hindu support; the two communities had drifted apart. There were communal riots in several places. Not knowing how to stem this tide of frustration, he undertook a fast if twenty-one days a to atone once again for the sins of his people. "It seems as if God has been dethroned," he said, announcing the fast. "Let us reinstate Him in our hearts." The fast caused considerable heart-searching, and long before it was over, pledges of amity poured in upon him from men of various communities. For the next five years Gandhi seemingly retired from active agitational politics and devoted himself to the propagation of what he regarded as the basic national needs, namely, Hindu-Muslim unity, removal of untouchability, equality of women, popularization of hand-spinning and the reconstruction of village economy in general. "I am not interested". He wrote in June 1923, "freeing India merely from the English yoke. I am bent upon freeing and social and economic freedom, must go together.

There was also the fact that Gandhi, on his release from prison, had found the Congress divided. By 1929, however, the various groups had once more rallied under his leadership, and when on the last day of that year he himself moved the Resolution in the Congress session declaring complete Independence as the goal of Congress policy, it was obvious that he was again ready to lead the nation in an open challenge which was taken by millions throughout the country on January 26, 1930, which day has been celebrated as Independence as the goal of Congress policy, it was obvious that he was again ready to lead the nation in an open challenge to British rule. He drew up a pledge of "Purna Swaraj" or complete independence which was taken by millions throughout the country on January 26, 1930, which day has been celebrated as Independence Day ever since. All eyes were now turned to Sabarmati. What will the wizard of nonviolence do next?

On March 12, 1930, after having duly informed the Viceroy, Gandhi, followed by seventy-eight members of his ashram, both men and women, began his historic 24-day march to the sea beach at Dandi to break the law which had deprived the poor man of his right to make his own salt.

This seemed a small issue, but the dramatic manner in which he announced and executed the plan, the march on foot of this unarmed man of God for 241 miles, with villagers flocking from miles around to kneel by the roadside, set the imagination of the nation aflame and roused enthusiasm such as no one had anticipated. Early in the morning of April 6, after prayers, he went to the beach and picked up a little lump of salt left by the waves.

This simple act was immediately followed by a nationwide defiance of the law. Men and women, simple villagers and sophisticated city folk, marched in thousands to invite arrest, police lathi charges and even shooting in many cases. Gandhi himself was arrested on May 4, soon after midnight. Within a few weeks about a hundred thousand men and women were in jail, throwing mighty machinery of the British Government out of gear.

When the First Round Table Conference met in November 1930, the Labour Government was faced with an embarrassing situation. At the closing session of the Conference, on January 19, 1931, Ramsay MacDonald expressed the hope that the Congress would be represented at the Second Round Tabie Conference. Gandhi and some other Congress leaders were therefore unconditionally released on January 26, exactly a year after the first independence pledge had been taken.

Soon after, on February 14, the Gandhi-Irwin talks began to the disgust of Winston Churchill, who was scandalized at "the nauseating and humiliating spectacle of this one-time Inner Temple Lawyer, now seditious fakir, striding half-naked up the steps of the Viceroy's palace, there to negotiate a parley on equal terms with the representative of the King-Emperor."

Interlude in England and a Christmas Gift

On March 5 was signed the Gandhi-Irwin Pact and on August 29 Gandhi sailed for London to attend the Second Round Table Conference as the delegate of the Congress. "There is every chance of my returning empty-handed", he said, as he embarked. He was right. But though he returned empty-handed, his visit was not without good results. He had by now become a legend and fantastic stories, some kind some malicious, had spread about him. It was good therefore for the British people to see for themselves how simple, kindly and irresistible was the charm of his personality, how universal his sympathies, how keen his humour and infectious his laughter.

In London, he declined to go to a hotel and stayed at Kingsley Hall, a social service centre in the East End, where he soon won the hearts of the young and old. His kindliness and his humour broke down the barriers of national and race prejudice. When asked why he chose to wear only a loin-cloth, he replied, "You people wear plus-fours, mine are minus-four." He went to Lancashire where his agitation against foreign cloth had caused unemployment. The workers cheered him and one of the unemployed said : "I am one of the unemployed, but if I was in India I would say the same thing that Mr. Gandhi is saying."

On his way back he visited Romain Rolland in Switzerland. It was at a meeting of the pacifists at Lausanne that he explained why rather than say, god is Truth, he would say, Truth is God.

The day he reached Bombay he said: "I am not conscious of a single experience throughout my three months stay in England and Europe that made me feel that after all East is East and West is West. On the contrary, I have been convinced more than ever that human nature is much the same, no matter under what clime it flourishes, and that if you approached people with trust and affection you would have ten-fold trust and thousand-fold affection returned to you."

But the immediate experience that awaited him hardly bore out this optimism. Even before he had reached India, the effect of the Gandhi-Irwin Pact had been destroyed by the repressive policy of the new Viceroy, Lord Willingdon. India was being ruled by Ordinances, and shooting and arrests had become the order of the day. Jawaharlal Nehru who was coming to Bombay to receive Gandhi was arrested on the way. "I take it", said Gandhi when he landed on December 28, 1931, "that these are Christmas gifts from Lord Willingdon, our Christian Viceroy." A week later Gandhi himself was arrested and locked up in Yervada Jail without trial.

Quit India

With the Outbreak of the war in 1939, Gandhi was dragged back into the political arena. He had loyally supported the Empire in the First World War. In the Boer War, even though his moral sympathies were with the Boers who were fighting for their independence, he had offered his services to the Empire out of a sense of loyalty. His feelings were different now, though, as stated, "my sympathies are wholly with the allies." He had came to believe "all war to be wholly wrong". He was also aware of the anomaly in Britain's position in fighting for freedom while denying India her. There were many patriots in India who felt that this was the hour to strike, since Britain's difficulty was India's opportunity. But Gandhi refused to countenance such an attitude. "We do not seek our independence out of Britain's ruin. That is not the way of nonviolence."

The majority of Congress leaders would have welcomed participation in the war effort, provided India could do so as an equal partner with Britain. Gandhi did not believe in conditional nonviolence, but he was realistic enough to know that he could not carry the majority of the Congress leaders, who were at best patriot-politicians, not saints, along the arduous path of absolute nonviolence. Nor was he vain enough to insist on the Congress accepting his terms as the price of his leadership, though he knew that in the impending political crisis the party could not do without him. He therefore effaced himself and advised the nation to accept the Congress stand and pleaded with the British on its behalf.

But the British Government was in no mood to listen and Winston Churchill was frank enough to say that he had not become "the King's First Minister in order to preside at the liquidation of the British Empire." In the meanwhile, the situation rapidly deteriorated. The British were unable to stem the Japanese advance to the Indian border.

The people were becoming increasingly restive and impatient, and Gandhi feared that if this excitement were not given an organized nonviolent expression, it would break out in sporadic disorder and violence. Since the British did not seem able at that time to ensure India's defence and were not willing to let India defend herself, Gandhi called upon them to "Quit India" and prepared to organize Satyagraha. Addressing historic session of the All India Congress Committee on August 7, 1942, he said : Our quarrel is not with the British people; we fight their imperialism. The proposal for the withdrawal of British power did not come out of anger. It came to enable India to play its due part at the present critical juncture."

He had not yet formulated any clear plan of action. In any case, he wanted to see the Viceroy before doing so. But the initiative was taken away from his hands, for in the early hours of the morning of August 9, he and other leaders of the Congress were arrested. Disorders broke out immediately all over India, many of them violent. The Government having deprived the people of nonviolent leadership answered violence with greater violence till India virtually became a country under armed occupation.

Gandhi was interned in the Aga Khan Palace near Poona. He was greatly perturbed by the terror reigning in the country and at the British Government's charge that he was responsible for violence. He entered into a long correspondence with the Government which ended in his fasting for twenty-one years. During the fast, which began on February 10, 1943, his condition grew very critical and it was feared that he would not survive. Fortunately he did. This period in prison was one of tribulation and tragedy for Gandhi. Six days after his arrest, Mahadev Desai, his secretary and companion for twenty-four years, died suddenly of heart failure. In December 1943, Kasturbai fell ill and in February of the following year she, too, died.

The mental strain he had gone through his arrest told on Gandhi's health and six weeks after Kasturbai's death he had a severe attack of malaria. On May 3, the doctor's bulletin described his general condition as "giving rise to anxiety." The Government, embarrassed by the public agitation caused by the news of his illness, released him unconditionally on May 6. For a long time after, he was so weak that to conserve his energy he was obliged to observe long periods of silence.

But weak or strong, he could not sit idle and watch the situation in the country rapidly deteriorate. He asked to see the Viceroy but Lord Wavell declined to meet him. He knew that the British were encouraging Muslim demands to keep the Hindus and Muslims divided and were using this difference as an excuse for their continued occupation of India. Although his political career he had worked passionately for Hindu-Muslim accord. In 1919, he had made the Khilafat cause his own and had later fasted to bring about communal harmony. But the more he tried to placate the Muslims the more adamant and extravagant grew their demands until their leader Jinnah would be satisfied with nothing less than a separate state for the Muslims.

Freedom and Martyrdom

The British were unable to control the situation in India which was steadily becoming worse. Famine and disorder had sapped the foundations of imperial prestige. Britain emerged from the war victorious but physically exhausted and morally sober. The general elections of 1945 returned Labour to power and Mr. Attlee, the British Prime Minister, unwilling to lose India altogether by persisting in the Church illian policy of blood and iron, promised "an early realization of self Government in India." In the meanwhile, elections were to be held and a Constituent Assembly convened to frame a constitution for a united India. A Cabinet Mission arrived from England to discuss with Indian leaders the future shape of a free and united India, but failed to bring the Congress and Muslims together. Having encouraged Muslims separatism the British were now unable to control it,

On August 12, 1946, the Viceroy invited Jawaharlal Nehru to form an interim government. Jinnah declared a "Direct Action Day" in Bengal which resulted in an orgy of bloodshed. Shootings and stabbing took place in many places in India. This blood-red prologue to freedom was pure agony for Gandhi. He was staying in the Bhangi colony (untouchable's quarters) in Delhi from where day after day he raised his voice against violence. But his voice seemed a voice in the wilderness.

Then came the news of a large-scale outbreak of violence against the Hindu minority In the Noakhali district of East Bengal. Gandhi could no longer sit quite. He must beard the lion in his own den and teach the two communities to live and let live if necessary at the cost of his life. If he could not do that his message of nonviolence had fallen on deaf at the ears and the freedom to which he had brought India so near was not the freedom he had dream of. And so, against the pleading of his Congress colleagues who did not wish that he should risk his life, he left for Noakhali in Bengal where the Muslim

League government was in power. While in Calcutta, he heard that the Hindus of Bihar had retaliated against the Muslims, repeating the outrages of Noakhali. Bitter sorrow filled Gandhi's heart, for he always felt the misdeeds of his co-religionists more acutely than he did of others, and Bihar was the land where he had launched his first Satyagraha in India. As penance, he resolved to keep himself "on the lowest diet possible" which would become "a fast unto death if the erring Biharis have not turned over a new leaf." Fortunately, "the erring Bihari's were restored to sanity by this warning and Gandhi proceeded to Noakhali.

In the noble book of Gandhi's life this chapter is the noblest. Just when political freedom was almost achieved and the State apparatus of power his for the asking, he renounced it and embraced the hazards of a lone pilgrimage to plant the message of love and courage in a wilderness of hatred and terror. In a region were 80 per cent of the people were Muslim, most of whom hostile, where there were hardly any roads and almost no means of modern communication, where hundreds of Hindus had been butchered, their women raped and thousands forcibly converted and where hordes of unruly fanatics still roamed the countryside in search of loot and fresh victims. Gandhi pitched his camp, refusing police protection and keeping only one Bengali interpreter and one stenographer with him. At the age of seventy-seven, he went barefoot from village to village, through a most difficult countryside, where low, marshy patches had to be crossed on precarious, improvised bridges of bamboo poles. He lived on local fruit and vegetables and worked day and night to plant courage in the hearts of the Hindus and love in the hearts of the Muslims. "I have only one object in view and it is a clear one : namely, that God should purify the hearts of Hindus and Muslims and the two communities should be free from suspicion and fear of one another."

Thus he lived and suffered and taught in Noakhali from November 7, 1946, to March 2, 1947, when he had to leave for Bihar in answer to persistent request. In Bihar also, he did what he had done in Noakhali. He went from village to village, mostly on foot, asking to people to make amends for the wrongs they had done to the Muslims. Unlike Noakhali, he was besieged by worshipping crowds wherever he went in Bihar. He collected money for the relief of the injured and homeless Muslims. Many women gave away their jewellery. Harrowing tales were pouring in of the massacre of the Hindus in Rawalpindi in the Punjab and but for Gandhi's presence the Biharis might have again lost their heads in a frenzy of retaliation. "If ever you become mad again, you must destroy me first", he told them.

In May 1947, he was called to Delhi where the new Viceroy, Lord Mountbatten had succeeded in persuading the Congress leaders to accept Jinnah's insistent demand for the partition of India as a condition precedent for British withdrawal. Gandhi was against partition at any cost but he was unable to convince the Congress leaders of the wisdom of his stand.

On August 15, 1947, India was partitioned and became free. Gandhi declined to attend the celebrations in the capital and went to Calcutta where communal riots were still raging. And then on the day of independence a miracle happened. A year-old riot stopped as if by magic and Hindus and Muslims began to fraternize with one another. Gandhi spent a day in fast and prayer.

Unfortunately, the communal frenzy broke loose again on August 31, and while he was staying in a Muslim house, the safety of his own persons was threatened. On the following day he went on a fast which was "to end only if and when sanity returns to Calcutta". The effect was magical. Those who had indulged in loot, arson and murder amid shouts of glee, came and knelt by his beside and begged for forgiveness. On September 4, the leaders of all communities in the city brought him a signed pledge that Calcutta would see no more of such outrages. Then Gandhi broke the fast. Calcutta kept the pledge even when many other cities were plunged in violence in the wake of Partition.

When Gandhi returned to Delhi in September 1947, the city was in the grip of communal hysteria. Ghastly tales of what had happened to Hindus and Sikhs in West Pakistan had kindled passions which burst into a conflagration when the uprooted victims of this tragedy poured into the city. In the frenzy of vengeance Hindu and Sikhs had taken the law into their hands and were looting Muslim houses, seizing mosques and stabbing innocent passer-by. The Government had taken stern measures but it was helpless without public cooperation. Into this chaos of fear and terror came this little man in the loin-cloth to bring courage to the frightened, comfort to the afflicted and sanity to the frenzied.

On his birthday October 2, when messages and greetings poured in from all over the world, he asked: "Where do congratulations come in? Would it not be more appropriate to send condolences? There is nothing but anguish in my heart... I cannot live while hatred and killing mar the atmosphere."

His anguish continued and increased. Though his presence had calmed the fury in Delhi, sporadic violence had occurred. The tension was still there and the Muslims could not move about freely in the streets. Gandhi was anxious to go to Pakistan to help the harassed and frightened minorities there but could not leave Delhi until the mood of the people was such as to assure him that the madness would not flare up again. He felt helpless and since, as he put it, "I have never put up with helplessness in all my life", he went on a fast on January 13, 1948. "God sent me the fast", he said. He asked people not to worry about him and to "turn the searchlight inward".

It was turned, although it is difficult to say how deep the light penetrated. On January 18, after a week of painful suspense and anxiety, representatives of various communities and organizations in Delhi including the militant Hindu organization known as R.S.S., came to Birla house where Gandhi lay on a cot, weak but cheerful, and gave him a written pledge that "we shall protect the life, property and faith of the Muslims and that the incidents which have taken place in Delhi will not happen again". Gandhi then broke the fast amid the chanting of passages from the various scriptures of the world.

Though the fast had touched the hearts of millions all over the world, its effect on the Hindu extremists was different. They were incensed at the success of the fast and felt that Gandhi had blackmailed the Hindu conscience to appease Pakistan.

On the second day after the fast while Gandhi was at his usual evening prayers, a bomb was thrown at him. Fortunately it missed the mark. Gandhi sat unmoved and continued his discourse.

It had been practice for many years to pray with the crowd. Every evening, wherever he was, he held his prayers in an open ground, facing a large congregation. No orthodox ritual was followed at these prayers. Verses from the scriptures of various religions were recited and hymns sung. At the end Gandhi would address a few words in Hindi to the congregation, not necessary on a religious theme but on any topic of the day. Whatever the topic, he raised it to a moral and spiritual plane so that even when he talked of a political issue it was as if a religious man were teaching the way of righteousness.

Sometimes these congregations were of a few hundred only and sometimes they ran into hundred of thousands, depending on the place where the prayers were held. Men of all faiths and of all political persuasions were free to come. There was no restriction. Sitting on a raise platform he was always an easy target. So far the only protection he needed was form the unbounded adulation of the adoring crowds anxious to touch his feet as is the Hindu way of showing reverence. But now the times were unhappy. Violent passions had been aroused. Hatred was in the air. Hindu fanatics were impatient with his doctrine of love and looked upon him as the main stumbling block to their lust for vengeance against Muslim atrocities in Pakistan. As in Pakistan, so here, the cry of religion in danger served as a cloak of idealism for the demon of barbaric passions. He had been warned.

The police were nervous. But Gandhi refused any kind of police protection. He care not to live except by the power of love. Forty years earlier when his life was threatened by a Pathan in South Africa, he had replied : "Death is appointed end of all life. To die by the hand of a brother, rather than by disease or in such other way, cannot be for me a matter of sorrow. And if, even in such a case, I am free from the thought of anger or hatred against my assailant, I know that will redound to my eternal welfare."

These sublime words proved to be prophetic. On January 30, 1948, ten days after the bomb incident, Gandhi hurriedly went up the few steps of the prayer ground in the large park of the Birla House. He had been detained by a conference with the Deputy Prime Minister, Sardar Vallabhbhai Patel, and was late by a few minutes. He loved punctuality and was worried that he had kept the congregation waiting. "I am late by ten minutes," he murmured. "I should be here at the stroke of five." He raised his hands and touched the palms together to greet the crowd that was waiting. Every one returned the greeting. Many came forward wanting to touch his feet. They were not allowed to do so, as Gandhi was already late. But a young Hindu from Poona forced his way forward and while seeming to do obeisance fired three point-blank shots from a small automatic pistol aimed at the heart. Gandhi fell, his lips uttering the name of God (He Ram). Before medical aid could arrive the heart had ceased to beat-the heart that had beat only love of man.

Thus died the Mahatma, at the hands of one of his own people, to the eternal glory of what he had lived for and to the eternal shame of those who failed to understand that he was the best representative of the religion for which he suffered martyrdom.

The nation's feeling was best expressed by Prime Minister Nehru when with a trembling voice and a heart full of grief he gave the news to the people on the radio:

> *"The light has gone out of our lives and there is darkness everywhere and I do not quite know what to tell you and how to say it. Our beloved leader, Bapu as we call him, the father of our nation, is no more... The light has gone out, I said, and yet I was wrong. For the light that shone in this country was no ordinary light. The light that has illumined this country for these many years, and the world will see it and it will give solace to innumerable hearts. For that light represented the living truth, and the eternal man was with us with his eternal truth reminding us of the right path, drawing us from error, taking this ancient country to freedom..."*

Such men cannot die, for they live in their achievements. His were many, each one of which, judged by the greatness of its execution or in its results for human welfare, would have made his name immortal anywhere in the world. He brought freedom from foreign subjection to a fifth of the human race. The freedom he wrought for India naturally includes that of Pakistan, for the latter was an offshoot of the former. Of no less importance was what he did for those who were once known as the untouchables. He freed millions of human beings from the shackles of caste tyranny and social indignity by his insistence that freedom was to be measured by the well-being of the millions who were living in the villages, he laid the foundation for a new way of life which may one day well provide an effective alternative to both a regiment and an acquisitive economy. His martyrdom shamed his people out of communal hysteria and helped to establish the secular and democratic character of the Indian State.

The moral influence of his personality and of his gospel and technique of nonviolence cannot be weighed in any material scale. Nor is its value limited to any particular country or generation it is his imperishable gift to humanity.

7

Gandhi's Philosophy of Education

EDUCATION AS PER MAHATMA GANDHI

Medium of Education

I find daily proof of the increasing & continuing wrong being done to the millions by our false de-Indianizing education.

We seem to have come to think that no one can hope to be like a Bose unless he knows English. I cannot conceive a grosser superstition than this. No Japanese feels so helpless as we seem to do....

The medium of instruction should be alerted at once, and at any cost, the provincial languages being given their rightful place. I would prefer temporary chaos in higher education to the criminal waste that is daily accumulating.

Education through a foreign Language entails a certain degree of strain, and our boys have to pay dearly for it. To a large extent, they lose the capacity of shouldering any other burden afterwards., for they become a useless lot who are weak of body, without any zest for work and imitators of the West. They have little interest in original research or deep thinking, and the qualities of courage, perseverance. bravery and fearlessness are lacking. That is why we are unable to make new plans or carry our projects to meet our problems. In case we make them to fail to implement them. A few who do show promise usually die young.......

We, the English educated people alone are unable to assess the great loss that this factor has caused. Some idea of its immensity would be had if we could estimate how little we have influenced the general mass of our people.

The school must be an extension of home there must be concordance between the impressions which a child gathers at home and at school, if the best results are to be obtained. Education through the medium of strange tongue breaks the concordance which should exist. Those who breaks this relationship are enemies of the people even though their motives may be honest. To be a voluntary victim of this system of education is as good as the betrayal of our duty towards our mothers. The harm done by this alien type of education does not stop here; it goes much further. It has produced a gulf between the educated classes and the masses. The people look on us as beings apart from them.

It is my considered opinion that English education in the manner it has been given has emasculated the English educated Indian, it has put a severe strain upon the Indian students' nervous energy and has made of us imitators. The process of displacing the vernaculars has been one of the saddest chapters in the British connection. Ram Mohan Rai would have been a greater reformer, and Lokmanya Tilak would have been a greater scholar, if they had not to start with the handicap of having to think in English and transmit their thoughts chiefly in English. Their effect on their own people, marvellous as it was, would have been greater if they would have been brought under a less unnatural system. No dought they both gained from their knowledge of the rich treasures of English literature. But these should have been accessible to them through their own vernaculars. No country can become a nation by producing a race of imitators.

English is today studied because of its commercial and so called political value. Our boys think and rightly in the present circumstances, that without English they cannot get Government service. Girls are taught English as a passport to marriage. I know several instances of women wanting to learn English so that they may be able to talk in English. I know families in which English is made a mother tongue. Hundreds of youth believe that without the Knowledge of English, freedom of India is practically impossible.

The canker has so eaten into the society that in many cases the only meaning of education is Knowledge of English. All these are for me signs of our slavery and degradation. It is unbearable to me that the vernaculars should be crushed and starved as they have been. I cannot tolerate the idea of parents writing to their children, or husbands writing to their wives, not in their own vernaculars but in English.

The foreign medium has caused brains fag, put an undue strain upon the nerves of our children, made them crammers and imitators, unfitted them for original work and thought, and disabled them for filtrating their learning to the family or the masses. The foreign medium has made our children practically foreigners in their own lands. It is the greatest tragedy of the existing system. The foreign medium has prevented the growth of our vernaculars. If I had the powers of a despot, I would today stop the tuitions of our boys and girls through a foreign medium and require all the teachers and professors on pain of dismissal to introduce the change forthwith. I would not wait for the preparation of Text books. They will follow the change. It is an evil that need a summary remedy.

Among the many evils of foreign rule, this blighting imposition of a foreign medium upon the youth of the country will be counted by history as one of the greatest. It has sapped the energy of the nation, it has estranged them for the masses, it has made education unnecessarily expensive. If this process is still persisted in, it bids fair to rob the nation of its soul. The sooner, therefore educated India shakes itself free from the hypnotic spell of the foreign medium, the better it would be for them and the people

Buniyadi Shiksha (Basic Education)

The ancient aphorism "Education is that which liberates", is as true as it was before. Education here does not mean mere spiritual knowledge, nor does liberation signify spiritual liberation after death. Knowledge includes all training that is useful for the service of mankind and liberation means freedom of all manner of servitude is of two kinds: slavery to domination from outside and to one's own artificial needs. The knowledge acquired in the pursuit of this ideal alone contributed true study.

Persistent questioning and healthy inquisitiveness are the first requisite for acquiring learning of any kind. Inquisitiveness should be tempered by humility and respectful regard for the teacher. It must not degenerate into impudence. The latter is the enemy of the receptivity of mind. There can be no knowledge without humility and the will to learn education must be of a new type for the sake of the creation of the new world. Everyone of us has good inherent in the soul it needs to be drawn out by the teachers, and only those teachers can perform this sacred function whose own character is unsullied, who are always ready to learn and to grow from perfection to perfection.

Useful manual labour, intelligently performed is the means par excellence for developing the intellect......

A balance intellect presupposes a harmonious growth of body mind & soul..... An intellect that is developed through the medium of socially useful labour will be an instrument for service and will not easily be led astray or fall into devious paths.

Craft, Art, Health and education should all be integrated into one scheme. Nai Taleem is a beautiful blend of all the four and covers the whole education of the individual from the time of conception to the moment of death...... Instead of regarding craft & industry as different from education. I will regard the former as the medium for the latter.

Our system of education leads to the development of the mind, body and soul. The ordinary system cares only for the mind.

The teachers earn what they take. It stands for the art of living. Therefore, both the teacher and the learning. It enriches life from the commencement. It makes the nation independent of the search for employment.

It is popularly and correctly described as education through handicrafts. This is part of the truth. The root of this new education goes much deeper. It lies in the application of the truth and love in every variety of human activity, weather in individual life or a corporate one. The notion of education through handicrafts rises from the contemplation of truth and love permeating life's activities. Love requires that true education should be easily accessible to all, and should be of use to every villager in his daily life, such education is not derived from nor does it depend upon books. It has no relation to sectional religion. If it can be called religious, it is universal religion from which all select religions are derived. Therefore it is learned from the book of life which costs nothing and which cannot be taken away from one by any force on earth.

I hold that the largest time is devoted of our time is devoted to labour for earning our bread, our children must from their infancy be taught the dignity of such labour. Our children should not be taught as to despise labour. There is no reason why a peasants son after having gone to school should become useless as he does become, as an agricultural labourer.

Gandhi's Views on Education

Character cannot be built with mortar and stone. It cannot be built by hands other than your own.

An education which does not teach us to discriminate between good and bad, to assimilate the one and eschew the other, is a misnomer.

Education should be so revolutionized as to answer the wants of the poorest villager, instead of answering those of an imperial exploiter.

Education in the understanding of citizenship is a short-term affair if we are honest and earnest.

Basic education links the children, whether of cities or the villages, to all that is best and lasting in India.

Is not education the art of drawing out full manhood of the children under training?

Literacy in itself is no education.

Literacy is not the end of education nor even the beginning.

Literacy education should follow the education of the hand-the one gift that visibly distinguishes man from beast.

Real education has to draw out the best from the boys and girls to be educated.

True education must correspond to the surrounding circumstances or it is not a healthy growth.

What is really needed to make democracy function is not knowledge of facts, but right education.

National education to be truly national must reflect the national condition for the time being.

The function of Nayee-Taleem is not to teach an occupation, but through it to develop the whole man.

I believe that religious education must be the sole concern of religious associations.

By education I mean an all-round drawing out of the best in the child and man-body, mind and spirit.

By spiritual training I mean education of the heart.

Experience gained in two schools under my control has taught me that punishment does not purify, if anything, it hardens children.

I consider writing as a fine art. We kill it by imposing the alphabet on little children and making it the beginning of learning.

I do regard spinning and weaving as the necessary part of any national system of education.

The aim of university education should be to turn out true ervants of the people who will live and die for the country's reedom.

A balanced intellect presupposes a harmonious growth of body, mind and soul.

Love requires that true education should be easily accessible to all and should be of use to every villager in this daily life.

The notion of education through handicrafts rises from the contemplation of truth and love permeating life's activities.

The fees that you pay do not cover even a fraction of the amount that is spent on your education from the public exchanger.

Persistent questioning and healthy inquisitiveness are the first requisite for acquiring learning of any kind.

If we want to impart education best suited to the needs of the villagers, we should take the Vidyapith to the villages.

In a democratic scheme, money invested in the promotion of learning gives a tenfold return to the people even as a seed sown in good soil returns a luxuriant crop.

All education in a country has got to be demonstrably in promotion of the progress of the country in which it is given.

The schools and colleges are really a factory for turning out clerks for Government.

The canker has so eaten into the society that in many cases the only meaning of education is a knowledge of English.

The emphasis laid on the principle of spending every minute of one's life usefully is the best education for citizenship

To Students

Character cannot be built with mortar and stone. It cannot be built by hands other than your own. The Principal and the professor cannot give you character from the pages of the books. Character building comes from their very lives and really speaking, it must come within yourselves.

Put all tour knowledge, learning & scholarship in one scale and truth and purity in the other and the latter will far outweigh the other. The miasma of moral impurity has today spread among our school going children and like a hidden epidemic is working havoc among them. All your scholarship, all your study of the scriptures will be in vain if you fail to translate their teachings into your daily life.....

If teachers impart all the knowledge in the world to their students but inculcate not truth and purity among them., they will have betrayed them and instead of raising them set them on the downward road to perdition. Knowledge without character is a power for evil only, as seen in the instances of so many talented thieves and gentlemen rascals in the world. As to use of the vacation by students, if will they approach the work with zeal, they can undoubtedly do many things. I enumerate a few of them:

1. Conduct night & day schools with just a short course, well conceived, to last the period of the vacation.
2. Visit Harijan quarters and clean them, taking the assistance of Harijan if they would give it.
3. Taking Harijan children for excursions, showing them sights near the villages and teaching them how to study nature, and generally interesting them in their surroundings giving them by the way a working knowledge of geography & history.
4. Reading to them simple stories from the Ramayana and the Mahabharata.
5. Teaching them simple Bhajans.
6. Cleaning the Harijan boys of all the dirt that they would find about their persons and giving both the grown ups and the children simple lessons in hygiene.
7. Taking a detailed census in selected areas of the conditions of the Harijans.
8. Taking medical aid to the ailing Harijans. This is but a sample of what is possible to do among the Harijans. It is a list hurriedly made, but a thoughtful student will, I have no doubt, add many other items.

You are at the hope of the future. You will be called upon, when you are discharged from your colleges and schools, to enter upon public life to lead the poor people of this country. I would, therefore like you students to have a sense of your responsibility and show it in a much tangible manner. It is a remarkable fact, and a regrettable fact, that in the case of the vast majority of the students, whilst they entertain noble impulses during their student days, these disappear when they finish their studies. The vast majority of them look out for loaves and fishes. Surely there is something wrong in this. There is one reason which is obvious. Every educational system is faulty. It dos not respond to the requirements of the country, certainly not to the requirements of pauper India. There is no correspondence between the education that is given and the home life and the village life.

These are not necessities of life. There are some who manage to take ten cups of coffee a day.. Is it necessary for their healthy development and for keeping them awake, let them not drink coffee or tea but go to sleep. We must not become slaves to these things. But the majority of the people who drink coffee or tea are slaves to them. Cigars and Cigarettes, wealth foreign or indigenous must be avoided.

Cigarette smoking is like an opiate and the cigars that you smoke have a touch of opium about them. They get to your nerves and you cannot leave them afterwards. How can a single student foul his mouth in converting it into a chimney.? If you give up these habits of smoking cigars and cigarettes and drinking coffee and tea you will find out for yourselves how much you are able to save.

A drunkard in Tolstoy's story is hesitating to execute his design of murder so long as he has not smoked his cigar. But he puffs it, and then gets up smiling and saying, "What a coward am I!" takes the dagger and does the deed. Tolstoy spoke from experience of it. And he is much more against cigars and cigarettes than against drinks. But do not make the mistake that between drink and tobacco, drink is a lesser evil. No. If cigarette is Beelzebub than drink is Satan. The students should be above all humble, and correct..... The greatest to remain great has to be the lowliest by choice. If I can speak from my knowledge of Hindu belief, the life of the student is to correspond to the life of the sanyasi up to the time his studies end. He is to be under the strictest discipline. He cannot marry, nor indulge in dissipation. He cannot indulge in drinks and the like. His behaviour is to be a pattern of exemplary self-resistant.

NAYEE TALEEM-A METHOD OF TEACHING ENUNCIATED BY MAHATMA GANDHI

Mahatma Gandhi came up with a novel manner of imparting education.

Even though, the system of education in the country was too nervous to experiment with his ideas at the national level, in pockets his method, called Nayee Taleem is being followed to yield impressive results.

Two introductions need to be made. The first one is easy. Meet Mohandas Karamchand Gandhi, the greatest leader of the twentieth century. The second one is to the method of teaching as enunciated by him. He called it Nayee Taleem, which literally translated means New Education. As you go through the ideas that form the basis of Nayee Taleem, you realize, Gandhi had indeed loved and understood children and the learning process.

I will begin my relating my first encounter with Nayee Taleem. I had gone to Kausani. This is a small quiet hill station in the state of Uttar Pradesh, northeast of Delhi. The majestic Himalayas as the backdrop and valleys hurling down as surprises were filled with stories of dynamic enterprising village women. They had protested against the opening of a liquor shop at one village. At another they had resisted deforestation. And the women were as conversant with the written as well as the spoken word.

The most revealing encounter was on one of our treks. We met two young women who had come in the traditional attire including the scarf on their heads. They also carried with them was carrying some bramble too. With the spirit of reformation high in city-bred me, I asked them if they were literate. They said they were not and that they did not see why they should study. For one hour I explained to them why. At the end of it, they casually revealed they were doing their Masters in Sociology. They were home on vacation! Imagine my shock and a feeling of utter foolishness. It took some time to reflect on the fact that all their education had not alienated them from their roots.

As I followed the source of such spirit in these women I was led to an uphill climb. No vehicle went up, you just had to trek it. It went up so many steps that I felt I would soon reach the heavens, and in a sense I did. I was at Laxmi Ashram at Kasauni. It was set up in 1946 by Katherine Helliman, better known in India as Sarla Behn, an ardent follower of

Gandhi. Working with the people while building awareness for the fight for independence, Sarla Behn noticed the amount of hardship a woman from that region underwent. She decided, under Gandhi's encouragement and insistence, that this was where an institution based on Nayee Taleem should be set up. Beginning with three students, Lakshmi Ashram began imparting education to the people along Gandhian lines. Today the names of some of our major reformers and grass root workers figure in the school's alumni.

When we entered the complex that is spread over many acres of open land, we saw some students and their teachers preparing a bed for vegetable sowing. One student, far out across the hill, was out grazing cows. A few others were in the kitchen making breakfast. Within half hour when we had gone around the neat but Spartan complex, we came across yet another student. This time she was with a teacher trying to record the temperature from a barometer. The diverse activities wee too distracting to the mind that went to see an ordinary school. So I sat down to hear and read about Nayee Taleem, which was what the school was all about.

Gandhi, on his return to India from South Africa, was struck by the failure of the modern system of education. He argued that beginning with the language in which children were and continue to be taught, the school syllabus based on Macaulays system, was irrelevant to the country's context. After accessing that kind of education, it alienated the student from his or her motherland and culture. Yet it did not make him vocationally any worthier. The student community that dominated the thinker leader's mind comprised eighty percent of India's rural folk.

As he ruminated the problem in his mind, he decided the way to go about education, true education, was to give literary training through vocational training. Quoting Gandhi, I hold that true education of the intellect can only come through a proper exercise and training of the bodily organs. In other words, the intelligent use of the bodily organs in a child provides the best and quickest way of developing his intellect. He went on to elaborate his idea with the example of a takli. The takli is the most primitive form of the spinning wheel. It is actually a tool that must have been fashioned before the discovery of the wheel. The use of the wheel for spinning came later in history. The initial taklis could have been fashioned out of clay or wet flour, dried and a bamboo splinter passed through it. In some parts of Bengal and Bihar, this kind of tool is spin is still used. Most cloth in India was made of the takli yarn and the cottage industries still uses it for finer counts of textiles.

There you are-that was just Gandhi's idea. Talk about the takli and you have perforce to talk of the wheel, science, the coming of mill cloth, the dying out of taklis, the regional variations of taklis, the areas where cotton is grown and so on. History, geography, science and arithmetic are all taught through practical experience.

The education system should go to the people, should lure them for its value, both economic and intellectual. He argued that primary education should be spread across seven years and should contain the entire syllabus that children study till they leave school. In addition they will pick up one vocational skill. The takli was an example, it could be anything. Another quote from Gandhi's writings would be in order: Then as to primary education, my confirmed opinion is that the commencement of training by teaching the alphabet and reading and writing, hampers their intellectual growth. I would not teach them the alphabet till they have had an elementary knowledge of history, geography, mental arithmetic and art.

Through these three I should develop their intelligence. Question may be asked how intelligence can be developed through the takli or the spinning wheel. It can to a marvellous degree if it is not taught mechanically. When you tell a child the reason for each process, when you explain the mechanism of the takli, when you give him/her the history of cotton and its connection with civilization itself and take him to the village field where it is grown and teach him to the village field where it is grown and teach him to the village field where it is grown and teach him to count the rounds he spins and the method of finding the evenness and strength of the yarn, you hold his interest and simultaneously train his eyes, hands and mind.

I should give six months to this preliminary training. The child is now probably ready for learning how to read the alphabet and, when he is able to do so rapidly he is ready to learn simple drawing and when he has learnt to draw geometric figures and the figures if birds, etc., he will draw not scrawl the figures of the alphabet. I consider writing as a fine art. We kill it by imposing the alphabet on little children and making it the beginning of learning.

Gradually vocation should serve a dual process; it should pay for the student's course and also develop his skill. Land, building and equipment are not to be covered by the student's labour. All crafts that are widely practiced in India can be taught with minimal investment. The self-supporting aspect of Gandhi's New Education formula was in his opinion the only way to carry education to the crores of children in India awaiting education.

Higher education should be left to private enterprises and for meeting national requirements. The state universities should be purely examining bodies.

So when I looked up and saw the child returning from grazing the cows, I wondered what she would have associated with it-different types of greenery, love towards animals, the food cycle, milk, dairy farming… or the young women emerging from the kitchen, what would they have learnt about fire, cooking, nourishment, nutrition, agriculture and the growth of rice and pulses. A new desire seemed to sprout in me. I wished I could go back in time and sit amidst nature to learn.

Gandhi's Views on Education

These were the words he used. When I was working in the university in Kerala and I saw the different types of disturbances occurring on campuses. I used to say that literally we have taken life out of education. Everybody is doubting the purpose of education. Education is for life, life in its entirety and then education through life. This is not happening at all today. Education is only being provided through our so-called lectures and in the laboratory. Education throughout life is not happening at all. Of course, we are trying to supplement this education by using artificial means. Education throughout life: As teachers, we can say that once we get the qualifications, once we get our degree, we stop our education and do away with further study. I think nowadays we have several different types of education, whatever adjective we put before the word education, it is a different discipline altogether. This definition of Mahatma Gandhi would comprise everything that can be conceived under education. Education for life, education through life, and education throughout life. That the concept of life has been taken away from education is precisely the reason for the dehumanizing, alienating aspect of education. I used to say that literally lives are taken away from the campuses because of the physical clashes among the members of the student body.

This is happening in India. Hence, when we give life in its entirety as part of education, Gandhiji's views on education are realized, and this act of instilling life into the education process is the solution for any kind of educational development for this country. I have just mentioned some random thoughts on his views of education and how these views are relevant for any society, any country for that matter.

To bring about a change in society, which is really a stupendous task, especially in a country where considerable disparities in income persist and ignorance and illiteracy widen the gulf between the elite and the masses. In a developing society like India, each one adopted a planned approach towards development, where education becomes a key agent of socioeconomic reform. As the famous education commission of 1964–66, the Radhakrishnan Commission, observed; "for achieving change on a grand scale the only effective instrument is education. Education does initiate changes in social institutions and sub-systems, and this affects the social situation of the country."

Gandhi's Scheme of Education

In the Gandhian constructive program, the most important element is *'Nai Taleem,'* or the new education, which in the words of Acharya Kriplani, "... is the coping stone of Gandhi's social and political edifice."

Gandhiji regarded his scheme of education as spearheading the silent social revolution and expected it to provide a healthy relationship between the city and the village, which would go a long way in eradicating the poisoned relationship between the classes. This view was affirmed by various other scholars and thinkers in the field of education.

Zakir Hussain once commented on Gandhi's views on education. He wrote, "... Gandhi socially considered the introduction of such practical productive work in education to be participated in by all." The children of the nation will tend to break down the existing barriers of prejudice between manual and intellectual workers and harmful elites to both. Such is the social significance of the so-called new educational concept of Gandhi, but it does not entail any sacrifice of the individual goal of education or its social goal. Gandhiji had said, "by education, I mean an overall all around drawing out of the best in child and man, in body, mind, and spirit." This concept of education serves both goals at the same time. The application of Gandhi's concept of education was first suggested for children between the ages of 7 and 14. This is called basic education. This was later on extended to all the stages. Gandhi felt that it should include the education of everybody, at every stage of life; including the university stage. The Sarvodaya thinkers accepted the whole idea underlying the new educational concept of Gandhi, including its social and individual aims.

Gandhi laid the foundation of a scheme of national education that was suited to our needs, requirements, genius, and aspirations for the future. It is left up to us to perfect it and extend it to cover the entire field of education. In this process, adjustment and adaptation may be necessary, but these actions must be undertaken in the spirit of the total philosophy of Gandhi, that is, for the individual and the society. Whatever may be its merits and demerits, we should not forget that education to Gandhi meant inspiring the children with a new ideology based upon personal purity and unselfish service, resulting in the creation of a society based upon truth and love. This is precisely the Buddha's concept also. Basic education stands for a new outlook, a new approach. The fountainhead of all the conflicts in the world is that knowledge has been separated from work. They have been separated in thoughts by a faulty psychology. They have been separated in life by a faulty sociology. They have been assigned different market values by faulty economics. One of the basic principles of education is that work and knowledge must never be separated. Separation of learning from labour results in social injustices. In dynamic societies, education has to equip individuals with the skills and attitudes necessary for them to adapt to changing conditions, and for constructive participation in the task of social change. This is possible only through the adoption of a suitable educational system.

Gandhi believed that education should be intimately related with human experience, "what better book can be there than the book of humanity?" he asked. The convergence of ideas and action was the key note of his approach, which was national in scope, as he wanted to present an alternative to the system introduced by the British colonial system. He stressed that the educational system must be one in which the highest development of mind and soul is possible and which instills courage and self-reliance in the individual, while at the same time, helping them cultivate the highest intellectual scientific, moral, and ethical accomplishments.

Gandhiji aimed at developing a society, "a socially conscious 'man' dedicated to truth and nonviolence." His educational scheme was nationalist in setting, idealist in nature and pragmatic on one hand while social in purpose and spiritual in intent on the other hand. It was also an essential instrument for materializing his dream of *Sarvodaya Samaj*, in which the vertical and horizontal distance between people is reduced to a minimum. Gandhi formulated his scheme of basic education in the context of poverty, illiteracy, backwardness, frustration, and the degeneration of our masses, resulting from the disruption of traditional social institutions and the destruction of the small-scale cottage industry.

He says that we must draw out the best in adult and child, as I mentioned earlier. This radical scheme was geared up, checking the progressive decay of our villages, reviving the village economy, laying the foundations of a just social order, in which there is no unnatural division between the 'haves' and the 'have-nots' and everybody is assured of achieving acceptable standards. The basic educational scheme was an essential ingredient of Gandhi's plan to eliminate the rural-urban divide and redress the structural and socioeconomic imbalances that were abound in Indian society. Gandhi also addressed the issue of free education.

By free education, Gandhi did not mean an education fully supported and subsidized by the state or other outside agencies. Instead, he implied a system that had the maximum possible capacity of self-support from the people's work experience, which is both an instrument of education and a source of income. The Gandhian system was free in another sense also: It did not regard formal, full-time schooling of the pupil as essential. He had very specific views about secondary and higher education. There is a feeling that Gandhi was against research, higher education, etc.

He had very specific ideas about research, higher education and the accumulation of knowledge. In Gandhi's scheme, higher education performed the essential function of providing training and properly motivating human power for national needs and there was an urgent need for the purposive expansion of such education. I would like to conclude with a quote from Gandhi. He declared, "... under my scheme, there will be more and better libraries, more and better research institutes. Under, it we should have an army of chemists, engineers, and other experts who will be the real servants of the nation and answer the varied and growing requirements of the people who are becoming increasingly conscious other rights and wants."

Several critics say that Gandhi was only concerned with primary and basic education. This was not true. He had very specific views of higher education. Of course, I have a few more points to cover, which I will take them up with you later during the discussion session.

EDUCATION THROUGH CRAFT

Speaking about education through a craft Gandhiji said:

"If such education is given, the direct result will be that it will be self-supporting. But the test of success is not its self-supporting character, but that the whole man has been drawn out through the teaching of the handicraft in a scientific manner. In fact I would reject a teacher who would promise to make it self-supporting under any circumstances. The self-supporting part will be the logical corollary of the fact that the pupil has learnt the use of every one of his faculties. If a boy who works at a handicraft for three hours a day will surely earn his keep, how much more a boy who adds to the work a development of his mind and soul!" (Harijan, 11 June 1938 (CW 67, p. 115))

BASIC EDUCATION

This Basic Education has grown out of the atmosphere surrounding us in the country and is in response to it. It is, therefore, designed to cope with that atmosphere. This atmosphere pervades India's seven hundred thousand villages and its millions of inhabitants. Forget them and you forget India. India is not to be found in her cities. It is in her innumerable villages.

The following are the fundamentals of Basic Education:

1. All education to be true must be self-supporting, that is to say, in the end it will pay its expenses excepting the capital which will remain intact.
2. In it the cunning of the hand will be utilized even up to the final stage, that is to say, hands of the pupils will be skilfully working at some industry for some period during the day.
3. All education must be imparted through the medium of the provincial language.
4. In this there is no room for giving sectional religious training. Fundamental universal ethics will have full scope.
5. This education, whether it is confined to children or adults, male or female, will find its way to the homes of the pupils.

6. Since millions of students receiving this education will consider themselves as of the whole of India, they must learn an interprovincial language. This common interprovincial speech can only be Hindustani written in Nagari or Urdu script. Therefore, pupils have to master both the scripts. *(Harijan, 2 November 1947 (CW 89, pp. 404–05))*

INTELLECTUAL DEVELOPMENT

During my recent wanderings in Travancore and Madras I found that most of the students and 'intellectuals' who came into touch with me were an instance of intellectual dissipation rather than intellectual development. The fault lies in the modern system of education which encourages this vicious tendency, misdirects the mind, and thereby hinders its development instead of helping it. My experiments in Segaon have only confirmed this impression. But they are as yet too incomplete to be cited as evidence. The views on education that I am now going to set forth have been held by me right from the time of the founding of the Phoenix Settlement in South Africa in the year 1904.

I hold that true education of the intellect can only come through a proper exercise and training of the bodily organs, *e.g* hands, feet, eyes, ears, nose, etc. In other words, an intelligent use of the bodily organs in a child provides the best and quickest way of developing his intellect. But unless the development of the mind and body goes hand in hand with a corresponding awakening of the soul, the former alone would prove to be a poor lopsided affair. By spiritual training I mean education of the heart. A proper and all-round development of the mind, therefore, can take place only when it proceeds pari passu with the education of the physical and spiritual faculties of the child. They constitute an indivisible whole. According to this theory, therefore, it would be a gross fallacy to suppose that they can be developed piecemeal or independently of one another.

The baneful effects of absence of proper coordination and harmony among the various faculties of body, mind and soul respectively are obvious. They are all around us; only we have lost perception of them owing to our present perverse associations. Take the case of our village folk. From their childhood upward they toil and labour in their fields, from morning till night, like their cattle in the midst of whom they live. Their existence is a weary endless round of mechanical drudgery unrelieved by a spark of intelligence or higher graces of life. Deprived of all scope for developing their mind and soul, they have sunk to the level of the beast. Life to them is a sorry bungle which they muddle through anyhow. On the other hand, what goes by the name of education in our schools and colleges in the cities today is in reality only intellectual dissipation.

Intellectual training is there looked upon as something altogether unrelated to manual or physical work. But since the body must have some sort of physical exercise to keep it in health, they vainly try to attain that end by means of an artificial and otherwise barren system of physical culture which would be ridiculous beyond words if the result was not so tragic. The young man who emerges from this system can in no way compete in physical endurance with an ordinary labourer. The slightest physical exertion gives him a headache; a mild exposure to the sun is enough to cause him giddiness. And what is more, all this is looked upon as quite 'natural'. As for the faculties of the heart, they are simply allowed to run to seed or to grow anyhow in a wild undisciplined manner. The result is moral and spiritual anarchy. And it is regarded as something laudable!

As against this, take the case of a child in whom the education of the heart is attended to from the very beginning. Supposing he is set to some useful occupation like spinning, carpentry, agriculture, etc., for his education and in that connection is given a thorough comprehensive knowledge relating to the theory of the various operations that he is to perform and the use and construction of the tools that he would be wielding. He would not only develop a fine healthy body but also a sound, vigorous intellect that is not merely academic but is firmly rooted in and is tested from day to day by experience. His intellectual education would include a knowledge of mathematics and various other sciences that are useful for an intelligent and efficient exercise of his avocation.

If to this is added literature by way of recreation, it would give him a perfect well-balanced, all-round education in which the intellect, the body and the spirit have all full play and develop together into a natural, harmonious whole. Man is neither mere intellect, nor the gross animal body, nor the heart of soul alone. A proper and harmonious combination of all the three is required for the making of the whole man and constitutes the true economics of education. To say that this kind of education can only be given after we have attained our independence would, I am afraid, be like putting the cart before the horse.

The advent of independence would be incredibly hastened if we could educate millions of our people through an intelligent exercise of their respective vocations like this and teach them that they live for the common good of all. *(Harijan, 8 May 1937 (CW 65, pp. 73–75))*

8

Gandhi and Nonviolence

Gandhi did not claim to be a prophet or even a philosopher. "There is no such thing as Gandhism," he warned, "and I do not want to leave any sect after me." There was only one Gandhian, he said, an imperfect one at that: himself.

The real significance of the Indian freedom movement in Gandhi's eyes was that it was waged non-violently. He would have had no interest in it if the Indian National Congress had adopted Satyagraha and subscribed to nonviolence. He objected to violence not only because an unarmed people had little chance of success in an armed rebellion, but because he considered violence a clumsy weapon which created more problems than it solved, and left a trail of hatred and bitterness in which genuine reconciliation was almost impossible.

This emphasis on nonviolence jarred alike on Gandhi's British and Indian critics, though for different reasons. To the former, nonviolence was a camouflage; to the latter, it was sheer sentimentalism. To the British who tended to see the Indian struggle through the prism of European history, the professions of nonviolence rather than on the remarkably peaceful nature of Gandhi's campaigns. To the radical Indian politicians, who had browsed on the history of the French and Russian revolutions or the Italian and Irish nationalist struggles, it was patent that force would only yield to force, and that it was foolish to miss opportunities and sacrifice tactical gains for reasons more relevant to ethics than to politics. Gandhi's total allegiance to nonviolence created a gulf between him and the educated elite in India which was temporarily bridged only during periods of intense political excitement. Even among his closest colleagues there were few who were prepared to follow his doctrine of nonviolence to its logical conclusion: the adoption of unilateral disarmament in a world armed to the teeth, the scrapping of the police and the armed forces, and the decentralization of administration to the point where the state would "wither away". Nehru, Patel and others on whom fell the task of organizing the administration of independent India did not question the superiority of the principle of nonviolence as enunciated by their leader, but they did not cope rider it practical politics. The Indian Constituent Assembly include a majority of members owing allegiance to Gandhi or at least holding him in high esteem, but the constitution which emerged from their labours in 1949 was based more on the Western parliamentary than on he Gandhian model. The development of the Indian economy during the last four decades cannot be said to have conformed to Gandhi's conception of "self-reliant village republics". On the other hand, it bears the marks of a conscious effort to launch an Indian industrial revolution.

Jawaharlal Nehru-Gandhi's "political heir"-was thoroughly imbued with the humane values inculcated by the Mahatma. But the man who spoke Gandhi's language, after his death, was Vinoba Bhave, the "Walking Saint", who kept out of politics and government, Bhave's Bhoodan (land gift) Movement was designed as much as a measure of land reform as that of a spiritual renewal. Though more than five million acres of land were distributed to the landless, the movement, despite its early promise, never really spiralled into a social revolution by consent. This was partly because Vinoba Bhave did not command Gandhi's extraordinary genius for organizing the masses for a national crusade, and partly because in independent India the tendency grew for the people to look up to the government rather than to rely on voluntary and cooperative effort for effecting reforms in society.

Soon after Gandhi's death in 1948, a delegate speaking at the United Nations predicted that "the greatest achievements of the Indian sage were yet to come" "Gandhi's times," said

Vinoba Bhave, "were the first pale dawn of the sun of Satyagraha." Forty years after Gandhi's death, this optimism would seem to have been too high-pitched. The manner in which Gandhi's techniques have sometimes been invoked even in the land of his birth in recent years would appear to be a travesty of his principles. And the world has been in the grip of a series of crises in Korea, the Congo, the Vietnam, the Middle East, and South Africa with a never-ending trail of blood and bitterness. The shadow of a thermo-nuclear war with its incalculable hazards continues to hang over mankind. From this predicament, Gandhi's ideas and techniques may suggest a way out. Unfortunately, his motives and methods are often misunderstood, and not only by mobs in the street, Not long ago, Arthur Koestler described Gandhi's attitude as one "of passive submission to bayonetting and raping, to villages without sewage, septic childhood's and trachoma." Such a judgement is of course completely with the same tenacity with which he battled with the British Raj. He advocated nonviolence not because it offered an easy way out, but because he considered violence a crude and in the long run, an ineffective weapon. His rejection of violence stemmed from choice, not from necessity.

Horace Alexander, who knew Gandhi and saw him in action, graphically describes the attitude of the nonviolent resister to his opponent: "On your side you have all the mighty forces of the modern State, arms, money, a controlled press, and all the rest. On my side, I have nothing but my conviction of right and truth, the unquenchable spirit of man, who is prepared to die for his convictions than submit to your brute force. I have my comrades in armlessness. Here we stand; and here if need be, we fall." Far from being a craven retreat from difficulty and danger, nonviolent resistance demands courage of a high order, the courage to resist injustice without rancour, to unite the utmost firmness with the utmost gentleness, to invite suffering but not to inflict it, to die but not to kill.

Gandhi did not make the facile division of mankind into "good" and "bad". He was convinced that every human being-even the "enemy"-had a kernel of decency: there were only evil acts, no wholly evil men. His technique of Satyagraha was designed not to coerce the opponent, but to set into motion forces which could lead to his conversion. Relying as it did on persuasion and compromise, Gandhi's method was not always quick in producing results, but the results were likely to be the more durable for having been brought about peacefully. "It is my firm conviction," Gandhi affirmed, "that nothing enduring can be built upon violence. " The rate of social change through the nonviolent technique was not in fact likely to be much slower than that achieved by violent methods; it was definitely faster than that expected from the normal functioning of institutions which tended to fossilize and preserve the status quo.

Gandhi did not think it possible to bring about radical changes in the structure of society overnight. Nor did he succumb to the illusion that the road to a new order could be paved merely with pious wishes and fine words. It was not enough to blame the opponent or bewail the times in which one's lot was cast. However heavy the odds, it was the Satyagrahi's duty never to feel helpless. The least he could do was to make a beginning with himself. If he was crusading for a new deal for peasantry, he could go to a village and live there, If he wanted to bring peace to a disturbed district, he could walk through it, entering into the minds and hearts of those who were going through the ordeal, If an age-old evil like untouchability was to be fought, what could be a more effective symbol of defiance for a reformer than to adopt an untouchable child? If the object was to challenge foreign rule, why not act on the assumption that the country was already free, ignore the alien government and build alternative institutions to harness the spontaneous, constructive and cooperative effort of the people? If the goal was world peace, why not begin today by acting peacefully towards the immediate neighbour, going more than half way to understand and win him over?

Though he may have appeared a starry-eyed idealist to some, Gandhi's attitude to social and political problems was severely practical. There was a deep mystical streak in him, but even his mysticism seemed to have little of the ethereal about it. He did not dream heavenly dreams nor see things unutterable in trance; when "the still small voice" spoke to him, it was often to tell how he could fight a social evil or heal a rift between two warring communities. Far from distracting him from his role in public affairs, Gandhi's religious quest gave him the stamina to play it more effectively. To him true religion was not merely the reading of scriptures, the dissection of ancient texts, or even the practice of cloistered virtue: it had to be lived in the challenging context of political and social life.

Gandhi used his nonviolent technique on behalf of his fellow-countrymen in South Africa and India, but he did not conceive it only as a weapon in the armoury of Indian nationalism. On the other hand, he fashioned it as an instrument for righting wrongs and resolving conflicts between opposing groups, races and nations. It is a strange paradox that though the stoutest and perhaps the most successful champion of the revolt against colonialism in our time, Gandhi was frees from the taint of narrow nationalism. As early as 1924, he had declared that "the better mind of the world desires today, not absolutely independent states, warring one against another, but a federation of independent, of friendly interdependent states".

Even before the First World War had revealed the disastrous results of the combination of industrialism and nationalism, he had become a convert to the idea that violence between nation-states must be completely abjured.

In 1931, during his visit to England, a cartoon in the Star depicted him in a loin cloth besides Mussolini, Hitler, de Valera and Stalin, who were clad in black, brown, green and red shirts respectively. The caption, "And he ain't wearing any blooming' shirt at all" was not only literally but figuratively true. For a man of nonviolence, who believed in the brotherhood of man, there was no superficial division of nations into good and bad, allies and adversaries. This did not, however, mean that Gandhi did not distinguish between the countries which inflicted and the countries which suffered violence. His own life had been one struggle against the forces of violence, and Satyagraha was designed at once to eschew violence and to fight injustice.

In the years immediately preceding the Second Word war, when the tide of Nazi and Fascist aggression was relentlessly rolling forward, Gandhi had reasserted his faith in nonviolence and commanded it to the smaller nation which were living in daily dread of being overwhelmed by superior force. Through the pages of his weekly paper the Harijan, he expounded the nonviolent approach to military aggression and political tyranny. He advised the weaker nations to defend themselves not by increasing their fighting potential, but by nonviolent resistance to the aggressor. When Czechoslovakia was black-mailed into submission in September 1938, Gandhi suggested to the unfortunate Czechs: "There is no bravery greater than a resolute refusal

To bend the knee to an earthly power, no matter how great, and that without bitterness of spirit, and in the fullness of faith that the spirit alone lives, nothing else does."

Seven years later when the first atomic bombs exploded over Hiroshima and Nagasaki, Gandhi's reaction was characteristic: "I did not move a muscle. On the contrary, I said to myself that unless now the adopts nonviolence, it will spell certain suicide for mankind." The irony of the very perfection of the weapons of war rendering them useless as arbiters between nations has become increasingly clear during the last forty years. The atomic stockpiles which the major nuclear powers have already built up are capable of destroying civilization, as we know it several time over and peace has been precariously preserved by, what has been grimly termed, "the balance of atomic terror." The fact is that with the weapons of mass destruction, which are at hand now, to attack another nation is tantamount to attacking oneself. This is a bitter truth which old habits of thought have prevented from going home. "This splitting of the atoms has changed everything" bewailed Einstein, "save our modes of thinking and thus we drift towards unparalleled catastrophe."

Nonviolence, as Gandhi expounded it, has ceased to be a pious exhortation, and become a necessity. The advice he gave to the unfortunate Abyssinians and Czechs during the twilight years before the Second Word War, may have seemed utopian thirty years ago. Today, it sounds commonsense. Even some hardheaded military strategists such as Sir Stephen King-Hall have begun to see in Gandhi's method a possible alternative to suicidal violence.

Gandhi would have been the first to deny that his method offered an instant or universal panacea for world peace. His method is capable of almost infinite evolution to suit new situations in a changing world. It is possible that "applied nonviolence" is at present at the same

Stage of development "as the invention of electricity was in the days of Edison and Marconi." The lives-and deaths-of Chief Lithuli and Dr. Martin Luther King have proved that there is nothing esoteric about nonviolence, limiting it to a particular country or a particular period.

Indeed Tagore, the great contemporary and friend of Gandhi, prophesies that the West would accept Gandhi before the East "for the West has gone through the cycle of dependence on force and material things of life and has become disillusioned. They want a return to the spirit. The East has not yet gone through materialism and hence has not become so disillusioned."

The Gospel of Nonviolence

The Law of Our Species

I am not a visionary. I claim to be a practical idealist. The religion of nonviolence is not meant merely for the rishis and saints. It is meant for the common people as well. Nonviolence is the law of our species as violence is the law of the brute. The spirit lies dormant in the brute and he knows no law but that of physical might. The dignity of man requires obedience to a higher law-to the strength of the spirit.... The rishis who discovered the law of nonviolence in the midst of violence were greater geniuses than Newton. They were themselves known the use of arms, they realized their uselessness, and taught a weary world that its salvation lay not through violence but through nonviolence. (YI, 11-8-1920, p3)

My Ahimsa

I know only one way-the way of ahimsa. The way of himsa

goes against my grain. I do not want to cultivate the power to inculcate himsa...The faith sustains me that He is the help of the helpless, that He comes to one's succour only when one throws himself on His mercy. It is because of that faith that I cherish the hope that God will one day show me a path which I may confidently commend to the people. (YI, 10-10-1928, p342)

I have been a 'gambler' all my life. In my passion for finding truth and in relentlessly following out my faith in nonviolence, I have counted no stake too great. In doing so I have erred, if at all, in the company of the most distinguished scientist of any age and any clime. (YI, 20-2-1930, p61)

I learnt the lesson of nonviolence from my wife, when I tried to bend her to my will. Her determined resistance to my will, on the one hand, and her quiet submission to the suffering my stupidity involved, on the other, ultimately made me ashamed of myself and cured me of my stupidity in thinking that I was born to rule over her and, in the end, she became my teacher in nonviolence. (H, 24-12-1938, p394)

The doctrine that has guided my life is not one of inaction but of the highest action. (H, 28-6-1942, p201)

I must not...flatter myself with the belief—nor allow friends...to entertain the belief that I have exhibited any heroic and demonstrable nonviolence in myself. All I can claim is that I am sailing in that direction without a moment's stop. (H, 11-1-1948, p504)

Character of Nonviolence

Non-violence is the law of the human race and is infinitely greater than and superior to brute force. In the last resort it does not avail to those who do not possess a living faith in the God of Love.

Nonviolence affords the fullest protection to one's self-respect and sense of honour, but not always to possession of land or movable property, though its habitual practice does prove a better bulwark than the possession of armed men to defend them. Nonviolence, in the very nature of things, is of no assistance in the defence of ill-gotten gains and immoral acts. Individuals or nations who would practice nonviolence must be prepared to sacrifice (nations to last man) their all except honour. It is, therefore, inconsistent with the possession of other people's countries, i.e., modern imperialism, which is frankly based on force for its defence.

Nonviolence is a power which can be wielded equally by all-children, young men and women or grown-up people, provided they have a living faith in the God of Love and have therefore equal love for all mankind. When nonviolence is accepted as the law of life, it must pervade the whole being and not be applied to isolated acts.

It is a profound error to suppose that, whilst the law is good enough for individuals, it is not for masses of mankind. (H, 5-9-1936, p236)

For the way of nonviolence and truth is sharp as the razor's edge. Its practice is more than our daily food. Rightly taken, food sustains the body; rightly practiced nonviolence sustains the soul. The body food we can only take in measured quantities and at stated intervals; nonviolence, which is the spiritual food, we have to take in continually. There is no such thing as satiation. I have to be conscious every moment that I am pursuing the goal and have to examine myself in terms of that goal.

Changeless Creed

The very first step in nonviolence is that we cultivate in our daily life, as between ourselves, truthfulness, humility, tolerance, loving kindness. Honesty, they say in English, is the best policy. But, in terms of nonviolence, it is not mere policy. Policies may and do change. Nonviolence is an unchangeable creed. It has to be pursued in face of violence raging around you. Nonviolence with a nonviolent man is no merit. In fact it becomes difficult to say whether it is nonviolence at all. But when it is pitted against violence, then one realizes the difference between the two. This we cannot do unless we are ever wakeful, ever vigilant, ever striving. (H, 2-4-1938, p64)

The only thing lawful is nonviolence. Violence can never be lawful in the sense meant here, i.e., not according to man-made law but according to the law made by Nature for man. (H, 27-10-1946, p369)

Faith in God

[A living faith in nonviolence] is impossible without a living faith in God. A nonviolent man can do nothing save by the power and grace of God. Without it he won't have the courage to die without anger, without fear and without retaliation. Such courage comes from the belief that God sits in the hearts of all and that there should be no fear in the presence of God. The knowledge of the omnipresence of God also means respect for the lives even of those who may be called opponents.... (H, 18-6-1938, p64)

Nonviolence is an active force of the highest order. It is soul force or the power of Godhead within us. Imperfect man cannot grasp the whole of that Essence-he would not be able to bear its full blaze, but even an infinitesimal fraction of it, when it becomes active within us, can work wonders.

The sun in the heavens fills the whole universe with its life-giving warmth. But if one went too near it, it would consume him to ashes. Even so it is with God-head. We become Godlike to the extent we realize nonviolence; but we can never become wholly God. (H, 12-11-1938, p326)

The fact is that nonviolence does not work in the same way as violence. It works in the opposite way. An armed man naturally relies upon his arms. A man who is intentionally unarmed relies upon the Unseen Force called God by poets, but called the Unknown by scientists. But that which is unknown is not necessarily non-existent. God is the Force among all forces known and unknown. Nonviolence without reliance upon that Force is poor stuff to be thrown in the dust. (H, 28-6-1942, p201)

Consciousness of the living presence of God within one is undoubtedly the first requisite. (H, 29-6-1947, p209)

Religious Basis

My claim to Hinduism has been rejected by some, because I believe and advocate nonviolence in its extreme form. They say that I am a Christian in disguise. I have been even seriously told that I am distorting the meaning of the Gita, when I ascribe to that great poem the teaching of unadulterated nonviolence. Some of my Hindu friends tell me that killing is a duty enjoined by the Gita under certain circumstances. A very learned shastri only the other day scornfully rejected my interpretation of the Gita and said that there was no warrant for the opinion held by some commentators that the Gita represented the eternal duel between forces of evil and good, and inculcated the duty of eradicating evil within us without hesitation, without tenderness.

I state these opinions against nonviolence in detail, because it is necessary to understand them, if we would understand the solution I have to offer....

I must be dismissed out of considerations. My religion is a matter solely between my Maker and myself. If I am a Hindu, I cannot cease to be one even though I may be disowned by the whole of the Hindu population. I do however suggest that nonviolence is the end of all religions. (YI, 29-5-1924, p175)

The lesson of nonviolence is present in every religion, but I fondly believe that, perhaps, it is here in India that its practice has been reduced to a science. Innumerable saints have laid down their lives in tapashcharya until poets had felt that the Himalayas became purified in their snowy whiteness by means of their sacrifice. But all this practice of nonviolence is nearly dead today. It is necessary to revive the eternal law of answering anger by love and of violence by nonviolence; and where can this be more readily done than in this land of Kind Janaka and Ramachandra? (H, 30-3-1947, p86)

Hinduism's Unique Contribution

Nonviolence is common to all religions, but it has found the highest expression and application in Hinduism. (I do not regard Jainism or Buddhism as separate from Hinduism).

Hinduism believes in the oneness not of merely all human life but in the oneness of all that lives. Its worship of the cow is, in my opinion, its unique contribution to the evolution of humanitarianism. It is a practical application of the belief in the oneness and, therefore, sacredness of all life. The great belief in transmigration is a direct consequence of that belief. Finally, the discovery of the law of Varnashrama is a magnificent result of the ceaseless search for truth. (YI, 20-10-1927, p352)

I have also been asked wherefrom in Hinduism I have unearthed ahimsa. Ahimsa is in Hinduism, it is in Christianity as well as in Islam. Whether you agree with me or not, it is my bounden duty to preach what I believe to be the truth as I see it. I am also sure that ahimsa has never made anyone a coward. (H, 27-4-1947, p126)

The Koran and Nonviolence

[Barisaheb] assured me that there was warrant enough for Satyagraha in the Holy Koran. He agreed with the interpretation of the Koran to the effect that, whilst violence under certain well-defined circumstances is permissible, self-restraint is dearer to God than violence, and that is the law of love. That is Satyagraha. Violence is concession to human weakness, Satyagraha is an obligation. Even from the practical standpoint it is easy enough to see that violence can do no good and only do infinite harm. (YI, 14-5-1919, quoted in Communal Unity, p985)

Some Muslim friends tell me that Muslims will never subscribe to unadulterated nonviolence. With them, they say, violence is as lawful and necessary as nonviolence. The use of either depends upon circumstances. It does not need Koranic authority to justify the lawfulness of both. That is the well-known path the world has traversed through the ages. There is no such thing as unadulterated violence in the world. But I have heard it from many Muslim friends that the Koran teaches the use of nonviolence. It regards forbearance as superior to vengeance. The very word Islam means peace, which is nonviolence. Badshahkhan, a staunch Muslim who never misses his namaz and Ramzan, has accepted out and out nonviolence as his creed. It would be no answer to say that he does not live up to his creed, even as I know to my shame that I do not one of kind, it is of degree. But, argument about nonviolence in the Holy Koran is an interpolation, not necessary for my thesis. (H, 7-10-1939, p296)

No Matter of Diet

Ahimsa is not a mere matter of dietetics, it transcends it. What a man eats or drinks matters little; it is the self-denial, the self-restraint behind it that matters. By all means practice as much restraint in the choice of the articles of your diet as you like. The restraint is commendable, even necessary, but it touches only the fringe of ahimsa. A man may allow himself a wide latitude in the matter of diet and yet may be a personification of ahimsa and compel our homage, if is heart overflows with love and melts at another's woe, and has been purged of all passions. On the other hand a man always over-scrupulous in diet is an utter stranger to ahimsa and pitiful wretch, if he is a slave to selfishness and passions and is hard of heart. (YI, 6-9-1928, pp300-1)

Road to Truth

My love for nonviolence is superior to every other thing mundane or supramundane. It is equaled only by my love for Truth, which is to me synonymous with nonviolence through which and which alone I can see and reach Truth. (YI, 20-2-1930, p61)

....Without ahimsa it is not possible to seek and find Truth. Ahimsa and Truth are so intertwined that it is practically impossible to disentangle and separate them. They are like the two sides of a coin, or rather of a smooth, unstamped, metallic disc. Who can say which is the obverse, and which is the reverse? Nevertheless ahimsa is the means; Truth is the end. Means to be means must always be within our reach, and so ahimsa is our supreme duty. If we take care of the means, we are bound to reach the end sooner of latter. When once we have grasped this point, final victory is beyond question. (FYM, pp12-3)

Ahimsa is not the goal. Truth is the goal. But we have no means of realizing truth in human relationships except through the practice of ahimsa. A steadfast pursuit of ahimsa is inevitably bound to truth—not so violence. That is why I swear by ahimsa. Truth came naturally to me. Ahimsa I acquired after a struggle.

But ahimsa being the means, we are naturally more concerned with it in our everyday life. It is ahimsa, therefore, that our masses have to be educated in. Education in truth follows from it as a natural end. (H, 23-6-1946, p199)

No Cover for Cowardice

My nonviolence does not admit of running away from danger and leaving dear ones unprotected. Between violence and cowardly flight, I can only prefer violence to cowardice. I can no more preach nonviolence to a coward than I can tempt a blind man to enjoy healthy scenes. Nonviolence is the summit of bravery. And in my own experience, I have had no difficulty in demonstrating to men trained in the school of violence the superiority of nonviolence. As a coward, which I was for years, I harboured violence. I began to prize nonviolence only when I began to shed cowardice. Those Hindus who ran away from the post of duty when it was attended with danger did so not because they were nonviolent, or because they were afraid to strike, but because they were unwilling to die or even suffer an injury. A rabbit that runs away from the bull terrier is not particularly nonviolent. The poor thing trembles at the sight of the terrier and runs for very life. (YI, 28-5-1924, p178)

Nonviolence is not a cover for cowardice, but it is the supreme virtue of the brave. Exercise of nonviolence requires far greater bravery than that of swordsmanship. Cowardice is wholly inconsistent with nonviolence. Translation from swordsmanship to nonviolence is possible and, at times, even an easy stage. Nonviolence, therefore, presupposes ability to strike. It is a conscious deliberate restraint put upon one's desire for vengeance. But vengeance is any day superior to passive, effeminate and helpless submission. Forgiveness is higher still. Vengeance too is weakness. The desire for vengeance comes out of fear of harm, imaginary or real. A dog barks and bites when he fears. A man who fears no one on earth would consider it too troublesome even to summon up anger against one who is vainly trying to injure him. The sun does not wreak vengeance upon little children who throw dust at him. They only harm themselves in the act. (YI, 12-8-1926, p285)

The path of true nonviolence requires much more courage than violence. (H, 4-8-1946, pp248-9)

The minimum that is required of a person wishing to cultivate the ahimsa of the brave is first to clear one's thought of cowardice and, in the light of the clearance, regulate his conduct in every activity, great or small. Thus the votary must refuse to be cowed down by his superior, without being angry. He must, however, be ready to sacrifice his post, however remunerative it may be. Whilst sacrificing his all, if the votary has no sense of irritation against his employer, he has ahimsa of the brave in him.

Assume that a fellow-passenger threatens my son with assault and I reason with the would-be-assailant who then turns upon me. If then I take his blow with grace and dignity, without harbouring any ill-will against him, I exhibit the ahimsa of the brave. Such instances are of every day occurrence and can be easily multiplied. If I succeed in curbing my temper every time and, though able to give blow for blow, I refrain, I shall develop the ahimsa of the brave which will never fail me and which will compel recognition from the most confirmed adversaries. (H, 17-11-1946, p404)

Inculcation of cowardice is against my nature. Ever since my return from South Africa, where a few thousand had stood up not unsuccessfully against heavy odds, I have made it my mission to preach true bravery which ahimsa means. (H, 1-6-1947, p175)

Humility Essential

If one has...pride and egoism, there is no nonviolence. Nonviolence is impossible without humility. My own experience is that, whenever I have acted non-violently, I have been led to it and sustained in it by the higher promptings of an unseen power. Through my own will I should have miserably failed. When I first went to jail, I quailed at the prospect. I had heard terrible things about jail life. But I had faith in God's protection. Our experience was that those who went to jail in a prayerful spirit came out victorious, those who had gone in their own strength failed. There is no room for self-pitying in it either when you say God is giving you the strength. Self-pity comes when you do a thing for which you expect recognition from others. But there is no question of recognition. (H, 28-1-1939 p442)

It was only when I had learnt to reduce myself to zero that I was able to evolve the power of Satyagraha in South Africa. (H, 6-5-1939, p113)

A STUDY OF THE MEANINGS OF NONVIOLENCE

"Nonviolence", "nonviolent resistance", "Satyagraha" and "pacifism" are words now frequently found in such newspapers as the Manchester Guardian, The Times, and the New York Times. The Negroes of Montgomery, Alabama, conduct a year-long nonviolent bus boycott. Danilo Dolci is jailed for leading hungry Sicilians in a nonviolent demonstration. Jehovah's Witnesses continue to gain adherents to their creed, which includes refusal of military duty. The word "pacifism" appears frequently in news reports from Germany. The crew of the ketch Golden Rule go to prison for attempting to stop U.S. nuclear tests by sailing into the Pacific "proving grounds". The Welsh Nationalists use nonviolent resistance in addition to educational and electoral methods in their struggle for Welsh self-government. Young Frenchmen begin their fifth year in prison as war resisters. London newspapers headline the arrest of 45 opponents of nuclear weapons for civil disobedience in nonviolently "invading" a rocket base site in an effort to halt construction.

In India, Vinoba Bhave redistributes land by "looting with love". A Mennonite father refuses to send his children to an Ohio school because they will be taught war-like and un-Godly ideas. Commander Sir Stephen King-Hall lectures to top British naval, army and air-force officers on "The Alternative to the Nuclear Deterrent: Nonviolent Resistance". Women of Budapest Stop Russian tanks by lying down in front of them. Film star Don Murray, as a religious pacifist, helps resettle World War II refugees still without homes. South African "Black Sash" women keep silent vigils to defend the Constitution. Hundreds in Britain march four days in rain, snow and sun to the

Aldermaston Atomic Weapons Research Establishment in protest against nuclear weapons. The All-African Peoples' Conference in Accra pledges support for nonviolent resistance, including civil disobedience, movements for the liberation of Africa. Although almost everyone says the world must end war forever or be destroyed, the ideas and ideals of "nonviolence" and methods of nonviolent social action are still espoused by only minorities.

But they have now risen to sufficient prominence that they must be reckoned with in world thinking and events. Gandhi is in large degree responsible for this. The impact of "nonviolence", however, is now felt in many parts of the world and arises from diverse sources. This increased awareness of "nonviolence" has come despite (or because of) the fact that many of the ideas, ideals and methods of "nonviolence" run counter to established orthodoxies and socially approved behaviour. They also stand in contrast to modern developments of violence: totalitarianism and nuclear weapons. Despite this growing awareness of "nonviolence" there is widespread confusion about just what "nonviolence" is. All the above examples and many more have been labelled with the terms "nonviolence" and "pacifism". This lack of clarity has its effect on the groups promoting nonviolent approaches, on criticisms by their opponents, and on the thinking of still others.

The usual degree of misunderstanding which may result from a varied and imprecise use of terms becomes plain confusion when the phenomena concerned are relatively little known. When these phenomena include unorthodox ideas, beliefs and methods of resistance-each of which may be associated with strong emotions among both proponents and opponents-the confusion may become chaos. At first glance, all that is "not violence" may seem to be of a single kind. In a society where such systems of ideas, beliefs and behaviour are usually regarded as esoteric, "crack-pot", impractical, dangerous or simply strange, few people undertake a sufficiently serious examination of these phenomena to make them aware that quite different types of belief and behaviour are involved. "Pacifism", "passive resistance" "nonviolence" and the other terms are commonly used either as broad generalities (glittering, scathing or just vague) or with a wide variety of more specific meanings for the same word. A failure, however, to discern the very real differences among the various types of "nonviolence" and to exercise more care in the use of the terms may have a number of undesirable consequences. Two of these are that evaluation of the merits and demerits of those approaches will be seriously handicapped, and that research in this area will face unnecessary difficulties.

Persons rejecting violence on grounds of principle have rarely analyzed the relation of their particular belief systems to others also rejecting violence. They have failed to do this largely because such analysis has seemed to them irrelevant: their duty was to follow the imperatives of their beliefs. However, some of them have recognized differences in motivation and behaviour among those rejecting violence. For example, Guy F. Hershberger, a Mennonite, distinguishes between "nonresistance" and "modern pacifism". Non-resistance, he says, describes the faith and life of those "who cannot have any part in warfare because they believe the Bible forbids it, and who renounce all coercion, even nonviolent coercion". Pacifism, he says, is "a term which covers many types of opposition to war". Some Western pacifists have seen Gandhi's approach as sufficiently different from their own that they have felt it was not genuinely "pacifist".

Reginald Reynolds writes: "A reading of 'official' [British] pacifist literature from, say, 1920 onwards would reveal some odd things which many pacifists would prefer to forget. People accepted as 'leading pacifists' were, as late as 1930, writing abusive articles about Gandhi and defending British Rule in India. Such articles and letters could be found in The Friend (weekly unofficial paper of the Quakers), in Reconciliation (monthly organ of the Fellowship of Reconciliation), and in No More War (the monthly organ of the [No More War] movement)." Western pacifists have sometimes distinguished between the "religious" pacifists and the "nonreligious" pacifists who base their pacifism on "humanitarian" or "philosophical" considerations. This distinction has also been made bynonpacifists. Pacifists have also recognized differences among themselves in their response to military conscription.

There have been: (a) the "absolutists" who believe in civil disobedience to such laws and refuse cooperation with the administrative agencies for military conscription even to obtain their personal exemption from military duty where the law allows for such exemption; (b) those who refuse entry into the armed forces (even as non-combatants) but are willing to cooperate with the conscription system to obtain their exemption from military duty and are willing to perform alternative civilian work where such alternative is allowed; and (c) those who refuse to bear arms but are willing to perform noncombatant (*e.g.* medical) duties within the armed forces. Although Gandhi never wrote systematic treatises on "nonviolence", he did distinguish between two or more types of "nonviolence" After first calling his South African protest movements "passive resistance", he discarded the term and adopted a new term, Satyagraha. "When in a meeting of Europeans I found that the term 'passive resistance' was too narrowly construed that it was supposed to be a weapon of the weak, that it could be characterized by hatred, and that it could finally manifest itself as violence, I had to demur to all these statements and explain the real nature of the Indian movement.

It was clear that a new word must be coined by the Indians to designate their struggle." Gandhi also seems to have assumed an implicit distinction between Western pacifism and Satyagraha, although explicit statements to this effect are difficult to find. Bharatan Kumarappa, in an introductory note to a small collection of Gandhi's writings prepared for the World Pacifist Conference in India, December 1949-January 1950, writes: "It is a far cry... from pacifism to Gandhiji's idea of nonviolence. While pacifism hopes to get rid of war chiefly by refusing to fight and by carrying on propaganda against war, Gandhiji goes much deeper and sees that war cannot be avoided, so long as the seeds of it remain in man's breast and grow and develop in his social, political and economic life.

Gandhiji's cure is, therefore, very radical and far-reaching. It demands nothing less than rooting out violence from oneself and from one's environment." The American sociologist Clarence Marsh Case in his study of such phenomena explicitly recognizes differences between various types, although he makes no attempt to develop a typology. He uses the terms "nonviolent resistance" and "passive resistance" interchangeably. Political scientist Dr. Mulford Sibley has distinguished three types of "nonviolence": Hindu pacifism (Satyagraha), Christian pacifism, and revolutionary secular pacifism. This classification, however, did not purport to encompass the field of "nonviolence" and was limited to those modern types of pacifism containing political theory. Professor Leo Kuper of the Sociology Department of Natal University has distinguished between nonviolent resistance movements aimed at achieving their goals by means of embarrassment and conversion of their opponents respectively; but, again, this does not purport to be a full typology. Theodore Paullin comes close to developing a typology of "nonviolence", although this was not his main intention. Paullin structured his discussion on the basis of six types resulting from a continuum "at one end of which we place violence coupled with hatred, and at the other, dependence only upon the application of positive love and goodwill.

In the intermediate positions we might place (1) violence without hatred, (2) nonviolence practiced by necessity rather than because of principle, (3) nonviolent coercion, (4) Satyagraha and nonviolent direct action, and (5) nonresistance." The nonviolence extremity of his continuum, "active goodwill and reconciliation", becomes the sixth type. Because Paullin's main objective in the booklet was to consider the application of "nonviolent means of achieving group purposes" his classification has suffered through lack of development and refinement. Some types of "nonviolence" have not been included, and some seem classified incorrectly. Paullin has, however, made a genuine contribution towards developing a typology.

GENERIC NONVIOLENCE

The whole gamut of behaviour and belief characterized by an abstention from physical violence is hereafter described by the term "generic nonviolence". This is the sense in which the term "nonviolence" has been hitherto used in this paper. 20

"Generic nonviolence" thus includes a wide variety of types of "nonviolence": all the examples briefly listed in the opening section of this paper and more. These vary widely on several points, such as whether "nonviolence" is viewed as intrinsically good or simply as an effective method of action, the degree of passivity and activity, the presence or absence of strategy, and whether the followers of the approach are "other worldly" or "this wordly". These phenomena have in common only the abstention from physical violence, either generally or in meeting particular conflict situations, or both. Not included in this broad classification are: (1) hermits and (2) cases of cowardice (both involving a de facto withdrawal, though for different reasons, from aspects of life involving physical violence rather than the offering of a nonviolent response in the situation); and (3) legislation, State decrees, etc. (backed by threat of physical violence, as imprisonment, execution, etc.).

Pacifism

The term 'pacifism' as here defined, includes the belief systems of those persons and groups who, as a minimum, refuse participation in all international or civil wars or violent revolutions and base this refusal on moral, ethical or religious principle. Such persons and groups are here called "pacifists". "Pacifism" is thus a narrower term than "generic nonviolence", and is an intermediary classification including several of the types of generic nonviolence described below. These are indicated below after the typology.

Nonviolent Resistance and Direct Action

"Nonviolent resistance and direct action" is another interim diary classification, being both narrower than "generic nonviolence" and broader than the specific types. The methods of "nonviolent resistance and direct action" fall on a continuum between personal exemplary behaviour and verbal persuasion at one end and sabotage and physical violence at the other.

"Nonviolent resistance and direct action" refers to those methods of resistance and direct action without physical violence in which the members of the nonviolent group perform either (1) acts of omission-that is, they refuse to perform acts which they usually perform, and are expected by custom to perform or are required by law or regulation to perform; or (2) acts of commission-that is, they insist on performing acts which they usually do not perform, are not expected by custom to perform or are forbidden by law or regulation from performing; or (3) both. These methods are "extra-constitutional": that is, they do not rely upon established procedures of the State (whether parliamentary or non-parliamentary) for achieving their objective. Such acts may be directed towards a change in, or abolition of, existing attitudes, values, social patterns, customs or social structure, or a combination of these.

Such change or abolition may take place whether these attitudes etc. are of the society as a whole or of only a section of it. Such acts may also be directed, in defense of attitudes, values, social patterns, customs, or social structure, or a combination of these, against attempts of the opponent to alter or to abolish them, whether by the introduction of particular or general innovations or both. In some cases of nonviolent resistance and direct action the primary intent is to change attitudes and values as a preliminary to changing policies. In other cases, the primary intent is to change policies (or thwart attempts to change policies) whether or not the opponents have first changed their attitudes and values. In other cases, the intent may be to change simultaneously attitudes and policies. Included in "nonviolent resistance and direct action" are those cases where violence has been rejected because of (1) religious, ethical or moral reasons; (2) considerations of expediency; and (3) mixed motivations of various types. Where the behaviour of the nonviolent group is primarily resistance, usually acts of omission, it can be described simply as "nonviolent resistance". Where the behaviour of the nonviolent group is primarily intervention, usually acts of commission, it can be described as "nonviolent direct action". The types of generic nonviolence which are included in the category "nonviolent resistance and direct action" are indicated below following the typology.

THE TYPES OF GENERIC NONVIOLENCE

In developing this typology, the writer has sought to observe the "natural" groupings or types as they seem to exist, rather than-reselecting certain criteria and then seeking to fit the phenomena into the pre-determined categories. After a classification of the-types had been made, the writer sought to examine what were the intrinsic characteristics possessed by the respective types which distinguish them from the others. The criteria which emerged include such factors as whether the motivation for nonviolence is expediency, principle, or mixed; whether the nonviolent group's belief system is "other worldly" or "this worldly" : whether or not the nonviolent group has a program of social change; what is the nonviolent group's attitude towards the opponents; whether all or only some physical violence is rejected; whether the nonviolent group is concerned with its own integrity; and others. Following the description of the types of generic nonviolence, appears a chart listing the main criteria which emerged. The nine types of generic nonviolence described below are: non-resistance, active reconciliation, moral resistance, selective nonviolence, passive resistance, peaceful resistance, nonviolent direct action, Satyagraha, and nonviolent revolution. These are listed roughly in the order of increasing activity There are no strict separations between some of these types, and particular cases may not seem to fit exactly into any one of them. This classification should be viewed simply as a tool to facilitate understanding and study of the phenomena, a tool which is neither perfect nor final, but may nevertheless be useful. The examples cited and statements used as illustrations for the respective types have been chosen from those available to the writer on the basis of their adequacy as illustrations and because of the presence of suitable documentation. There is no pretence that the examples cited are geographically representative or exhaustive of the cases belonging to each type. Further research on each of these types could provide abundant additional examples and illustrative statements.

Non-Resistance

The non-resistant reject on principle all physical violence, whether on an individual, State or international level. There are various Christian sects of this type, such as the Mennonites and the Amish. They refuse participation in war; and also in the State by holding government office, voting or having recourse to the courts. They pay their taxes, however, and do what the State demands, as long as it is not inconsistent with what they consider to be their duty to God. They refuse to resist evil situations even by nonviolent techniques, and in times of oppression simply hold to their beliefs and follow them-ignoring the evil as much as possible, and suffering their lot as part of their religious duty.

The non-resistant are concerned with being true to their-beliefs and maintaining their own integrity, rather than with attempts at social reconstruction, many even opposing attempts to create a good society here on earth. A common belief of the-non-resistant is that it is not possible for the world as a whole to become free from sin, and therefore, the Christian should withdraw from evil. Such influence as they have on society results from their acts of goodwill (such as relief work), their exhortations and their example. The non-resistants have their roots in early Christianity. With very few exceptions, the early Christians refused all military service and subservience to the Roman emperor. 'The crucial change began under the reign of Constantine, who was converted to Christianity in 312 A.D. and declared it to be the State religion in 321 A.D. After the main Christian groups began to turn towards the State for support and no longer refused participation in war, small heretical groups perpetuated the pacifist interpretation of Christianity.

They were cruelly persecuted. Some of their names have been lost. In the Middle Ages and later there were many sects which sought a return to what they believed to be the basic gospel. Among these were the Albigenses or Cathari; "Christ's Poor"; the Waldenses, or "The Poor Men of Lyons"; the "Humilates"; the Bohemian Brethren, of the Church of the Unitas Fratrum: the revived Unitas Fratrum or the Moravian Church; the Schwenkfelders; the German Baptists or Dunkers; the Obbenites; the Mennonites; the Collegiants (which represented a movement for a creedless spiritual worship within the existing denominations); the Simonians; the Socinians; and the Brownists. Some of these were Anabaptist sects.

Hershberger describes these sects thus: "Alongside the mediaeval church there were certain small, intimate groups of Christians who refused to accept a compromise with the social order. They stood aloof and maintained that indifference or hostility to the world which characterized the primitive church. These groups are known as the sects.

They generally refused to use the law, to take the oath, to exercise domination over others, or to participate in war. Theirs was not an ascetic emphasis on heroic and vicarious achievement. It was not an opposition, in most cases, to the sense life or the average life of humanity, but simply an opposition to the social institutions of the world. "The sects generally emphasized lay religion, personal ethical achievement, religious equality, brotherly love, indifference to the state and the ruling classes, dislike of the law and oath, and the ideal of poverty and frugality, direct personal religious relationship, appeal to the primitive church, criticism of the theologians. They always demanded a high standard of moral performance. This made for small groups, of course, but what they lost in the spirit of universalism, they made up for in intensity of life. This tradition of the sects was carried down from the Montanists and Dontanists through the Waldensians to the followers of Wycliff and Huss to the Anabaptists." Describing one of the non-resistant sects, the Mennonites, C. Henry Smith writes: "They adopted bodily the faith of the peaceful type of Anabaptists, and that was a rejection of all civil and a great deal of the prevailing ecclesiastical government as unnecessary for the Christian". They "went no further, however, in their opposition to the temporal authority than to declare that the true church and the temporal powers had nothing in common and must be entirely separate; not only must the state not interfere with the church, but the true Christian must be entirely free from participating in civil matters.

The temporal authority must needs exist, since it was instituted of God to punish the wicked, but in that work the Christian had no hand. This position they reached from a literal interpretation of the Sermon on the Mount, where Christ taught his disciples, among other things, to 'love their enemies' and to 'swear not at all'. Hence their position involved opposition to the oath, holding of office, and bearing of arms." In 1917 in America the general conference and various branches of the Mennonite Church united in addressing a signed "Appeal to the President" in which they said: "Because of our understanding of the teachings of Christ and New Testament generally against war in any form, we can render no service, either combatant or non-combatant, under the military establishment, but will rather be amenable to any punishment the government sees fit to lay upon us as a penalty".

Active Reconciliation

The nonviolence of this group, favouring the use of active goodwill and reconciliation, is based upon principle. It refers not only to outward actions, but to personal reconciliation and improvement of one's own life before attempting to change others. "Its proponents seek to accomplish a positive alteration in the attitude and policy of the group or person responsible for some undesirable situation; but they never use coercion-even nonviolent coercion. Rather they seek to convince their opponent..... They place their emphasis on the positive action of goodwill which they will use rather than upon a catalogue of violent actions which they will not use." A large part of the basis of this approach is the importance placed on the worth of very individual and the belief that he can change. Direct action and strategy are not involved. Tolstoy and many of his followers, and much of the present Society of Friends (Quakers), are proponents of this type of generic nonviolence. So also are many other individual pacifists. Tolstoy rejected the use of violence under all circumstances and also private property and association with institutions which practise coercion over men. Tolstoy depended upon the power of example and goodwill to influence men. He sought a regeneration of society as a whole through the practice of love in all one's relationships, simple living, self-service, and the persuasion of others to follow this way of life. In Tolstoy's own words: ".....it is this acknowledgement of the law of love as the supreme law of human life, and this clearly expressed guidance for conduct resulting from the Christian teaching of love, embracing enemies and those who hate, offend and curse us, that constitute the peculiarity of Christ's teaching, and by giving to the doctrine of love, and to the guidance flowing there from, an exact and definite meaning, inevitably involve a complete change of the established organization of life, not only in Christendom, but among all the nations of the earth."

"The time will come-it is already coming-when the Christian principles of equality and fraternity, community of property, non-resistance of evil by force, will appear just as natural and simple as the principles of family or social life seem to us now." "The Christian will not dispute with any one, nor attack any one, nor use violence against any one. On the contrary, he will bear violence without opposing it. But by this very attitude to violence, he will not only himself be free, but will free the whole world from all external power." George Fox and the early Quakers recognized religious experience as the final authority in religion, in place of the Scriptures which were the authority of the non-resistant sects and other Protestants. The Friends believe that the life of every person, however degraded, has worth and is guided by an Inner Light (sometimes called "the spirit of Christ"). This rules out any right to constrain men by means of violence. Also involved in it is the conviction that men should live the kind of life which removes the occasion for wars and builds a world of peace. Friends in general have not completely rejected the use of force by a civil government and often today work for the adoption of legislation and sometimes hold office, even as judges. Early Quakers, believing in the imminence of the spiritual regeneration of the world, eventually identified themselves with the civil government, expecting to administer to affairs of state on the principles of love, kindness and goodwill. With most Quakers there was a fundamental difference between the use of force in personal relations and by the military on one hand, and by a civil government on the other. After some years of Quaker administration in Pennsylvania, the Quakers withdrew from the government.

There is variation in opinion on the matter among present day Quakers, many of whom are not pacifists. Quakers have made large efforts at international relief and reconstruction, international conciliation and peace education, social reform activities and conscientious objection. Quakers describe their belief in peace in such terms as these: "The conviction that the spirit of Christ dwells in the souls of all men is the source of our refusal to take part in war, and of our opposition to slavery and oppression in every form. We believe that the primary Christian duty in relation to others is to appeal to that of God in them and, therefore, any method of oppression or violence that renders such an appeal impossible must be set out on one side." "There is a right and possible way for the family of nations to live together at peace.... It is the way of active, reconciling love, of overcoming evil with good. We feel an inward compulsion, which we cannot disregard, to strive to follow the way of constructive goodwill, despite the sense of our own shortcomings and despite the failure, in which we have shared, to labour sufficiently for the Kingdom of God on earth." "The fundamental ground of our opposition to war is religious and ethical.

It attaches to the nature of God as revealed in Christ and to the nature of man as related to Him.... The only absolute ground for an unalterable and inevitable opposition to war is one which attaches to the inherent nature of right and wrong, one which springs out of the consciousness of obligation to what the enlightened soul knows ought to be." This peace testimony "never was 'adopted'". For "it is not a policy; it is a conviction of the soul. It cannot be followed at one time and surrendered at another time.... The Christian way of life revealed in the New Testament, the voice of conscience revealed in the soul, the preciousness of personality revealed in the transforming force of love, and the irrationality revealed in modern warfare, either together or singly, present grounds which for those who feel them make participation in war under any conditions impossible." Friends "do not rest their case on sporadic texts. They find themselves confronted with a Christianity, the Christianity of the Gospels, that calls for a radical transformation of man, for the creation of a new type of person and for the building of a new social order, and they take this with utmost seriousness as a thing to be ventured and tried."

Persons sharing the "active reconciliation" beliefs often prefer a rather quietist approach to social problems, disliking anything akin to "agitation" or "trouble".

Some of them may thus oppose nonviolent resistance and direct action (including strikes, boycotts, etc.,) and even outspoken verbal statements, believing such methods to be violent in spirit, perhaps even immoral, and harmful in their effects on the opponent. They would prefer much more quiet methods, such as personal representations, letters and private deputations.

THE POWER NONVIOLENCE

Nonviolence in its dynamic condition means conscious suffering. It does not mean meek submission to the will of the evildoer, but it means the pitting of one's whole soul against the will of the tyrant. Working under this law of our being, it is possible for a single individual to defy the whole might of an unjust empire to save his honour, his religion, his soul and lay the foundation for that empire's fall or its regeneration. (YI, 1-8-1920, p3)

Active Force

The nonviolence of my conception is a more active and more real fighting against wickedness than retaliation whose very nature is to increase wickedness. I contemplate a mental and, therefore, a moral opposition to immoralities. I seek entirely to blunt the edge of the tyrant's sword, not by putting up against it a sharper-edged weapon, but by disappointing his expectation that I would be offering physical resistance. The resistance of the should that I should offer instead would elude him. It would at first dazzle him, and at last compel recognition from him, which recognition would not humiliate him but would uplift him. It may be urged that this again is an ideal state. And so it is.

The propositions from which I have drawn my arguments are as true as Euclid's definitions, which are none the less true because in practice we are unable to even draw Euclid's line on a blackboard. But even a geometrician finds it impossible to get on without bearing in mind Euclid's definitions. Nor may we...dispense with the fundamental propositions on which the doctrine of Satyagraha is based. (YI, 8-10-1925, p346)

I admit that the strong will rob the weak and that it is sin to be weak. But this is said of the soul in man, not of the body. If it be said of the body, we could never be free from the sin of weakness. But the strength of soul can defy a whole world in arms against it. This strength is open to the weakest in body. (YI, 6-5-1926, p164)

Nonviolence is the greatest force at the disposal of mankind. It is mightier than the mightiest weapon of destruction devised by the ingenuity of man. Destruction is not the law of the humans. Man lives freely by his readiness to die, if need be, at the hands of his brother, never by killing him. Every murder or other injury, no matter for what cause, committed or inflicted on another is a crime against humanity. (H, 20-7-1935, pp180-1)

Nonviolence is like radium in its action. An infinitesimal quantity of it embedded in a malignant growth acts continuously, silently and ceaselessly till it has transformed the whole mass of the diseased tissue into a healthy one. Similarly, even a little of true nonviolence acts in a silent, subtle, unseen way and leavens the whole society. (H, 12-11-1938, p327)

Matchless Bravery

An armed soldier relies on his weapons for his strength. Take away from him his weapons-his gun or his sword, and he generally becomes helpless. But a person who has truly realized the principle of nonviolence has the God-given strength for his weapon and the world has not known anything that can match it. (H, 19-11-1938, pp341-2)

A small body of determined spirits fired by an unquenchable faith in their mission can alter the course of history. (ibid, p343)

Nonviolence of the strong is any day stronger than that of the bravest soldier fully armed or a whole host. (H, 12-5-1946, p128)

Exercise in Faith

The hardest metal yields to sufficient heat. Even so the

hardest heart must melt before sufficiency of the heat of nonviolence. And there is no limit to the capacity of nonviolence to generate heat.

Every action is a resultant of a multitude of forces even of a contrary nature. There is no waste of energy. So we learn in the books on mechanics. This is equally true of human actions. The difference is that in the one case we generally know the forces at work, and when we do, we can mathematically foretell the resultant. In the case of human actions, they result from a concurrence of forces of most of which we have no knowledge. But our ignorance must not be made to serve the cause of disbelief in the power of these forces. Rather is our ignorance a cause for greater faith. And nonviolence being the mightiest force in the world and also the most elusive in its working, it demands the greatest exercise of faith. Even as we believe in God in faith, so have we to believe in nonviolence in faith. (H, 7-1-1939, p417)

Violence like water, when it has an outlet, rushes forward furiously with an overwhelming force. Nonviolence cannot act madly. It is the essence of discipline. But, when it is set going, no amount of violence can crush it. For full play, it requires unsullied purity and an unquenchable faith... (H, 21-3-1939, p433)

A Science

Ahimsa is a science. The word 'failure' has no place in the vocabulary of science. Failure to obtain the expected result is often the precursor to further discoveries. (H, 6-5-1939, p113)

If the function of himsa is to devour all it comes across, the function of ahimsa is to rush into the mouth of himsa. In an atmosphere of ahimsa one has no scope to put his ahimsa to the test. It can be tested only in the face of himsa. (H, 13-5-1939, p121)

Violence can only be effectively met by nonviolence. This is an old, established truth...that the weapon of violence, even if it was the atom bomb, became useless when matched against nonviolence. That very few understand how to wield this mighty weapon is true. It requires a lot of understanding and strength of mind. It is unlike what is needed in military schools and colleges. The difficulty one experiences in meeting himsa with ahimsa arises from weakness of mind. (H, 1-6-1947, p172)

The Deed, not Doer

'Hate the sin and not the sinner' is a precept which, though easy enough to understand, is rarely practised, and that is why the poison of hatred spreads in the world.

This ahimsa is the basis of the search for truth. I am realizing every day that the search is vain unless it is founded on ahimsa as the basis. It is quite proper to resist and attack a system, but to resist and attack its author is tantamount to resisting and attacking oneself. For we are all tarred with the same brush, and are children of one and the same creator, and as such, the divine powers within us are infinite. To slight a single human being is to slight those divine powers, and thus to harm not only that Being but with Him the whole world. (A, p203)

Man and his deed are two distinct things. Whereas a good deed should call forth approbation and a wicked deed disapprobation, the doer of the deed, whether good or wicked, always deserves respect or pity as the case may be. (ibid)

Those who seek to destroy men rather than manners adopt the latter and become worse than those whom they destroy under the mistaken belief that the manners will die with the men. They do not know the root of the evil. (YI, 17-3-1927, p85)

It is the acid test of nonviolence that, in a nonviolent conflict, there is no rancour left behind, and in the end the enemies are converted into friends. That was my experience in South Africa, with General Smuts. He started with being my bitterest opponent and critic. Today he is my warmest friend. (H, 12-11-1938, p327)

The principal implication of ahimsa is that the ahimsa in us ought to soften and not to stiffen our opponents' attitude to us; it ought to melt him; it ought to strike a responsive chord in his heart.

As ahimsa-ites, can you say that you practice genuine ahimsa? Can you say that you receive the arrows of the opponent on your bare breasts without returning them? Can you say that you are not angry, that you are not perturbed by his criticism? (H, 13-5-1939, p121)

By reason of life-long practice of ahimsa, I claim to be an expert in it, though very imperfect. Speaking in absolute terms, the more I practice it the clearer I see how far I am from the full expression of ahimsa in my life. It is his ignorance of this, the greatest duty of man in the world, which makes him say that in this age nonviolence has little scope in the face of violence, whereas I make bold to say that in this age of the Atom Bomb unadulterated nonviolence is the only force that can confound all the tricks put together of violence. (H, 16-11-1947, p412)

TRAINING FOR NONVIOLENCE

"How are we to train individuals or communities in this difficult art?" There is no royal road, except through living the creed in your life which must be a living sermon. Of course, the expression in one's own life presupposes great study, tremendous perseverance, and thorough cleansing of one's self of all the impurities.

If for mastering of the physical sciences you have to devote a whole life-time, how many lifetimes may be needed for mastering the greatest spiritual force that mankind has known? But why worry even if it means several lifetimes? For, if this is the only permanent thing in life, if this is the only thing that counts, then whatever effort you bestow on mastering it is well spent. Seek ye first the Kingdom of Heaven and everything else shall be added unto you. The Kingdom of Heaven is ahimsa. (H, 14-3-1936, p39)

Arms are surely unnecessary for a training in ahimsa. In fact the arms, if any, have to be thrown away, as the Khansaheb did in the Frontier Province. Those who hold that it is essential to learn violence before we can learn nonviolence, would hold that only sinners can be saints.

Fearlessness the Prerequisite

Just as one must learn the art of killing in the training for violence, so one must learn the art of dying in the training for nonviolence. Violence does not mean emancipation from fear, but discovering the means of combating the cause of fear. Nonviolence, on the other hand, has no cause for fear. The votary of nonviolence has to cultivate the capacity for sacrifice of the highest type in order to be free from fear. He racks not if he should lose his land, his wealth, his life. He who has not overcome all fear cannot practice ahimsa to perfection.

The votary of ahimsa has only one fear, that is of God. He who seeks refuge in God ought to have a glimpse of the Atman that transcends the body; and the moment one has a glimpse of the Imperishable Atman, one sheds the love of the perishable body. Training in nonviolence is thus diametrically opposed to training in violence. Violence is needed for the protection of things external, nonviolence is needed for the protection of the Atman, for the protection of one's honour.

This nonviolence cannot be learnt by staying at home. It needs enterprise. In order to test ourselves we should learn to dare danger and death, mortify the flesh, and acquire the capacity to endure all manner of hardships. He who trembles or take to his heels the moment he sees two people fighting is not nonviolent, but a coward. A nonviolent person will lay down his life in preventing such quarrels. The bravery of the nonviolent is vastly superior to that of the violent. The badge of the violent is his weapon-spear, or sword, or rifle. God is the shield of the nonviolent.

This is not course of training for one intending to learn nonviolence. But it is easy to evolve one from the principles I have laid down. (H, 1-9-1940, p268)

Nonviolence of the Brave

Nonviolence does not require any outside or outward training. It simply requires the will not to kill even in retaliation and the courage to face death without revenge. This is no sermon on ahimsa but cold reason and the statement of a universal law. Given the unquenchable faith in the law, no provocation should prove too great for the exercise of forbearance. This I have described as the nonviolence of the brave. (H, 8-9-1946, p296)

That nonviolence which only an individual can use is not of much use in terms of society. Man is a social being. His accomplishments to be of use must be such as any person with sufficient diligence can attain. That which can be exercised only among friends is of value only as a spark of nonviolence. It cannot merit the appellation of ahimsa. 'Enmity vanishes before ahimsa' is a great aphorism. It means that the greatest enmity requires an equal measure of ahimsa for its abatement.

Cultivation of this virtue may need long practice, ever extending to several births. It does not become useless on that account. Travelling along the route, the pilgrim will meet richer experiences from day to day, so that he may have a glimpse of the beauty he is destined to see at the top. This will add to his zest. No one is entitled to infer from this that the path will be a continuous carpet of roses without thorns. A poet has sung that the way to reach God accrues only to the very brave, never to the fainthearted. The atmosphere today is so much saturated with poison that one refuses to recollect the wisdom of the ancients and to perceive the varied little experience of ahimsa in action. 'A bad turn is neutralized by a good' ,is a wise saying of daily experience in practice. Why can we not see that if the sum total of the world's activities was destructive, it would have come to an end long ago? Love, otherwise, ahimsa, sustains this planet of ours. This much must be admitted. The precious grace of life has to be strenuously cultivated, naturally so because it is uplifting. Descent is easy, not so ascent. A large majority of us being undisciplined, our daily experience is that of fighting or swearing at one another on the slightest pretext.

This, the richest grace of ahimsa, will descend easily upon the owner of hard discipline. (H, 14-12-1947, p468)

APPLICATION OF NONVIOLENCE

If one does not practice nonviolence in one's personal relations with others, and hopes to use it in bigger affairs, one is vastly mistaken. Nonviolence like charity must begin at home.

But if it is necessary for the individual to be trained in nonviolence, it is even more necessary for the nation to be trained likewise. One cannot be nonviolent in one's own circle and violent outside it. Or else, one is not truly nonviolent even in one's own circle; often the nonviolence is only in appearance. It is only when you meet with resistance, as for instance, when a thief or a murderer appears, that your nonviolence is put on its trail. You either try or should try to oppose the thief with his own weapons, or you try to disarm him by love. Living among decent people, your conduct may not be described as a nonviolent. Mutual forbearance is nonviolence. Immediately, therefore, you get the conviction that nonviolence is the law of life, you have to practice it towards those who act violently towards you, and the law must apply to nations as individuals. Training no doubt is necessary. And beginnings are always small. But if the conviction is there, the rest will follow. (H, 28-1-1939, pp441-2)

Universality of Nonviolence

Nonviolence to be a creed has to be all-pervasive. I cannot be nonviolent about one activity of mine and violent about others. (H, 12-10-1935, p376)

It is a blasphemy to say that nonviolence can only be practiced by individuals and never by nations which are composed of individuals. (H, 12-11-1938, p328)

In my opinion, nonviolence is not passivity in any shape or form. Nonviolence, as I understand it, is the most active force in the world...Non-violence is the supreme law. During my half a century of experience, I have not yet come across a situation when I had to say that I was helpless, that I had no remedy in terms of nonviolence. (H, 24-12-1938, p393)

Cultivation of Nonviolence

I am an irrepressible optimist. My optimism rests on my belief in the infinite possibilities of the individual to develop nonviolence. The more you develop it in your own being, the more infectious it becomes till it over-whelms your surroundings and by and by might over sweep the world. (H, 28-1-1939, p443)

I have known from early youth that nonviolence is not a cloistered virtue to be practiced by the individual for his peace and final salvation, but it is a rule of conduct for society if it is to live consistently with human dignity and make progress towards the attainment of peace for which it has been yearning for ages past. (GCG, pp42-44, pp170-1)

To practice nonviolence in mundane matters is to know its true value. It is to bring heaven upon earth. There is no such thing as the other world. All works are one. There is no 'here' and no 'there'. As Jeans has demonstrated, the whole universe including the most distant stars, invisible even through the most powerful telescope in the world, is compressed in an atom.

I hold it, therefore, to be wrong to limit the use of nonviolence to cave-dwellers and for acquiring merit for a favoured position in the other world. All virtue ceases to have use if it serves no purpose in every walk of life. (H, 26-7-1942, p248)

Use on Mass Scale

Unfortunately for us, we are strangers to the nonviolence of the brave on a mass scale. Some even doubt the possibility of the exercise of nonviolence by groups, much less by masses of people. They restrict its exercise to exceptional individuals. Only, mankind can have no use of it if it is always reserved only for individuals. (H, 8-9-1946, p296)

Efficacy

I have been practicing with scientific precision nonviolence and its possibilities for an unbroken period of over fifty years. I have applied it in every walk of life, domestic, institutional, economic and political. I know of no single case in which it has failed. Where it has seemed sometimes to have failed, I have ascribed it to my imperfections. I claim no perfection for myself. But I do claim to be a passionate seeker after Truth, which is but another name for God. In the course of that search, the discovery of nonviolence came to me. Its spread is my life mission. I have no interest in living except for the prosecution of that mission. (H, 6-7-1940, pp185-6)

There is no hope for the aching world except through the narrow and straight path of nonviolence. Millions like me may fail to prove the truth in their own lives, that would be their failure, never of the eternal law. (H, 29-6-1947, p209)

THE NONVIOLENT SOCIETY

I hold that nonviolence is not merely a personal virtue. It is also a social virtue to be cultivated like the other virtues. Surely society is largely regulated by the expression of nonviolence in its mutual dealings. What I ask for is an extension of it on a larger, national and international scale. (H, 7-1-1939, p417)

All society is held together by nonviolence, even as the earth is held in her position by gravitation. But when the law of gravitation was discovered, the discovery yielded results of which our ancestors had no knowledge.

Even so, when society is deliberately constructed in accordance with the law of nonviolence, its structure will be different in material particulars from what it is today. But I cannot say in advance what the government based on nonviolence will be like.

What is happening today is disregard of the law of nonviolence and enthronement of violence as if it were an eternal law. (H, 11-12-1939, p8)

Society based on nonviolence can only consist of groups settled in villages in which voluntary cooperation is the condition of dignified and peaceful existence. (H, 13-1-1940, pp410-11)

The Government

The Government cannot succeed in becoming entirely nonviolent, because it represents all the people. I do not today conceive of such a golden age. But I do believe in the possibility of a predominantly nonviolent society. And I am working for it. (H, 9-3-1940, p31)

There remains the question as to whether in an ideal society, there should be any or no government. I do not think we need worry ourselves about this at the moment. If we continue to work for such a society, it will slowly come into being to an extent, such that the people can benefit by it. Euclid's line is one without breadth, but no one has so far been able to draw it and never will. All the same, it is only by keeping the ideal line in mind that we have made progress in geometry. What is true here is true of every ideal.

Anarchy

It must be remembered that nowhere in the world does a State without government exist. If at all it could ever come into being, it would be in India; for, ours is the only country where the attempt has, at any rate, been made.

We have not yet been able to show that bravery to the degree which is necessary and for the attainment of which there is only one way. Those who have faith in the latter have to demonstrate it. In order to do so, the fear of death has to be completely shed, just as we have shed the fear of prisons. (H, 15-9-1946, p309)

Democracy and Nonviolence

Science of war leads one to dictatorship pure and simple. Science of nonviolence can alone lead one to pure democracy. (H, 15-10-1938, p290)

Democracy and violence can ill go together. The State that are today nominally democratic have either to become frankly totalitarian, or if they are to become truly democratic, they must become courageously nonviolent. (H, 12-11-1938, p328)

Holding the view that, without the recognition of nonviolence on a national scale, there is no such thing as a constitutional or democratic government, I devote my energy to the propagation of nonviolence as the law of our life, individual, social, political, national and international.

I fancy that I have seen the light, though dimly. I write cautiously for I do not profess to know the whole of the Law. If I know the success of my experiments, I know also my failures. But the successes are enough to fill me with undying hope.

I have often said that if one takes care of the means, the end will take care of itself. Nonviolence is the means, the end for everyone is complete independence. There will be an international League only when all the nations, big or small, composing it are fully independent. The nature of that independence will correspond to the extent of nonviolence assimilated by the nations concerned. One thing is certain. In a society based on nonviolence, the smallest nation will feel as tall as the tallest. The idea of superiority and inferiority will be wholly obliterated.

...The conclusion is irresistible that for one like me, wedded to nonviolence, constitutional or democratic government is a distant dream so long as nonviolence is not recognized as a living force, an inviolable creed, not a mere policy. While I prate about universal nonviolence, my experiment is confined to India. If it succeeds, the world will accept it without effort. There is however a bit BUT. The pause does not worry me. My faith is brightest in the midst of impenetrable darkness. (H, 11-12-1939, p8)

Use of Power

By its very nature, nonviolence cannot 'seize' power, nor can that be its goal. But nonviolence can do more; it can effectively control and guide power without capturing the machinery of government. That is its beauty.

There is an exception, of course. If the nonviolent noncooperation of the people is so complete that the administration ceases to function or if the administration crumbles under the impact of a foreign invasion and a vacuum results, the people's representatives will then step in and fill it. Theoretically that is possible.

But the use of power need not necessarily be violent. A father wields power over his children; he may even punish but not by inflicting violence. The most effective exercise of power is that which irks least. Power rightly exercised must sit light as a flower; no one should feel the weight of it.

The people accepted the authority of the Congress willingly. I was on more than one occasion invested with the absolute power of dictatorship. But everybody knew that my power rested on their willing acceptance. They could set me aside at any time and I would have stepped aside without a murmur.

Prophets and supermen are born only once in an age. But if even a single individual realizes the ideal of ahimsa in its fullness, he covers and redeems the whole society. Once Jesus had blazed the trail, his twelve disciples could carry on his mission without his presence.

It needed the perseverance and genius of so many generations of scientists to discover the laws of electricity, but today everybody, even children use electric power in their daily life. Similarly, it will not always need a perfect being to administer an ideal State once it has come into being. What is needed is a thorough social awakening to begin with. The rest will follow.

To take an instance nearer home, I have presented to the working class the truth that true capital is not silver or gold, but the labour of their hands and feet and their intelligence. Once labour develops that awareness, it would not need my presence to enable it to make use of the power that it will release. (TNH, pp91-93)

APPLICATIONS OF NONVIOLENCE

The nonviolent approach is in one aspect based on the use and efficacy of moral force (Gandhi's term was "soul-force") as against physical force or violence. President Johnson has made on the whole an admirable record in the matter of civil rights. He has even ventured into places like Atlanta to plead that integration is a moral issue. He has exerted moral force in this way. Subsequently he was urged in various quarters to send troops into Mississippi. Sending troops is an essentially political act. An essentially moral act would have been for President Johnson not to send troops but to take upon himself responsibility for going to Jackson personally in order to confer with Governor Paul B. Johnson, Jr., to meet the editors of the State, the clergy, perhaps the lawyers, the civil rights volunteers, and so on. This would not be primarily on the technical issue of law enforcement, but on the basic human and moral issue with which not only Mississippi but the whole nation is now confronted; according to Mr. Johnson's own declarations.

It is foreign to nonviolence to seek a victory over other human beings in a war in which one group of humans is arrayed against another. The aim is not to conquer and humiliate the "enemy" but to change his mind and will. The system or institutional pattern in which people are involved-whatever the prevailing pattern of domination and subordination may be at a given time-is conceived as something which traps, harms, degrades all who live under it. This means, as Martin Luther King, Jr. has put it more than once, that the aim of the civil rights movement is to "liberate" the South, not only to liberate Negroes. I am well aware that there are many in the current movement in Mississippi who share these views. However, they are by no means universally held and I am suggesting that more effort be put into cultivating this attitude in all civil rights workers and in trying to communicate to Mississippians that this is the spirit which motivates the movement for equality.

I take it that Quakers are doing this to some extent, but my own experiences recently in Georgia in some sections of which conditions are not too dissimilar from Mississippi, have given me a strong conviction that more effort should be put into attempts to set up communication between members of the white and Negro communities. This involves a patient effort to locate the members of the white community, clergy and lay, who have a measure of sensitivity and intelligence. They are consequently inwardly disturbed, but ordinarily for motives creditable and not creditable, they do not act and speak. Yet time and thought need to begin reaching these people. They will largely determine in the end what happens in the local community. I do not mean by that to rule out or deprecate the role of the "outside agitator", having been one most of my life. The polarization and absence of communication are to be reckoned with as a fact; they must not be accepted as the basis on which warfare is to be waged.

One hesitates to raise the point of "protection" and "defence" in face of the brutality so often witnessed in many Southern ocalities. And I have repeatedly pointed out that it is the duty of the authorities, by their own professed standards and the law of the land, to provide peaceful demonstrators with protection. It is legitimate for citizens who accept these premises to insist that the protection be provided. But it is not a part of the nonviolent strategy or ethos to ask for protection which ultimately rests on violence to restrain violence. nonviolence means to go unarmed and in that sense to be defenceless. This also means not having arms-one's own or that of the police or the army, in reserve somewhere. It means to take suffering upon oneself and to avoid inflicting it in any way on others.

I am, therefore, proposing that the practice of calling on the police and especially on troops for protection be abandoned by the civil rights movement. To be consistent I think we have to adopt that course in relation to Mississippi. Let the authorities face up to their own responsibilities but let us operate on our own assumptions and our own nonviolent ethic. I firmly believe myself that it may well be the only way in which Mississippi can in fact be disarmed and transformed.

There is a sense in which young people ought to have "protection", though they have made it magnificently clear that they are not looking for an easy life. Is it out of the question to ask decent Mississippians to act as escorts for each team of volunteers? Or the parents or other relatives of the volunteers might act in that capacity. Or clergy in pairs from various parts of the country. I gather that some of these ideas are already being considered.

MORE AGGRESSIVE NONVIOLENCE

There are two final observations. One of the reasons, in my opinion, why nonviolence has become obnoxious to many Negroes is a pattern often followed in civil rights struggles. When the struggle in a city like Birmingham reaches the point where a significant breakthrough seems imminent, the powers that be become tougher and more violent. They accuse the nonviolent leaders of provoking violence and that any blood if it is shed will be on their hands. The latter are deeply troubled. The outcome is the setting up of a bi-racial committee which is to work out steps toward integration. The struggle is thus relaxed or even initially abandoned. And nothing happens. I suggest this pattern be avoided in the future. The struggle should be maintained until some specific steps towards integration are assured. Secondly, the typical struggle involves large numbers but is usually at a low level of intensity, in the sense that leaders and rank and file expect to be bailed out promptly, with the result that very large amounts of money are tied up indefinitely which has a crippling effect financially on future activities. A sounder nonviolent strategy would be to refuse to put up bail or spend large sums on trials, to remain in jail, for those able to do so to fast or go on hunger strike, and so on. This in turn would deeply stir the community, Negro and, at least to some extent, also the white, and would contribute towards the political force and effectiveness of the movement.

What has appeared up to this point was written before the adoption of the civil rights bill. It is obviously too early to make a definite analysis of the effects of its adoption and of the way it is or is not being enforced. Nevertheless the first impact of the new situation, the post-adoption period, has occurred and we cannot avoid trying to make a provisional assessment of what this means for future strategy.

It seems to me clear that the adoption of the bill, whatever its shortcomings, is a notable gain. We have only to think for a moment where we should now be if a filibuster were on and the bill had failed of adoption. By no stretch of the imagination can the adoption be laid to violence on the part of the integration movement. It is the fruit of a militantly nonviolent struggle.

There are dramatic instances such as that of the businessmen and Mayor Allen C. Thompson of Jackson, Mississippi, standing together "against the White Citizen's Council in a decision to comply with the Civil Rights Act". Peaceful integration of hotels, motels and restaurants has, "to the surprise of many of the Mississippians", as the New York Times reports, actually taken place. I think of another example, close to myself and the whole nonviolent movement, in which such organizations as the War Resister's League and the Committee for Nonviolent Action are involved, *viz.* Albany, Georgia. Reports from the scene there reveal that there also integration of hotels and eating places has taken place without incident, and the atmosphere is on the whole relaxed! It is difficult for anyone who was close to the ordeal which the Quebec-Washington-Guantanamo Peace Walkers experienced in Albany earlier in 1964 to believe that this could possibly be true; yet it is.

Without going into further detail, it is clear that in so far as any conclusion can be drawn from the latest developments they point to the application of a militant and imaginative strategy of nonviolence. They certainly give no support to an abandonment of that strategy.

VIOLENCE AS THE ENEMY

The civil rights movement has its own task and must deal with the problems and dilemmas which spring directly from it. However, its leaders and many of its members already are aware of the fact that civil rights in a meaningful and decisive degree can be achieved only in the context of a Triple Revolution which will also solve the problem of jobs and the problem of peace. Both have to be solved, obviously. for all; there is no such thing as a solution for some and not for others.

The problem of "peace" relates to the relations between nations in the era of nuclear technology. But it relates to much more. Any force of "violence" that has social dimensions and implications takes on new evil meaning because it may "escalate" into war, get out of hand and bring on the danger of extinguishing civilization, if not the race itself. Furthermore, as daily events testify, alongside refinements in modern culture, we are confronted with frustration, alienation, swift change apparently beyond human control, and consequently with violence in many forms. It can no longer be considered a minor matter for those seeking to combat the "anti-human" in any form whether violence is to be resorted to for the sake of a seemingly good and necessary end or whether a decision for or against violence itself is now basic for every human being and especially for committed devotees of any "cause".

The great French novelist, philosopher and hero of the Resistance, Albert Camus, some time ago came to the conclusion that the latter is indeed the case. In 1947 he wrote an essay which states the challenge to break with murder and violence and suggests how that may be done. His is a voice that will be listened to not without a measure of respect on both or all sides of the lines that divide men into warring camps and sometimes lead to a proliferation of violence on many levels which make us wonder whether mankind is dominated by a wish to die. The essay is entitled "Neither Victims Nor Executioners". Crudely put, it points out that in a world saturated in violence we may not have a choice as to whether or not to be victims but we can still choose not to be executioners. "For my part", he concludes, "I am fairly sure that I have made the choice.... I will never again be one of those, whoever they be, who compromise with murder." The basic decision that must be made, he elaborates, is "whether Humanity's lot must be made still more miserable in order to achieve far-off and shadowy ends, whether we should accept a world bristling with arms where brother kills brother; or whether, on the contrary, we should avoid bloodshed and misery as much as possible so that we give a chance for survival to later generations better equipped than we are".

Camus in 1947 assumed that only a few at first would take the course of rejecting murder as a social instrument and embracing nonviolence, the course of "discovering a style of life". Even so he felt that precisely such a minority would exhibit a "positively dazzling realism". But may it not be that in the nuclear age multitudes on both sides of barriers may indeed be driven both by necessity-the need for bare survival-and by moral passion, to commit themselves to nonviolence?

Even Camus a decade or so ago could not reject the possibility of such a development and accordingly concluded his essay with this beautiful expression of-hope that "the thirst for fraternity which burns in Western man" might be satisfied. He wrote: "Over the expanse of five continents throughout the coming years an endless struggle is going to be pursued between violence and friendly persuasion, a struggle in which granted, the former has a thousand times the chance of success than the latter. But I have always held that, if he who bases his hope on human nature is a fool, he who gives up in the face of circumstances is a coward."

NONVIOLENCE AND LABOUR

The vital role which organized labour must necessarily play in highly industrialized societies makes its attitude to violence and nonviolence of unusual importance. Two contradictory tendencies have been present in American labour. On the one hand, its lack of political sophistication and difficulty of gaining recognition have all too frequently involved it in the violence of a capitalist culture. On the other hand, it is from certain leaders of labour, active as they are in the practical day-to-day problems of negotiating agreements and considering strikes, that some of the best insights into the power of nonviolence have come. Legal recognition and protection of the right to organize and bargain collectively were won only after much travail: the story begins early in the nineteenth century, when labour organization was ruled a "conspiracy" under common law, and extends to the passage of the National Labour Relations Act during the presidency of Franklin D. Roosevelt. Since Roosevelt, problems of large-scale organisation and bureaucracy, jurisdictional conflicts, and leadership issues have provided new temptations to violence.

During the period between the Civil War and the New Deal, business corporations often stooped to almost any methods to control labour, not excluding private police, professional strike breakers, and actual physical force. It is not surprising that in this context workers often resorted to violence in retaliation, particularly since the corporations were so frequently supported by public authority.

In part, the tendency of labour to sometimes turn to violence was, as Robert Hunter argued, the result of its lack of political sophistication. Despite the arguments of Socialists within its ranks, it refused to develop an independent political movement which might have related its own immediate interests to long-run considerations of fundamental public policy. Its very lack of commitment to revolutionary change subjected it to the imperatives of an often violent culture. Even the sit-down strikes of the thirties (in industrial Michigan), which might have become the inspiration for a philosophy of nonviolent power, were marred by acts of violence. Although the industrial union movement (Congress of Industrial Organizations) helped remove some of the frustrations of an American labour organization hitherto dominated by narrow craft unionism, the very rapidity of growth which resulted, combined with continued absence of an over-all political philosophy for guidance, subjected post-World-War II American labour to many stresses. Sometimes labour organizations were allied with the underworld of violent crime; and on occasion certain leaders resorted to violence to maintain their own power or that of their organizations.

But the other side of the picture is also important. In the early days, many were impressed by the way in which German socialists resisted-largely by nonviolent methods-the repressive legislation of Bismarck; and they noted the comment of Wilhelm Liebknecht that "moral force" had preserved the integrity of the labour and socialist movement. To some extent, the ideology of the general strike, which had its devotees in the United States, exalted the principle of nonviolent coercion. The novelist Jack London, in a graphic essay, portrayed a vision of what the general strike might do to paralyse the whole machinery of industry and government without firing a shot, thus inaugurating a truly nonviolent revolution.

Several American anarchist theorists, too, thought that both labour and society in general were to be emancipated primarily through political enlightenment and passive resistance to social wrong. Thus Benjamin Tucker, a well-known individualist anarchist, maintained that while governments can usually quell violent resistance, no army can in the long run defeat men who simply stay home from the polling booths, refuse to enter the army, firmly and peacefully demonstrate, or decline to pay taxes.

From a more orthodox point of view, Tom Mooney, a well known American labour martyr, observed: "Violence is the weapon used by the employers. Violence wins no strike... only education and organization." Other labour leaders from time to time have repeated his sentiments, contending that the greater the violence, the less likely it is that a strike will be successful. And in post-World-War II America, as a matter of fact, most spokesmen for labour would undoubtedly have endorsed this position.

Although American labour itself had not by the postwar epoch developed a general philosophy of nonviolence (as contrasted with more or less pragmatic observations), the idea of the perfectly nonviolent and self-disciplined strike had become a model for the thinking of those, like R.B. Gregg (himself a lawyer interested in labour matters), who had worked out such a philosophy. To the student of nonviolence observing labour in the sixties of the twentieth century, a number of questions might occur. Was there a chance that, under stress of rapid technological change, labour might at long last develop an overall political philosophy that would embrace a theory of nonviolence? Could it re-think its position vis-a-vis an American State so committed to preparation for war? Could it come to realize its vast potentialities for leading American society away from notions of military defence to conceptions of nonviolent resistance to invasion-conceptions that might well rely on its own experience of the strike? The possibilities appeared so great; yet the vision, on the whole, remained so narrow.

SOCIAL JUSTICE: THE NEGRO STRUGGLE AND NONVIOLENCE

As for nonviolence and the struggle for racial justice, it had its antecedents in earlier movements and particularly in the conflict for the emancipation of women. After first turning to respectable methods without many results, women like Alice Paul, who had been brought up in the Quaker tradition, suggested more dramatic and less orthodox action. A recent writer has thus described the methods used after Alice Paul's techniques came to be adopted: "The militants staged massive parades and kept them marching while the women were subjected to obscene insults, spat upon, slapped in the face, tripped up and pelted with burning cigar stubs. Early in 1917, Alice Paul launched her most belligerent effort-the day-after-day picketing of the White House with purple-white-and-gold banners shrilling: Mr. President, How Long Must Women Wait for Democracy?"

Negroes, like women, had been exploited, denied human dignity and for many years been kept in a condition of near-servitude. In the fifties of the twentieth century, they decided that they had enough and in effect asked the same question as the early feminists, How Long Must We Wait for Democracy? They turned to direct nonviolent action, aided and abetted by such legal decisions as that of the Supreme Court declaring, in 1954, that racial segregation in the public schools (a common practice in many States) was a violation of the constitution of the United States. By nonviolent direct action they began not merely to undermine the structure of racial injustice but also to develop a sense of self-confidence and dignity. Just as Gandhi found that the Indian masses had first to eliminate their own slavish attitudes before they could effectively oppose imperialism, so Martin Luther King, a leader of the Negro struggle, emphasized destruction of the "Uncle Tom" mentality. He observed: "The nonviolent approach does not immediately change the heart of the oppressor. It first does something to the hearts and souls of those committed to it. It gives them new self-respect; it calls up resources of strength and courage that they did not know they had."

The power of nonviolence to develop a sense of dignity and self confidence as well as to accomplish social results was demonstrated in the Montgomery, Alabama bus boycott of the fifties and in such later examples of nonviolent direct action as freedom rides, sit-ins, wade-ins, and street demonstrations. In the bus boycott, thousands of Negroes walked to work, often over long distances, rather than surrender their objective, the desegregation of buses. In sit-ins, mixed Negro and white groups would deliberately order food in segregated restaurants and, if ill-used physically, would refuse to retaliate in kind. Wade-ins involved similar action in segregated swimming pools. As for freedom rides, groups of Negroes and whites helped break down segregation patterns in buses. Street demonstrations, which were unusually well disciplined considering provocations, sought among other objectives to affect patterns of employment and to secure implementation of and respect for equal opportunity laws already on the statute books.

Although there were many frustrations and full Negro freedom may involve struggles for another generation, nonviolent direct action helped revive the conscience of the United States, provided implementing power for court decisions and statutes, and built up the courage of Negroes for future action. In terms of immediate results, too, it appeared to be effective. Thus the Montgomery bus boycott did break down segregation in the buses of the city; and Martin Luther King tells us that between 1959 and 1961, lunch counters in more than 150 cities were actually desegregated by "sit-in" direct actionists.

The major stream of Negro action, moreover, was animated by principled nonviolence and not merely by expediency. Men like Martin Luther King and Ralph Abernathy were deeply influenced by Gandhi, as well as by their interpretation of Christian teaching. Although King at no point in his life had wondered whether there was validity to the thesis that group action could not or need not abstain from violence, Gandhi's teaching appeared to remove any doubts he may have had.

Negro nonviolence did not lack its challengers, however. Some doubted whether it could be "effective" in the long run. Others frankly thought of it as a mere expediency, at best. It was by no means certain, as this is written, that the exponents of principled nonviolence would continue to occupy the centre of the stage.

Were nonviolence to be repudiated by the American Negro, it would be a sad day for the Negro, for America, and for the world. For the Negro, it would cut off a promising development in midstream and almost certainly help frustrate the quest for freedom: repudiation of nonviolence would restore the initiative to segregation leaders and alienate public opinion as well. America as a whole would lose, since the abandonment of nonviolence would probably strengthen the many forces of authoritarianism and militarism undoubtedly present in the United States. Finally, the world would find compromised and clouded the case studies on the Negro emancipation movement which it might otherwise have used as bases for the development of principled nonviolence elsewhere, especially in international relations.

9

Gandhi and the Gospel of Truth

What...is Truth? A difficult question; but I have solved it for myself by saying that it is what the voice within tells you. How then, you ask, [do] different people think of different and contrary truths? Well, seeing that the human mind works through innumerable media and that the evolution of the human mind is not the same for all, it follows that what may be truth for one may be untruth for another, and hence those who have made these experiments have come to the conclusion that there are certain conditions to be observed in making those experiments... It is because we have at the present moment everybody claiming the right of conscience without going through any discipline whatsoever, and there is so much untruth being delivered to a bewildered world. All that I can in true humility present to you is that Truth is not to be found by anybody who has not got an abundant sense of humility. If you would swim on the bosom of the ocean of Truth, you must reduce yourself to a zero. YI, 31-12-1931, p428)

Truth and Love-ahimsa-is the only thing that counts. Where this is present, everything rights itself in the end. This is a law to which there is no exception. (YI, 18-8-1927, p265)

Sovereign Principle

For me truth is the sovereign principle, which includes numerous other principles. This truth is not only truthfulness in word, but truthfulness in thought also, and not only the relative truth of our conception, but the Absolute Truth, the Eternal Principle, that is God. There are innumerable definitions of God, because His manifestations are innumerable. They overwhelm me with wonder and awe and for a moment stun me.

But I worship God as Truth only. I have not yet found Him, but I am seeking after Him. I am prepared to sacrifice the things dearest to me in pursuit of this quest. Even if the sacrifice demanded be my very life, I hope I may be prepared to give it.

But as long as I have not realized this Absolute Truth, so long must I hold by the relative truth as I have conceived it. That relative truth must, meanwhile, be my beacon, my shield and buckler. Though this path is strait and narrow and sharp as the razor's edge, for me it has been the quickest and easiest. Even my Himalayan blunders have seemed trifling to me because I have kept strictly to this path. For the path has saved me from coming to grief, and I have gone forward according to my light. Often in my progress I have had faint glimpses of the Absolute Truth, God, and daily the conviction is growing upon me that He alone is real and all else is unreal.

Quest for Truth

.....The further conviction has been growing upon me that whatever is possible for me is possible even for a child, and I have found sound reasons for saying so. The instruments for the quest of Truth are as simple as they are difficult. They may appear quite impossible to an arrogant person, and quite possible to an innocent child.

The seeker after Truth should be humbler than the dust. The world crushes the dust under its feet, but the seeker after Truth should so humble himself that even the dust could crush him. Only then, and not till then, will he have a glimpse of Truth. (A, p xv)

Truth is like a vast tree, which yields more and more fruit the more you nurture it. The deeper the search in the mine of truth the richer the discovery of the gems buried there, in the shape of openings for an even greater variety of service. (ibid, p159)

I think it is wrong to expect certainties in this world, where all else but God that is Truth is an uncertainty. All that appears and happens about and around is uncertain, transient. But there is a Supreme Being hidden therein as a Certainty, and one would be blessed if one could catch a glimpse of that certainty and hitch one's wagon to it. The quest for that Truth is the summum bonum of life. (ibid, p184)

In the march towards Truth, anger, selfishness, hatred, etc., naturally give way, for otherwise Truth would be impossible to attain. A man who is swayed by passions may have good enough intentions, may be truthful in word, but he will never find the Truth. A successful search for Truth means complete deliverance from the dual throng such as of love and hate, happiness and misery. (ibid, pp254-5)

Vision of Truth

To see the universal and all-pervading spirit of Truth face to face one must be able to love the meanest of creation as oneself. And a man who aspires after that cannot afford to keep out of any field of life. That is why my devotion to Truth has drawn me into the field of politics; and I can say without the slightest hesitation, and yet in all humility, that those who say that religion has nothing to do with politics do not know what religion means. (ibid, pp370-1)

My uniform experience has convinced me that there is no other God than Truth... The little fleeting glimpses... that I have been able to have of Truth can hardly convey an idea of the indescribable luster of Truth, a million times more intense than that of the sun we daily see with our eyes. (YI, 7-2-1929, p42)

In fact, what I have caught is only the faintest gleam of that mighty effulgence. But this much I can say with assurance, as a result of all my experiments, that a perfect vision of Truth can only follow a complete realization of ahimsa. (ibid)

Truth resides in every human heart, and one has to search for it there, and to be guided by truth as one sees it. But no one has a right to coerce others to act according to his own view of truth. (H, 24-11-1933, p6)

Absolute Truth

It is not given to man to know the whole Truth. His duty lies in living up to the truth as he sees it, and in doing so, to resort to the purest means, i.e., to nonviolence. (ibid)

God alone knows absolute truth. Therefore, I have often said, Truth is God. It follows that man, a finite being, cannot know absolute truth. (H, 7-4-1946, p70)

Nobody in this world possesses absolute truth. This is God's attribute alone. Relative truth is all we know. Therefore, we can only follow the truth as we see it. Such pursuit of truth cannot lead anyone astray.

(H, 2-6-1946, p167)

Truth and I

I have in my life never been guilty of saying things I did not mean-my nature is to go straight to the heart and, if often I fail in doing so for the time being, I know that Truth will ultimately make itself heard and felt, as it has often done in my experience. (YI, 20-8-1925, pp285-6)

Let hundreds like me perish, but let Truth prevail. Let us not reduce the standards of Truth even by a hair's breadth for judging erring mortals like myself. (A, p xv)

In judging myself I shall try to be as harsh as truth, as I want others also to be. Measuring myself by that standard I must exclaim with Surdas.

Where is there a wretch?
So wicked and loathsome as I?
I have forsaken by Maker,
So faithless have I been. (ibid, p xvi)

My Errors

I may be a despicable person, but when Truth speaks through me, I am invincible. (EF, p71)

I am devoted to none but Truth and I owe no discipline to anybody but Truth. (H, 25-5-1935, p115)

I have no God to serve but Truth. (H, 15-4-1939, p87)

I have no strength except what comes from insistence on truth. Nonviolence, too, springs from the same insistence. (H, 7-4-1946, p70)

I am a humble but very earnest seeker after Truth. And in my search, I take all fellow-seekers in uttermost confidence so that I may know my mistakes and correct them. I confess that I have often erred in my estimates and judgments... And inasmuch as in every case I retraced my steps, no permanent harm was done. On the contrary, the fundamental truth of nonviolence has been made infinitely more manifest than it ever has been, and the country has in no way been permanently injured. (YI, 21-4-1927, p126)

I am a learner myself, I have no axe to grind, and wherever I see a truth, I take it up and try to act up to it. (YI, 11-8-1927, p250)

I believe that, if in spite of the best of intentions, one is led into committing mistakes, they do not really result in harm to the world or, for the matter of that, any individual. God always saves the world from the consequences of unintended errors or men who live in fear of Him.

Those who are likely to be misled by my example would have gone that way all the same even if they had not known of my action. For, in the final analysis, a man is guided in his conduct by his own inner promptings, though the example of others might sometimes seem to guide him. But be it as it may, I know that the world has never had to suffer on account of my errors because they were all due to my ignorance. It is my firm belief that not one of my known errors was willful. (YI, 3-1-1929, p6)

Indeed, what may appear to be an obvious error to one may appear to another as pure wisdom. He cannot help himself even if he is under a hallucination.

Truly as Tulsidas said: 'Even though there never is silver in mother o' pearl nor water in the sunbeams, while the illusion of silver in the shinning shell or that of water in the beam lasts, no power on earth can shake the deluded man free from the spell.' Even so must it be with men like me who, it may be, are labouring under a great hallucination. Surely God will pardon them and the world should bear with them. Truth will assert itself in the end. (ibid)

Truth never damages a cause that is just. (H, 10-11-1946, p389)

Life is an aspiration. Its mission is to strive after perfection, which is self-realization. The ideal must not be lowered because of our weaknesses or imperfections. I am painfully conscious of both in me. The silent cry daily goes out to Truth to help me to remove these weakness and imperfections of mine. (H, 22-6-1935, p145)

No Abandonment of Truth

Believe me when I tell you, after 60 years of personal experience, that the only real misfortune is to abandon the path of truth. If you but realize this, your one prayer to God will always be to enable you to put up, without flinching, with any number of trials and hardships that may fall to your lot in the pursuit of truth. (H, 28-7-1946, p243)

Truth alone will endure, all the rest will be swept away before the tide of time. I must, therefore, continue to bear testimony to Truth even if I am forsaken by all. Mine may today be a voice in the wilderness, but it will be heard when all other voices are silenced, if it is the voice of Truth. (H, 15-8-1946, p284)

A man of faith will remain steadfast to truth, even-though the whole world might appear to be enveloped in falsehood. (H, 22-9-1946, p322)

When it is relevant, truth has to be uttered, however unpleasant it may be. Irrelevance is always untruth and should never be uttered. (H, 21-12-1947, p473)

TRUTH IS GOD

God Is

There is an indefinable mysterious Power that pervades everything. I feel it, though I do not see it. It is this unseen Power which makes itself felt and yet defies all proof, because it is so unlike all that I perceive through my senses. It transcends the senses. But it is possible to reason out the existence of God to a limited extent.

I do dimly perceive that whilst everything around me is ever changing, ever-dying, there is underlying all that change a Living Power that is changeless, that holds all together, that creates, dissolves, and recreates. That informing Power or Spirit is God. And since nothing else I see merely through the senses can or will persist, He alone is.

And is this Power benevolent or malevolent? I see it as purely benevolent. For I can see, that in the midst of death life persists, in the midst of untruth truth persists, in the midst of darkness light persists. Hence I gather that God is Life, Truth, Light. He is Love. He is the Supreme Good.

I confess... that I have no argument to convince... through reason. Faith transcends reason. All I can advise... is not to attempt the impossible. I cannot account for the existence of evil by any rational method. To want to do so is to be co-equal with God. I am, therefore, humble enough to recognize evil as such; and I call God long-suffering and patient precisely because He permits evil in the world. I know that He has no evil in Him and yet if there is evil, He is the author of it and yet untouched by it.

I know, too, that I shall never know God if I do not wrestle with and against evil even at the cost of life itself. I am fortified in the belief by my own humble and limited experience. The purer I try to become the nearer to God I feel myself to be. How much more should I be near to Him when my faith is not a mere apology, as it is today, but has become as immovable as the Himalayas and as white and bright as the snows on their peaks? (YI, 11-10-1928, pp340-1)

My Faith

I can easily put up with the denial of the world, but any denial by me of my God is unthinkable. (YI, 23-2-1922, p112)

I know that I can do nothing. God can do everything. O God, make me Thy fit instrument and use me as thou wilt! (YI, 9-10-1924, p329)

I have not seen Him, neither have I known Him. I have made the world's faith in God my own and as my faith is ineffaceable, I regard that faith as amounting to experience. However, as it may be said that to describe faith as experience is to tamper with truth, it may perhaps be more correct to say that I have no word for characterizing my belief in God. (A, p206)

I am surer of His existence than of the fact that you and I are sitting in this room. Then I can also testify that I may live without air and water but not without Him. You may pluck out my eyes, but that cannot kill me. You may chop off my nose, but that will not kill me. But blast my belief in God, and I am dead.

You may call this a superstition, but I confess it is a superstition that I hug, even as I used to hug the name of Rama in my childhood when there was any cause of danger or alarm. That was what an old nurse had taught me. (H, 14-5-1938, p109)

I believe that we can all become messengers of God, if we cease to fear man and seek only God's Truth. I do believe I am seeking only God's Truth and have lost all fear of man.

...I have no special revelation of God's will. My firm belief is that He reveals Himself daily to every human being, but we shut our ears to the 'still small voice'. We shut our eyes to the Pillar of Fire in front of us. I realize His omnipresence. (YI, 25-5-1921, pp161-2)

Some of my correspondents seem to think that I can work wonders. Let me say as a devotee of truth that I have no such gift. All the power I may have comes from God. But He does not work directly. He works through His numberless agencies. (H, 8-10-1938, p285)

Nature of God

To me God is Truth and Love; God is ethics and morality; God is fearlessness. God is the source of Light and Life and yet He is above and beyond all these. God is conscience. He is even the atheism of the atheist. For in His boundless love God permits the atheist to live. He is the searcher of hearts. He transcends speech and reason. He knows us and our hearts better than we do ourselves. He does not take us at our word, for He knows that we often do not mean it, some knowingly and others unknowingly.

He is a personal God to those who need His personal presence. He is embodied to those who need His touch. He is the purest essence. He simply is to those who have faith. He is all things to all men. He is in us and yet above and beyond us...

He cannot cease to be because hideous immoralities or inhuman brutalities are committed in His name. He is long-suffering. He is patient but He is also terrible. He is the most exacting personage in the world and the world to come. He metes out the same measure to us that we mete out to our neighbors-men and brutes.

With Him ignorance is no excuse. And withal He is ever forgiving, for He always gives us the chance to repent.

He is the greatest democrat the world knows, for He leaves us 'unfettered' to make our own choice between evil and good. He is the greatest tyrant ever known, for He often dashes the cup from our lips and under cove of free will leaves us a margin so wholly inadequate as to provide only mirth for Himself at our expense.

Therefore it is that Hinduism calls it all His sport-lila, or calls it all an illusion-maya. We are not, He alone Is. And if we will be, we must eternally sing His praise and do His will. Let us dance to the tune of His bansi-lute, and all would be well. (YI, 5-3-1925, p81)

God is the hardest taskmaster I have known on this earth, and He tries you through and through. And when you find that your faith is failing or your body is failing you and you are sinking, He comes to your assistance somehow or other and proves to you that you must not lose your faith and that He is always at your beck and call, but on His terms, not on your terms. So I have found. I cannot really recall a single instance when, at the eleventh hour, He has forsaken me. (SW, p1069)

In my early youth I was taught to repeat what in Hindu

scriptures are known as one thousand names of God. But these one thousand names of God were by no means exhaustive. We believe-and I think it is the truth-that God has as many names as there are creatures and, therefore, we also say that God is nameless and, since God has many forms, we also consider Him formless, and since He speaks to us through many tongues, we consider Him to be speechless and so on.

And so when I came to study Islam, I found that Islam too had many names for God.

I would say with those who say God is Love, God is Love. But deep down in me I used to say that though God may be Love, God is Truth, above all. If it is possible for the human tongue to give the fullest description of God, I have come to the conclusion that, for myself, God is Truth.

But two years ago I went a step further and said that Truth is God. You will see the fine distinction between the two statements, viz., that God is Truth and Truth is God. And I came to the conclusion after a continuous and relentless search after Truth which began nearly fifty years ago.

I then found that the nearest approach to Truth was through love. But I also found that love has many meanings in the English language at least and that human love in the sense of passion could become a degrading thing also. I found too that love in the sense of ahimsa had only a limited number of votaries in the world. But I never found a double meaning in connection with truth and not even atheists had demurred to the necessity or power of truth.

But, in their passion for discovering truth, the atheists have not hesitated to deny the very existence of God-from their own point of view, rightly. And it was because of this reasoning that I saw that, rather than say that God is Truth, I should say that Truth is God. (YI, 31-12-1931, p427-8)

God is Truth, but God is many other things also. That is why I say Truth is God.... Only remember that Truth is not one of the many qualities that we name. It is the living embodiment of God, it is the only Life, and I identify Truth with the fullest life, and that is how it becomes a concrete thing, for

God is His whole creation, the whole Existence, and service of all that exists-Truth-is service of God. (H, 25-5-1935, p115)

Perfection is the attribute of the Almighty, and yet what a great democrat He is! What an amount of wrong and humbug He suffers on our part! He even suffers us insignificant creatures of His to question His very existence, though He is in every atom about us, around us and within us. But He has reserved to Himself the right of becoming manifest to whomsoever He chooses. He is a Being without hands and feet and other organs, yet he can see Him to whom He chooses to reveal Himself. (H, 14-11-1936, p314)

God Through Service

If I did not fee the presence of God within me, I see so much of misery and disappointment every day that I would be a raving maniac and my destination would be the Hooghli. (YI, 6-8-1925, p275)

If I am to identify myself with the grief of the least in India, aye, if I have the power, the least in the world, let me identify myself with the sins of the little ones who are under my care. And so doing in all humility, I hope some day to see God-Truth-face to face. (YI, 3-12-1925, p422)

I am endeavoring to see God through service of humanity, for I know that God is neither in heaven, nor down below, but in every one. (YI, 4-8-1927, p247-8)

I am a part and parcel of the whole, and I cannot find Him apart from the rest of humanity. My countrymen are my nearest neighbors. They have become so helpless, so resourceless, so inert that I must concentrate on serving them. If I could persuade myself that I should find Him in a Himalayan cave, I would proceed there immediately. But I know that I cannot find Him apart from humanity. (H, 29-8-1936, p226)

I claim to know my millions. All the 24 hours of the day I am with them. They are my first care and last because I recognize no God except the God that is to be found in the hearts of the dumb millions. They do not recognize His presence; I do. And I worship the God that is Truth or Truth which is God through the service of these millions. (H, 11-3-1939, p44)

Guide and Protector

I must go... with God as my only guide. He is a jealous Lord. He will allow no one to share His authority. One has, therefore, to appear before Him in all one's weakness, empty-handed and in a spirit of full surrender, and then He enables you to stand before a whole world and protects you from all harm. (YI, 3-9-1931, p247)

I have learned this one lesson-that what is impossible with man is child's play with God and if we have faith in that Divinity which presides on the destiny of the meanest of His creation, I have no doubt that all things are possible; and in that final hope, I live and pass my time and endeavor to obey His will. (YI, 19-11-1931, p361)

Even in darkest despair, where there seems to be no helper and no comfort in the wide, wide world, His Name inspires us with strength and puts all doubts and despairs to flight. The sky may be overcast today with clouds, but a fervent prayer to Him is enough to dispel them. It is because of prayer that I have known no disappointment.

...I have known no despair. Why then should you give way to it? Let us pray that He may cleanse our hearts of pettiness, meanness and deceit and He will surely answer our prayers. Many I know have always turned to that unfailing source of strength. (H, 1-6-1935, p123)

I have seen and believe that God never appears to you in person, but in action which can only account for your deliverance in your darkest hour. (H, 10-12-1938, p373)

Individual worship cannot be described in words. It goes on continuously and even unconsciously. There is not a moment when I do not feel the presence of a Witness whose eye misses nothing and with whom I strive to keep in tune.

I have never found Him lacking in response. I have found Him nearest at hand when the horizon seemed darkest in my ordeals in jails when it was not all-smooth sailing for me. I cannot recall a moment in my life when I had a sense of desertion by God. (H, 24-12-1938, p395)

Self-realization

I believe it to be possible for every human being to attain to that blessed and indescribable, sinless state in which he feels within himself the presence of God to the exclusion of everything else. (YI, 17-11-1921, p368)

What I want to achieve, what I have been striving and pining to achieve..., is self-realization, to see God face to face, to attain moksha. I live and move and have my being in pursuit of this goal. All that I do by way of speaking and writing and all my ventures in the political field are directed to this same end. (A, p xiv)

For it is an unbroken torture to me that I am still so far from Him, who, as I fully know, governs every breath of my life, and whose offspring I am. I know that it is the evil passions within that keep me so far from Him, and yet I cannot get away from them. (ibid, p xvi)

This belief in God has to be based on faith, which transcends reason. Indeed, even the so-called realization has at bottom an element of faith without which it cannot be sustained. In the very nature of things it must be so. Who can transgress the limitations of his being? I hold that complete realization is impossible in this embodied life. Nor is it necessary. A living immovable faith is all that is required for reaching the full spiritual height attainable by human beings. God is not outside this earthly case of ours. Therefore, exterior proof is not of much avail, if any at all. We must ever fail to perceive Him through the senses, because He is beyond them. We can feel Him if we will but withdraw ourselves from the senses. The divine music is incessantly going on within ourselves, but the loud senses drown the delicate music, which is unlike and infinitely superior to anything we can perceive or hear with our senses. (H, 13-6-1936, pp140-1)

TRUTH AND BEAUTY

Inwardness of Art

There are two aspects of things - the outward and the inward....The outward has no meaning except in so far as it helps the inward. All true Art is thus an expression of the soul. The outward forms have value only in so far as they are the expression of the inner spirit of man. (YI, 13-11-1924, p.377)

I know that many call themselves artists, and are recognized as such, and yet in their works there is absolutely no trace of the soul's upward urge and unrest. (ibid)

All true Art must help the soul to realize its inner self. In my own case, I find that I can do entirely without external forms in my soul's realization. I can claim, therefore, that there is truly efficient Art in my life, though you might not see what you call works of Art about me. My room may have blank walls; and I may even dispense with the roof, so that I may gaze out at the starry heavens overhead that stretch in an unending expanse. What conscious Art of man can give me the panoramic scenes that open out before me, when I look up to the sky above with all its shining stars?

This, however, does not mean that I refuse to accept the value of productions of Art, generally accepted as such, but only that I personally feel how inadequate these are compared with the eternal symbols of beauty in Nature. These productions of man's Art have their value only in so far as they help the soul onward towards self-realization. (ibid)

Truth First

Truth is the first thing to be sought for, and Beauty and Goodness will then be added unto you. Jesus was, to my mind, a supreme artist because he saw and expressed Truth; and so was Muhammad, the Koran being, the most perfect composition in all Arabic literature - at any rate, that is what scholars say. It is because both of them strove first for Truth that the grace of expression naturally came in and yet neither Jesus not Muhammad wrote on Art. That is the Truth and Beauty I crave for, live for, and would die for. (YI, 20-11-1924, p.386)

Art for the Millions

Here too, just as elsewhere, I must think in terms of the millions. And to the millions we cannot give that training to acquire a perception of Beauty in such a way as to see Truth in it. Show them Truth first and they will see Beauty afterwards... Whatever can be useful to those starving millions is beautiful to my mind. Let us give today first the vital things of life and all the graces and ornaments of life will follow. (ibid)

I want art and literature that can speak to the millions. (H, 14-11-1936, p.135)

Art to be art must soothe. (YI, 27-5-1926, p.196)

After all, Art can only be expressed not through inanimate power-driven machinery designed for mass-production, but only through the delicate living touch of the hands of men and women. (YI, 14-3-1929, p.86)

Inner Purity

True art takes note not merely of form but also of what lies behind. There is an art that kills and an art that gives life... True art must be evidence of happiness, contentment and purity of its authors. (YI, 11-8-1921, p. 253)

True beauty after all consists in purity of heart. (A, p. 228)

I love music and all the other arts, but I do not attach such value to them as is generally done. I cannot, for example, recognize the value of those activities which require technical knowledge for their understanding.

Life is greater than all art. I would go even further and declare that the man whose life comes nearest to perfection is the greatest artist; for what is art without the sure foundation and framework of a noble life? (AG, pp. 65-66)

We have somehow accustomed ourselves to the belief that art is independent of the purity of private life. I can say with all the experience at my command that nothing could be more untrue. As I am nearing the end of my earthly life, I can say that purity of life, is the highest and truest art. The art of producing good music from a cultivated voice can be achieved by many, but the art of producing that music from the harmony of a pure life is achieved very rarely. (H, 19-2-1938, p 10)

Beauty in Truth

I see and find Beauty in Truth or through Truth. All Truths, not merely true ideas, but truthful faces, truthful pictures, or songs, are highly beautiful. People generally fail to see Beauty in Truth, the ordinary man runs away from it and becomes blind to the beauty in it. Whenever men begin to see Beauty in Truth, then true Art will arise. (YI, 13-11-1924, p. 377)

To a true artist only that face is beautiful which, quite apart from its exterior, shines with the Truth within the soul. There is... no Beauty apart from Truth. On the other hand, Truth may manifest itself in forms, which may not be outwardly beautiful at all. Socrates, we are told, was the most truthful man of his time, and yet his features are said to have been the ugliest in Greece. To my mind he was beautiful, because all his life was a striving after Truth, and you may remember that his outward form did not prevent Phidias from appreciating the beauty of Truth in him, though as an artist he was accustomed to see Beauty in outward forms also. (ibid)

Truth and Untruth often coexist; good and evil are often found together. In an artist also not seldom [do] the right perception of things and the wrong coexist. Truly beautiful creations come when right perception is at work. If these monuments are rare in life, they are also rare in Art. (ibid)

These beauties ['a sunset or a crescent moon that shines amid the stars at night'] are truthful, inasmuch as they make me think of the Creator at the back of them. How else could these be beautiful, but for the Truth that is in the centre of creation? When I admire the wonder of a sunset or the beauty of the moon, my soul expands in worship of the Creator. I try to see Him and His mercies in all these creations. But even the sunsets and sunrises would be mere hindrances if they did not help me to think of Him. Anything which is a hindrance to the flight of the soul is a delusion and a snare; even like the body, which often does hinder you in the path of salvation. (H, 13-11-1924, p. 379)

Why can't you see the beauty of colour in vegetables? And then, there is beauty in the speckles sky. But no, you want the colours of the rainbow, which is a mere optical illusion. We have been taught to believe that what is beautiful need not be useful and what is useful cannot be beautiful. I want to show that what is useful can also be beautiful. (H, 7-4-1946, p. 67)

THE ROOTS OF TRUTH

Among the delusions which at different periods have afflicted mankind, perhaps the gretest-certainly the least creditable-is modern economics based on the idea that an advantageous code of action may be determined irrespectively of the influence of social affection.

Of course, as in the case of other delusions, political economy has a plausible idea at the root of it. 'The social affections,' says the economist, 'are accidental and disturbing elements in human nature ; but avarice and the desire for progress are constant elements. Let us eliminate the inconstants, and considering man merely as a money-making machine, examine by what laws of labour, purchase and sale, the greatest amount of wealth can be accumulated. Those laws once determined, it will be for each individual afterwards to introduce as much of the disturbing affectionate element as he chooses.'

This would be a logical method of analysis if the accidentals afterwards to be introduced were of the same nature as the powers first examined. Supposing a body in motion to be influenced by constant and inconstant forces, it is the simplest way of examining its course to trace it first under the persistent conditions and afterwards introduce the causes of variation. But the disturbing elements in the social problem are not of the same nature as the constant ones; they alter the essence of the creature under examination the moment they are added. They operate not mathematically but chemically, introducing conditions which render all our previous knowledge unavailable.

I do not doubt the conclusions of the science of its terms are accepted. I am simply uninterested in them, as I should be in those of a science of gymnastics which assumed that men had no skeletons. It might be shown on that supposition that it would be advantageous to roll the students up into pellets, flatten them into cakes, or stretch them into cables; and that when these results were effected, the reinsertion of the skeleton would be attended with various inconveniences to their constitution. The reasoning might be admirable, the conclusions true, and the science deficient only in applicability. Modern political economy stands on a precisely similar basis. It imagines that man has a body but no soul to be taken into account and frames its laws accordingly. How can such laws possibly apply to man in whom the soul is the predominant element?

Political economy is no science at all. We see how helpless it is when labourers go on a strike. The masters take one view of the matter, the operatives another; and no political economy can set them at one. Disputant after disputant vainly strives to show that the interests of the masters are not antagonistic to those of the men. In fact it does not always follow that the persons must be antagonistic because their interests are. If there is only a crust of bread in the house, and mother and children are starving, their interests are not the same. If the mother eats it, the children want it; if the children eat it, the mother must go hungry to her work. Yet it does not follow that there is antagonism between them, that they will fight for the crust, and the mother, being strongest, will get it and eat it. Similarly it cannot be assumed that because their interests are diverse, persons must regard one another with hostility and use violence or cunning to obtain the advantage.

Even if we consider men as actuated by no other moral influences than those which affect rats or swine, it can never be shown generally either that the interests of master and labourer are alike or that they are opposed; for according to circumstances they may be either. It is indeed the interest of both that the work should be rightly done and a just price obtained for it ; but in the division of profits, the gain of the one may or may not be the loss of the other. It is not the master's interest to pay wages so low as to leave the men sickly and depressed, nor the workman's interest to be paid high wages if the smallness of the master's profit hinders him from conducting it in a safe and liberal way. A stoker ought not to desire high pay if the company is too poor to keep the engine-wheels in repair.

All endeavour, therefore, to deduce rules of action from balance of expediency is in vain. And it is meant to be in vain. For no human actions ever were intended by the Maker of men to be guided by balances of expediency but by balances of justice. He has therefore rendered all endeavours to determine expediency futile for evermore. No man can know what will be the ultimate result to himself or others of any given line of conduct. But every man may know and most of us do know what is a just and unjust act. And all of us may know also that the consequences of justice will be ultimately the best possible, both to others and ourselves, though we can neither say what is best, or how it is likely to come about.

I have meant in the term justice to include affection-such affection as one man owes to another. All right relations between master and operative ultimately depend on this.

As an illustration let us consider the position of domestic servants.

We will suppose that the master of a household tries only to get as much work out of his servants as he can, at the rate of wages he gives. He never allows them to be idle ; feeds them as poorly and lodges them as ill as they will endure. In doing this, there is no violation on his part of what is commonly called 'justice'. He agrees with the domestic for his whole time and service and takes them, the limits of hardship in treatment being fixed by the practice of other masters in the neighbourhood. If the servant can get a better place, he is free to take one.

This is the politico-economical view of the case according to the doctors of that science who assert that by this procedure the greatest average of work will be obtained from the servant, and therefore the greatest benefit to the community, and through the community, to the servant himself.

That however is not so. It would be so if the servant were an engine of which the motive power was steam, magnetism or some such agent of calculable force. But on the contrary he is an engine whose motive power is the Soul. Soul force enters into all the economist's equations without his knowledge and falsifies every one of their results.

The largest quantity of work will not be done by this curious engine for pay or under pressure. It will be done when the motive force, that is to say, the will or spirit of the creature, is brought to its greatest strength by its own proper fuel, namely by the affections. It does happen often that if the master is a man of sense and energy, much material work may be done under pressure ; also it does happen often that if the master is indolent and weak, a small quantity of work, and that bad, may be produced by his servant. But the universal law of the matter is that, assuming any given quantity of energy and sense in master and servant, the greatest material result obtainable by them will be not through antagonism to each other, but through affection for each other.

Nor is this one whit less generally true because indulgence will be frequently abused, and kindness met with ingratitude. For the servant who, gently treated, is ungrateful, treated ungently, will be revengeful ; and the man who is dishonest to a liberal master will be injurious to an unjust man.

In any case and with any person, this unselfish treatment will produce the most effective return. I am here considering the affections wholly as a motive power ; not at all as things in themselves desirable or noble. I look at them simply as an anomalous force, rendering every one of the ordinary economist's calculations nugatory. The affections only become a true motive power when they ignore every other motive and condition of economics. Treat the servant kindly with the idea of turning his gratitude to account, and you will get, as you deserve, no gratitude nor any value for your kindness ; but treat him kindly without any economical purpose, and all economical purposes will be answered ; here as elsewhere whoever will save his life shall lose it, whoso loses it shall find it.

The next simplest example of relation between master and operative is that which exists between the commander of a regiment and his men.

Supposing the officer only desires to apply the rules of discipline so as, with least trouble to himself, to make the regiment most effective, he will not be able, by any rules, on this selfish principle, to develop the full strength of his subordinates. But if he has the most direct personal relations with his men, the most care for their interests, and the most value for their lives, he will develop their effective strength, through their affection for his own person and trust in his character, to a degree wholly unattainable by other means. This applies more stringently as the numbers concerned are larger : a charge may often be successful though the men dislike their officers ; a battle has rarely been won, unless they loved their general.

A body of men associated for the purposes of robbery (as a Highland clan in ancient times) shall be animated by perfect affection, and every member of it be ready to lay down his life for the life for the life of his chief. But a band of men associated for purpose of legal production is usually animated by no such emotions, and none of them is willing to give his life for the life of his chief. For a servant or a soldier is engaged at a definite rate of wages for a definite period ; but a workman at a rate of wages variable according to the demand for labour, and with the risk of being at any time thrown out of employment by chances of trade. Now as under these conditions no action of the affections can take place, but only an explosive action of disaffections, two points offer themselves of consideration in the matter :

1. How far the rate of wages may be so regulated as not to vary with the demand for labour ;
2. How far it is possible that bodies of workmen may be engaged and maintained at such fixed rate of wages (whatever the state of trade may be), without enlarging or diminishing their number, so as to give them permanent interest in the establishment with which they are connected, like that of the domestic servants in an old family, or an esprit de corps, like that of the soldiers in a crack regiment.

A curious fact in the history of human error is the denial by the economist of the possibility of so regulating wages as not to vary with the demand for labour.

We do not sell our prime-minister by Dutch auction. Sick, we do not inquire for a physician who takes less than a guinea ; litigious, we never think of reducing six-and-eightpence to four-and-sixpence ; caught in a shower we do not canvass the cabmen to find one who value his driving at less than sixpence a mile.

The best labour always has been, and is, as all labour ought to be, paid by an invariable standard.

'What !' the reader perhaps answers amazedly : 'to pay good and bad workman alike ?'

Certainly. You pay with equal fee, contentedly, the good and bad preachers (workmen upon your soul) and the good and bad physicians (workmen upon your body) ; much more may you pay, contentedly, with equal fees, the good and bad workmen upon your house.

'Nay, but I choose my physician, thus indicating my sense of the quality of their work.' By all means choose your bricklayer ; that is the proper reward of the good workman, to be 'chosen'. The right system respecting all labour is, that it should be paid at a fixed rate, but the good workman employed, and the bad workman unemployed. The false system is when the bad workman is allowed to offer his work at half-price, and either take the place of the good or to force him by his competition to work for an inadequate sum. This equality of wages, then, being the first object towards which we have to discover the road, the second is that of maintaining constant numbers of workmen in employment, whatever may be the accidental demand for the article they produce.

The wages which enable any workman to live are necessarily higher if his work is liable to intermission, than if it is assured and continuous. In the latter case he will take low wages in the form of a fixed salary. The provision of regular labour for the workman is good for him as well as for his master in the long run, although he cannot then make large profits or take big risks or indulge in gambling. The soldier is ready to lay down his life for his chief and therefore he is held in greater honour than an ordinary workman. Really speaking, the soldier's trade is not slaying, but being slain in the defence of others. The reason the world honours the soldier is, because he holds his life at the service of the State.

Not less is the respect we pay to the lawyer, physician and clergyman, founded ultimately on their self-sacrifice. Set in a judge's seat, the lawyer will strive to judge justly, come of it what may. The physician will treat his patients with care, no matter under what difficulties. The clergyman will similarly instruct his congregation and direct it to the right path.

All the efficient members of these so-called learned professions are in public estimate of honour preferred before the head of a commercial firm, as the merchant is presumed to act always selfishly. His work may be very necessary to the community ; but the motive of it is understood to be wholly personal. The merchant's first object in all his dealings must be (the public believe) to get as much for himself and leave as little to his customer as possible. Enforcing this upon him, by political statute, as the necessary principle of his action ; recommending it to him, and themselves reciprocally adopting it, proclaiming for law of the universe that a buyer's function is to cheapen, and a seller's to cheat,-the public, nevertheless, involuntarily condemn the man of commerce for his compliance with their own statement, and stamp him for ever as belonging to an inferior grade of human personality.

This they must give up doing. They will have to discover a kind of commerce which is not excluselfish. Or rather they must discover that there never was or can be any other kind of commerce ; and that this which they have called commerce was not commerce at all but cozening. In true commerce, as in true preaching or true fighting, it is necessary to admit the idea of occasional voluntary loss ;-that sixpences have to be lost, as well as lives, under a sense of duty ; that the market may have its martyrdoms as well as the pulpit ; and trade its heroism as well as war.

Five great intellectual professions exist in every civilized nation :

The Soldier's profession is to defend it.

The Pastor's to teach it.

The Physician's to keep it in health.

The Lawyer's to enforce justice in it.

The Merchant's to provide for it.

And the duty of all these men is on due occasion to die for it. For truly the man who does not know when to die does not know how to live.

Observe, the merchant's function is to provide for the nation. It is no more his function to get profit for himself out of that provision than it is a clergyman's function to get his stipend. This stipend is a necessary adjunct but not the object of his life if he be a true clergyman, any more than his fee (or honorarium) is the object of life to a true physician. Neither is his fee the object of life to a true merchant. All three, if true men, have a work to be done irrespective of fee-to be done even at any cost, or for quite the contrary of fee ; the pastor's function being to teach, the physician's to heal and the merchant's to provide. That is to say, he has to apply all his sagacity and energy to the producing the thing he deals in perfect state and distributing it at the cheapest possible price where it is most needed.

And because the production of any commodity involves the agency of many lives and hands, the merchant becomes in the course of his business the master and governor of large masses of men in a more direct way than a military officer or pastor, so that on him falls, in great part, the responsibility for the kind of life they lead ; and it becomes his duty not only to produce goods in the purest and cheapest forms, but also to make the various employments involved in the production most beneficial to the men employed.

And as into these two functions, requiring for their right exercise the highest intelligence as well as patience, kindness and tact, the merchant is bound to put all his energy, so for their just discharge he is bound, as solier or physican is to give up, if need be, his life, in such way as it may be demanded of him.

Two main points he has to maintain ; first his engagement ; and secondly the perfectness and purity of the thing provided by him ; so that rather than fail in any engagement or consent to any deterioration, adulteration, or unjust or exorbitant price of that which he provides, he is bound to meet fearlessly any form of distress, poverty or labour which may through maintenance of these points come upon him.

Again in his office as governor of the men employed by him, the merchant is invested with a paternal authority and responsibility. In most cases a youth entering a commercial establishment is withdrawn altogether from home influence ; his master must become his father; else he has, for practical and constant help, no father at hand. So that the only means which the master has of doing justice to the men employed by him is to ask himself sternly whether he is dealing with such subordinate as he would with his own son, if compelled by circumstances to take such a position.

Supposing the captain of a frigate were obliged to place his own son in the position of a common sailor ; as he would then treat his son, he is bound always to treat every one of the men under him. So also supposing the master of a factory were obliged to place his own son in the position of an ordinary workman ; as he would then treat his son, he is bound always to treat every one of his men. This is the only effective, true or practical Rule which can be given in this point of economics.

And as the captain of a ship is bound to be the last man to leave his ship in case of wreck and to share his last crust with the sailors in case of famine, so the manufacturer, in any commercial crisis, is bound to take the suffering of it with his men, and even to take more of it for himself than he allows his men to feel ; as a father would in a famine, shipwreck or battle, sacrifice himself for his son.

All this sounds very strange; the only real strangeness in the matter being, nevertheless, that it should so sound. For all this is true everlastingly and practically ; all other doctrine than this being impossible in practice, consistently with any progressive state of national life ; all the life which we now possess as a nation showing itself in the denial by a few strong minds and faithful hearts of the economic principles taught to our multitudes, which principles, so far as accepted, lead straight to national destruction.

10

Gandhi and the Gospel of Satyagraha

Passive Resistance

Passive resistance is an all-sided sword; it can be used anyhow; it blesses him who uses it and him against whom it is used. Without drawing a drop of blood it produces far-reaching results. It never rusts and cannot be stolen. (Hs, p. 82)

I am quite sure that the stoniest heart will be melted by passive resistance...This is a sovereign and most effective remedy...It is a weapon of the purest type. It is not the weapon of the weak. It needs far greater courage to be a passive resister than a physical resister. It is the courage of a Jesus, a Daniel, a Crammer, a Latimer and a Ridley who could go calmly to suffering and death, and the courage of a Tolstoy who dared to defy the Czars of Russia, that stands out as the greatest.

Indeed, one PERFECT resister is enough to win the battle of Right against Wrong. (YI, 10-11-1921, p. 362)

I claim...that the method of passive resistance...is the clearest and safest, because, if the cause is not true, it is the resisters and they alone who suffer.

Jesus Christ, Daniel and Socrates represented the purest form of passive resistance or soul force. All these teachers counted their bodies as nothing in comparison to their soul.

Tolstoy was the best and brightest (modern) exponent of the doctrine. He not only expounded it, but lived according to it. In India, the doctrine was understood and commonly practiced long before it came into vogue in Europe.

It is easy to see that soul force is infinitely superior to body force. If people in order to secure redress of wrongs resort to soul force, much of the present suffering will be avoided.

In any case, the wielding of the force never causes suffering to others. So that whenever it is misused, It only injures the users and not those against whom it is used. Like virtue it has its own reward. There is no such thing as failure in the use of this kind of force. (SW, p. 165)

The Buddha fearlessly carried the war into the enemy's camp and brought down on its knees an arrogant priesthood. Christ drove out the money-changers from the temple of Jerusalem and drew down curses from Heaven upon he hypocrites and the Pharisees. Both were for intensely direct action.

But even as the Buddha and Christ chastised, they showed unmistakable gentleness and love behind every act of theirs. They would not raise a finger against their enemies, but would gladly surrender themselves rather than the truth for which they lived. The Buddha would have died resisting the priesthood, if the majesty of his love had not proved to be equal to the task of bending the priesthood. Christ died on the cross with a crown of thorns on his head, defying the might of a whole empire. And if I raise resistances of a nonviolent character, I simply and humbly follow in the footsteps of the great teachers... (YI, 12-5-1920, p. 3)

Civil Disobedience

Disobedience to be civil must be sincere, respectful, restrained, never defiant, must be based upon some well-understood principle, must not be capricious and, above all, must have no ill-will or hatred behind it. (YI, 24-3-1920, p. 4)

I hold the opinion firmly that civil disobedience is the purest type of constitutional agitation. Of course, it becomes degrading and despicable, if its civil, i.e., nonviolent character is a mere camouflage. If the honesty of nonviolence be admitted, there is no warrant for condemnation even of the fiercest disobedience, because of the likehood of its leading to violence. No big or swift movement can carried on without bold risks, and life will not be worth living if it is not attended with large risks. Does not the history of the world show that there would have been no romance in life if there had been no risks? (YI, 15-12-1921, p. 419)

Civil disobedience is the inherent right of a citizen. He dare not give it up without ceasing to be a man. Civil disobedience is never followed by anarchy. Criminal disobedience can lead to it. Every state puts down criminal disobedience by force. It perishes if it does not. (YI, 5-1-1922, p. 5)

A Satyagrahi obeys the laws of society intelligently and of his own free will, because he considers it to be his sacred duty to do so. It is only when a person has thus obeyed the laws of society scrupulously that he is in a position of judge as to which particular laws are good and just and which unjust and iniquitous. Only when does the right accrue to him of civil disobedience of certain laws in well-defined circumstances. (A, p. 347)

Condition Precedent

The first indispensable condition precedent to any civil resistance is that there should be surety against any outbreak of violence, whether on the part of those who are identified with civil resistance or on the part of the general public. It would be no answer in the case of an outbreak of violence that it was instigated by the State or other agencies hostile to civil resisters.

It should be obvious that civil resistance cannot flourish in an atmosphere of violence. This does not mean that the resources of a satyagrahi have come to an end. Ways other than civil disobedience should be found out. (H, 18-3-1939, p. 53)

Character of Satyagraha

That is the beauty of Satyagraha. It comes up to oneself, one has not to go out in search for it. That is a virtue inherent in the principle itself.

A dharmayuddha, in which there are no secrete to be guarded, no scope for canning and no place for untruth, comes unsought; and a man of religion is ever ready for it. A struggle which has to be previously planned is not and it is only when the Satyagrahi feels quite helpless, is apparently on his last legs and finds utter darkness all around him, that God comes to the rescue. (SSA, p. xiv)

In the application of Satyagraha, I discovered, in the earliest stages, that pursuit of Truth did not admit of violence being inflicted on one's opponent, but that he must be weaned from error by patience and sympathy. For, what appears to be truth to the one may appear to be error to the other. And patience means self-suffering. So the doctrine came to mean vindication of Truth, not by infliction of suffering on the opponent but one's own self. (RCPS)

Satyagraha and its off-shoots, noncooperation and civil resistance, are nothing but new names for the law of suffering. (YI, 11-8-1920, p. 3)

With satya combined with ahimsa, you can bring the world to your feet. Satyagraha in its essence is nothing but the introduction of truth and gentleness in the political, i.e., the national, life. (YI, 10-3-1920, p. 3)

Satyagraha is utter self-effacement, greatest humiliation, greatest patience and brightest faith. It is its own reward. (YI, 26-2-1925, p. 73)

Satyagraha is a relentless search for truth and a determination to reach truth. (YI, 19-3-1925, p. 95)

It is a force that works silently and apparently slowly. In reality, there is no force in the world that is so direct or so swift in working. (YI, 4-6-1925, p. 189)

The word Satyagraha is often most loosely used and is made to cover veiled violence. But, as the author of the word, I may be allowed to say that it excludes every form of violence, direct or indirect, veiled or unveiled, and whether in thought, word or deed. It is breach of Satyagraha to with ill to an opponent or to say a harsh word to him or of him with the intention of harming him...

Satyagraha is gentle, it never wounds. It must not be the result of anger or malice. It is never fussy, never impatient, never vociferous. It is the direct opposite of compulsion. It was conceived as a complete substitute for violence. (H, 15-4-1933, p. 8)

The fight of Satyagraha is for the strong in spirit, not the doubter or the timid. Satyagraha teaches us the art of living as well as dying. Birth and death are inevitable among mortals. What distinguishes the man from the brute is his conscious striving to realize the spirit within. (H, 7-4-1946, p. 74)

Evolving Science

I am myself daily growing in the knowledge of Satyagraha. I have no text-book to consult in time of need, not even the Gita which I have called my dictionary. Satyagraha as conceived by me is a science may prove to be no science at all and well prove to be the musings and doings of a fool, if not a madman.

It may be that what is true in Satyagraha is as ancient as the hills. But it has not yet been acknowledged to be of any value in the solution of world problems or, rather, the one supreme problem or war. It may be that what is claimed to be new in it will prove to be really of no value in terms of that supreme problem. It may be that what are claimed to be victories of Satyagraha i.e., ahimsa, were really victories not of truth and nonviolence but of fear of violence. These possibilities have always been in front of me. I am helpless. All I present to the nation for adoption is an answer to prayer or, which is the same thing, constantly waiting on God. (H, 24-9-1938, p. 266)

The Technique of Satyagraha

Not to yield your soul to the conqueror means that you will refuse to do that which your conscience forbids you to do. Suppose the 'enemy' were to ask you to rub your nose on the ground or to pull your ears or to go through such humiliating performances, you would not submit to any of these humiliations. But if he robs you of your possessions, you will yield them because, as a votary of ahimsa, you have from the beginning decided that earthly possessions have nothing to do with your soul. That which you look upon as your own you may keep only so long as the world allows you to own it.

Not to yield your mind means that you will not give way to any temptation. Man is oftentimes weak-minded enough to be caught in the snare of greed and honeyed words. We see this happening daily in our social life. A weak-minded man can never be a Satyagrahi. The latter's 'no' is invariably a 'no' and his 'yes' an eternal 'yes'. Such a man alone has the strength to be a devotee of truth and ahimsa. But here one must know the difference between steadfastness and obstinacy. If, after having said 'yes' or 'no', one finds out that the decision was wrong and in spite of that knowledge clings to it, that is obstinacy and folly. It is necessary to think things out carefully and thoroughly before coming to any decision. The meaning of refusal to own allegiance is clear. You will not bow to the supremacy of the victor, you will not help him to attain his object. Herr Hitler has never dreamt of possessing Britain. He wants the British to admit defeat. The victor can then demand anything he likes from the vanquished, and the latter has perforce to yield. But if defeat is not admitted, the enemy will fight until he has killed his opponent. A Satyagrahi, however, is dead to his body even before the enemy attempts to kill him, i.e., he is free from attachment to his body and only lives in the victory of the soul.

Therefore, when he is already thus dead, why would be yearn to kill anyone? To die in the act of killing is in essence to die defeated. Because, if the enemy is unable to get it after killing you. If, on the other hand, he realizes that you have not the remotest thought in your mind of raising your hand against him even for the sake of your life, he will lack the zest to kill you. Every hunter has had this experience. No one has ever heard of anyone hunting cows. (H, 18-8-1940, pp. 253-4)

Power of Suffering

The hardest heart and the grossest ignorance must disappear before the rising sun of suffering without anger and without malice. (YI, 19-2-1925, p. 61)

Suffering has its well-defined limits. Suffering can be both wise and unwise, and when the limit is reached, to prolong it would be not unwise but the height of folly. (YI, 12-3-1931, p. 30)

True suffering does not know itself and never calculates. It brings its own joy which surpasses all other joys. (YI, 19-3-1931, p. 41)

The conviction has been growing upon me that things of fundamental importance to the people are not secured by reason alone, but have to be purchased with their suffering. Suffering is the law of human beings; war is the law of the jungle. But suffering is infinitely more powerful than the law of the jungle for converting the opponent and opening his ears, which are otherwise shut, to the voice of reason. (YI, 5-11-1931, p. 341)

Code of Satyagraha

A Satyagrahi bids good-bye to fear. He is therefore, never afraid of trusting the opponent. Even if the opponent plays him false twenty times, the Satyagrahi is ready to trust him the twenty-first time, for an implicit trust in human nature is the very essence of his creed. (SSA, p. 159)

A Satyagrahi is nothing if not instinctively law-abiding, and it is his law-abiding nature which exacts from him implicit obedience to the highest law, that is the voice of conscience which overrides all other laws. (SW, p. 465)

Since Satyagraha is one of the most powerful methods of direct action, a Satyagrahi exhausts all other means before he resorts to Satyagraha. He will, therefore, constantly and continually approach the constituted authority, he will appeal to public opinion, educate public opinion, state his case calmly and coolly before everybody who wants to listen to him, and only after he has exhausted all these avenues will he resort to Satyagraha. But when he has found the impelling call of the inner voice within him and launches out upon Satyagraha, he has burnt his boats and there is no receding. (YI, 20-10-1927, p. 353)

The Satyagrahi, whilst he is ever ready for fight, must be equally eager for peace. He must welcome any honourable opportunity for peace. (YI, 19-3-1931, p. 40)

My advice is Satyagraha first and Satyagraha last. There is no other or better road to freedom. (H, 15-9-1946, p. 312)

In the code of the Satyagrahi there is no such thing as surrender to brute force. Or the surrender then is the surrender of suffering and not to the wielder of the bayonet. (YI, 30-4-1931, p. 93)

As a Satyagrahi I must always allow my cards to be examined and re-examined at all times and make reparation if an error is discovered. (H, 11-3-1939, p. 44)

Qualifications of a Satyagrahi

...The following qualifications....I hold are essential for every Satyagrahi in India:

He must have a living faith in God, for He is his only Rock.

He must believe in truth and nonviolence as his creed and, therefore, have faith in the inherent goodness of human nature which he expects to evoke by his truth and love expressed through his suffering.

He must be leading a chaste life and be ready and willing, for the sake of his cause, to give up his life and his possessions.

He must be a habitual Khadi-wearer and spinner. This is essential for India.

He must be a teetotaler and be free from the use of other intoxicants in order that his reason may be always unclouded and his mind constant.

He must carry out with a willing heart all the rules or discipline as may be laid down from time to time.

He should carry out the jail rules unless they are specially devised to hurt his self-respect.

The qualifications are not to be regarded as exhaustive. They are illustrative only. (H, 25-3-1939, p. 64)

A Satyagrahi may not even ascend to heaven on the wings of Satan. (H, 15-4-1939, p. 86)

In Satyagraha there is no place for fraud or falsehood, or any kind of untruth. (BC, 9-8-1942)

A Satyagrahi never misses, can never miss, a chance of compromise on honourable terms, it being always assumed that, in the event of failure, he is ever ready to offer battle.

He needs no previous preparation, his cards are always on the table. (YI, 16-4-1931, p. 77)

It is often forgotten that it is never the intention of a Satyagrahi to embarrass the wrongdoer. The appeal is never to his fear; it is, must, always to his heart. The Satyagrahi's object is to convert, not to coerce, the wrongdoer. He should avoid artificiality in all his doings. He acts naturally and from inward conviction. (H, 25-3-1939, p. 64)

Satyagraha is essentially a weapon of the truthful. A Satyagrahi is pledged to nonviolence and, unless people observe it in thought, word and deed, I cannot offer Satyagraha. (A, p. 345)

I have always held that it is only when one sees one's own mistakes with a convex lens, and does just the reverse in the case others, that one is able to arrive at a just relative estimate of the two. I further believe that a scrupulous and conscientious observance of this rule is necessary for one who wants to be a Satyagrahi. (ibid, p. 346)

A Satyagrahi relies upon God for protection against the tyranny of brute force... (H, 7-4-1946, p. 73)

No confirmed Satyagrahi is dismayed by the dangers, seen or unseen, from his opponent's side. What he must fear, as every army must, is the danger from within. (H, 14-7-1946, p. 220)

Satyagraha and Repression

Repression itself affords a training in Satyagraha, even as an unsought war affords a training for the soldier. Satyagrahis should discover the causes repression. They will find that repressed people are easily frightened by the slightest show of force and are unprepared for suffering and self-sacrifice. This is then the time for learning the first lessons of Satyagraha.

Those who know anything of this matchless force should teach their neighbours to bear repression not weakly and helplessly, but bravely and knowingly.....

And yet they [the unexciting rules of preparation] are much the most important part of Satyagraha training.

Potent and active nonviolence cannot be cultivated unless the candidate goes through the necessary stages which require a lot of plodding. (H, 8-4-1939, p. 80)

POWER OF SATYAGRAHA

Victory of Satyagraha

A clear victory of Satyagraha is impossible so long as there is ill-will. But those who believe themselves to be weak are incapable of loving. Let, then, our first act every morning be to make the following resolve for the day: 'I shall not fear any one on earth. I shall fear God only; I shall not bear ill-will towards any one. I shall not submit to injustice from any one. I shall conquer untruth by truth and in resisting untruth I shall put up with all suffering. (SL NO. 14, 4-5-1919)

There is no time-limit for a Satyagrahi nor is there a limit to his capacity for suffering. Hence there is no such thing as defeat in Satyagraha. (YI, 19-2-1925, p.61)

It is not because I value life low that I countenance with joy thousands voluntarily losing their lives for Satyagraha, but because I know that it results, in the long run, in the least loss of life and, what is more, it ennobles those who lose their lives and morally enriches the world for their sacrifice. (YI, 8-10-1925, p. 345)

And when once it is set in motion, its effect, if it is intensive enough, can overtake the whole universe. It is the greatest force because it is the highest expression of the soul. (YI, 23-9-1926, p. 332)

My experience has taught me that a law of progression applies to every righteous struggle. But in the case of Satyagraha the law amounts to an axiom. As a Satyagraha struggle progresses onward, many another element helps to swell its current and there is a constant growth in the results to which it leads. This is really inevitable, and is bound up with the first principles of Satyagraha. For in Satyagraha the minimum is also the maximum, and as it is the irreducible minimum, there is no question of retreat, and the only movement possible is an advance. In other struggles, even when they are righteous, the demand is first pitched a little higher so as to admit of future reduction, and hence the law of progression does not apply to all of them without exception. (S, p. 319)

To me it is one of the most active forces in the world, It is like the sun that rises upon us unfailingly from day to day. Only if we would but understand it, it is infinitely greater than a million suns put together. It radiates life and light and peace and happiness. (YI, 18-4-1929, p. 126)

One True Satyagrahi

If a single Satyagrahi holds out to the end, victory is certain. (SSA, p. xiv)

Self-sacrifice of one innocent man is a million times more potent than the sacrifice of a million men who die in the act of killing others. The willing sacrificed of the innocent is the most powerful retort to insolent tyranny that has yet been conceived by God or man. (YI, 12-2-1925, p. 60)

I have maintained that, even if there is one individual who is almost completely nonviolent, he can put out the conflagration...In this age of democracy, it is essential that desired results are achieved by the collective effort of the people. It will no doubt be good to achieve an objective through the effort of a supremely powerful individual, but it can never make the community conscious of its corporate strength. (H, 8-9-1940, p. 277)

I believe in walking alone. I came alone in this world, I have walked alone in the valley of the shadow of death and I shall quit alone when the time comes. I know I am quite capable of launching Satyagraha even if I am all alone. I have done so before. (YI, 21-7-1946, p. 227)

Application of Satyagraha

It is a force that may be used by individuals as well as by communities. It may be used as well in political as in domestic affairs. Its universal applicability is a demonstration of its permanence and invincibility. It can be used alike by men, women and children.

It is totally untrue to say that it is a force to be used only by the weak so long as they are not capable of meeting violence by violence.... This force is to violence and, therefore, to all tyranny, all injustice, what light is to darkness. In politics, its use is based upon the immutable maxim that government of the people is possible only so long as they consent either consciously or unconsciously to be governed. (YI, 3-11-1927, 369)

I have never claimed to be the one original Satyagrahi. What I have claimed is the application of that doctrine on an almost universal scale, and it yet remains to be seen and demonstrated that it is a doctrine which is capable of assimilation by thousands upon thousands of peoples in all ages and climes. (YI, 22-9-1927, p. 317)

The Nonviolent Sanction

Satyagraha is a law of universal application. Beginning with the family, its use can be extended to every other circle.

Supposing a landowner exploits his tenants and mulcts them of the fruit of their toil by appropriating it to his own use. When they expostulate with him he does not listen and raises objections that he requires so much for his wife, so much for his children and so on. The tenants or those who have espoused their cause and have influence will make an appeal to his wife to expostulate with her husband. She would probably say that for herself she does not need his exploited money. The children will say likewise that they would earn for themselves what they need.

Supposing further that he listens to nobody or that his wife and children combine against the tenants, they will not submit. They will quit if asked to do so, but they will make it clear that the land himself and he will have to give in to their just demands.

It may, however, be that the tenants are replaced by others. Agitation short of violence will then continue till the replacing tenants see their error and make common cause with the evicted tenants.

Thus Satyagraha is a process of educating public opinion, such that it covers all elements of society and in the end makes itself irresistible. Violence interrupts the process and prolongs the real revolution of the whole social structure. The conditions necessary for the success of Satyagraha are: (1) The Satyagrahi should not have any hatred in his heart against the opponent. (2) The issue must be true and substantial. (3) The Satyagrahi must be prepared to suffer till the end for his cause. (H, 31-3-1946, p. 64)

Training for Self-defence

I believe that every man and woman should learn the art of self-defence in this age. This is done through arms in the West. Every adult man is conscripted for army training for a definite period. The training for Satyagraha is meant for all, irrespective of age or sex. The more important part of the training here is mental, not physical. There can be no compulsion in mental training. The surrounding atmosphere no doubt acts on the mind, but that cannot justify compulsion...

Satyagraha is always superior to armed resistance. This can only be effectively proved by demonstration, not by argument. It is the weapon that adorns the strong. It can never adorn the weak. By weak is meant the weak in mind and spirit, not in body. That limitation is a quality to be prized and not defect to be deplored.

One ought also to understand one of its other limitations. It can never be used to defend a wrong cause.

Satyagraha brigades can be organized in every village and in every block of buildings in the cities. Each brigade should be composed of those persons who are well-known to the organizers. In this respect Satyagraha differs from armed defence. For the latter the State impresses the service of everybody. For a Satyagraha brigade only those are eligible who believe in ahimsa and satya. Therefore, an intimate knowledge of the persons enlisted is necessary for the organizers. (H, 17-3-1946, pp. 45-46)

Duragraha

I can see nothing but catastrophe for India from methods of violence. Workmen would be committing suicide and India would have to suffer indescribable misery if workingmen were to vent their anger by criminal disobedience of the laws of the land.... When I began to preach Satyagraha and civil disobedience, it was never meant to cover criminal disobedience. My experience teaches me that truth can never be propagated by doing violence.

Those who believe in the justice of their cause need to possess boundless patience, and those alone are fit to offer civil disobedience who are above committing criminal disobedience or doing violence.

A man cannot commit both civil and criminal disobedience at the same time, even as he cannot be both temperate and furious at the same time, and just as self-restraint is acquired only after one has been able to master his passions, so is the capacity for civil disobedience acquired after one has disciplined oneself in complete and voluntary obedience of the laws of the land.

Again, just as he alone can be said to be proof against temptations who, having been exposed to them, has succeeded in resisting them, so may we be said to have conquered anger when, having sufficient cause for it, we have succeeded in controlling ourselves. (YI, 28-4-1920, pp. 7-8)

Some students have revived the ancient form of barbarity in the form of 'sitting dhurna'...I call it 'barbarity' for it is a crude way of using coercion. It is also cowardly, because one who sits dhurna knows that he is not going to be trampled over. It is difficult to call the practice violent, but it is certainly worse.

If we fight our opponent, we at least enable him to return the blow. But when we challenge him to walk over us, knowing that he will not, we place him in a most awkward and humiliating position. I know that the over-zealous students who sat dhurna never thought of the barbarity of the deed. But one who is expected to follow the voice of conscience and stand even single-handed in the face of odds cannot afford to be thoughtless.

There must be no impatience, no barbarity, no insolence, no undue pressure. If we want to cultivate a true spirit of democracy, we cannot afford to be intolerant. Intolerance betrays want of faith in one's cause. (YI, 2-2-1921, p. 33)

I have not been able to understand the cause of so much excitement and disturbance that followed my detention. It is not Satyagraha. It is worse than Durgraha.

Those who join Satyagraha demonstrations were bound one and all to refrain at all hazard from violence, not to throw stones or in anyway whatever to injure anybody. But in Bombay we have been throwing stones. We have obstructed tram-cars by putting obstacles in the way. This is not Satyagraha. We have demanded the release of about 50 men who had been arrested for deeds of violence. Our duty is chiefly to get ourselves arrested. It is breach of religious duty to endeavour to secure the release of those who have committed deeds of violence. (SW, p. 474)

I have said times without number that Satyagraha admits of no violence, no pillage, no incendiarism; and still, in the name of Satyagraha, we have burnt buildings, forcibly captured weapons, extorted money, stopped trains, cut off telegraph wires, killed innocent people and plundered shops and private houses. If deeds such as these could save me from the prison-house or the scaffold, I should not like to be so saved. (ibid, p. 476)

....Heroism and sacrifice in a bad cause are so much waste of splendid energy and hurt the good cause by drawing away attention from it by the glamour of the misused heroism and sacrifice in a bad cause. (YI, 12-12-1925, p. 60)

....Indiscriminate resistance to authority must lead to lawlessness and unbridled license and consequent self-destruction. (YI, 2-4-1931, p. 58)

FASTING AND SATYAGRAHA

Weapon of Satyagraha

Fasting is a potent weapon in the Satyagraha armoury. It cannot be taken by every one. Mere physical capacity to take it is no qualification for it. It is of no use without a living faith in God. It should never be a mechanical effort or a mere limitation. It must come from the depth of one's soul. It is, therefore, always rare. (H, 18-3-1939, p. 56)

There can be no room for selfishness, anger, lack of faith or impatience in a pure fast....Infinite patience, firm resolve, single-mindedness of purpose, perfect calm, and no anger must of necessity be there. But since it is impossible for a person to develop all these qualities all at once, no one who has not devoted himself to following the laws of ahimsa should undertake a Satyagrahi fast. (H, 13-10-1940, p. 322)

[Fasting] is...fierce and not altogether free from danger. I myself have before condemned fasting when it seemed to me to be wrong or morally unjustified. But to shirk a fast where there is a clear moral indication is a dereliction of duty. Such a fast has to be based on unadulterated truth and ahimsa. (H, 28-7-1946, p. 235)

Fasting and Death

Fasting unto death is the last and the most potent weapon in the armoury of Satyagraha. It is a sacred thing. But it must be accepted with all its implication. It is not the fast itself, but what it implies that matters. (H, 18-8-1846, p. 262)

Fasting and the Way of Christ

Fasting cannot be undertaken mechanically. It is a powerful thing but a dangerous thing, if handled amateurishly. It requires complete self-purification, much more than what is required in facing death with retaliation even in mind. One such act of perfect sacrifice would suffice for the whole world. Such is held to be Jesus' example. (H, 27-10-1946, p. 272)

Of course, it is not to be denied that fasts can be really coercive. Such are fasts to attain a selfish object. A fast undertaken to wring money from a person or for fulfilling some such personal end would amount to the exercise of coercion or undue influence. I would unhesitatingly advocate resistance of such undue influence. I have myself successfully resisted it in the fasts that have been undertaken or threatened against me.

And if it is argued that the dividing line between a selfish and unselfish end is often very thin, I would urge that a person who regards the end of a fast to be selfish or otherwise base should resolutely refuse to yield to it, even though the refusal may result in the death of the fasting person.

If people will cultivate the habit of disregarding fasts which, in their opinion, are taken for unworthy ends, such fasts will be robbed of the taint of coercion and undue influence. Like all human institutions, fasting can be both legitimately and illegitimately used. (H, 9-9-1931, p. 5)

If a man, however popular and great he may be, takes up an improper cause and fasts in defence of the impropriety, it is the duty of his friends (among whom I count myself), fellow-workers and relatives to let him die rather than that an improper cause should triumph so that he may live. Fairest means cease to be fair when the end sought is unfair. (H, 17-3-1946, p. 43)

Last Resort

One general principle, however, I would like to enunciate. A Satyagrahi should fast only as a last resort when all other avenues of redress have been explored and have failed. There is no room for imitation in fasts. He who has no inner strength should not dream of it, and never with attachment to success.

But if a Satyagrahi once undertakes a fast from conviction, he must stick to his resolve whether there is a chance of his action bearing fruit or not. This does not mean that fasting cannot or can bear fruit. He who fasts in the expectation of fruit generally fails. And even if he does not seemingly fail, he loses all the inner joy which a true fast holds...

Ridiculous fasts spread like plague and are harmful. But, when fasting becomes a duty, it cannot be given up. Therefore, I do fast when I consider it to be necessary and cannot abstain from it on any score. What I do myself I cannot abstain from it on any score. What I do myself I cannot prevent others from doing under similar circumstances. It is common knowledge that the best of good things are often abused. We see this happening every day. (H, 21-4-1946, p. 93)

...When human ingenuity fails, the votary fasts. This fasting quickens the spirit of prayer, that is to say, the fasting is a spiritual act, and therefore, addressed to God. The effect of such action on the life of the people is that, where the person fasting is at all known to them, their sleeping conscience is awakened.

But there is the danger that the people through mistaken sympathy may act against their will in order to save the life of the loved one. This danger has got to be faced. One ought not to be deterred from right action when one is sure of the rightness. It can best promote circumspection. Such a fast is undertaken in obedience to the dictates of the inner voice and, therefore, prevents haste. (H, 21-12-1947, p. 476)

11

Gandhi and the Gospel of Sarvodaya

Unity of Man

I do not believe...that an individual may gain spiritually and those who surround him suffer. I believe in advaita, I believe in the essential unity of man and, for that matter, of all that life's.

Therefore, I believe that if one man gains spiritually, the whole world gains with him and, if one man falls, the whole world falls to that extent. (YI, 4-12-1924, p. 398)

I do not believe that the spiritual law works on a field of its own. On the contrary, it expresses itself only through the ordinary activities of life. It thus affects the economic, the social and the political fields. (YI, 3-9-1925, p. 304)

If we would serve Him or become one with Him, our activity must be as unwearied as His. There may be momentary rest in store for the drop which is separated from the ocean, but not for the drop in the ocean, which knows no rest. The same is the case with ourselves.

As soon as we become one with the ocean in the shape of God, there is no more rest for us, nor indeed do we need rest any longer. Our very sleep is action. For we sleep with the thought of God in our hearts. This restlessness constitutes true rest. This never-ceasing agitation holds the key to peace ineffable. This supreme state of total surrender is difficult to describe, but not beyond the bounds of human experience. It has been attained by many dedicated souls, and may be attained by ourselves as well. (FYM, p. 47)

Identification with Poor

I cannot imagine anything nobler or more national than that for, say, one hour in the day, we should all do the labour that the poor must do, and thus identify ourselves with them and through them with all mankind. I cannot imagine better worship of God than that, in His name, I should labour for the poor even as they do. (YI, 20-10-1921, p. 329)

God demands nothing less than self-surrender as the price for the only real freedom that is worth having. And when a man thus loses himself, he immediately finds himself in the service of God's creation. (YI, 20-12-1928, p. 420)

All our activity should be centred in Truth. Truth should be the very breath of our life. When once this stage in the pilgrim's progress is reached, all other rules of correct living will come without effort, and obedience to them will be instinctive. But without Truth it is impossible to observe any principles or rules in life. (FYM, p. 2)

Faith in Providence

A seeker after Truth, a follower of the Law of Love, cannot hold anything against tomorrow. God never provides for the morrow; He never creates more than what is strictly needed from day to day.

If, therefore, we repose faith in His Providence, we should rest assured that He will give us every day our daily bread, supplying enough that we require. (YI, 4-9-1930, p. 1)

Service of Man

Man's ultimate aim is the realization of God, and all his activities, social, political, religious, have to be guided by the ultimate aim of the vision of God. The immediate service of all human beings becomes a necessary part of the endeavour simply because the only way to find God is to see Him in His creation and be one with it. This can only be done by service of all. I am a part and parcel of the whole and I cannot find Him apart from the rest of humanity. My countrymen are my nearest neighbours.

They have become so helpless, so resourceless, so inert that I must concentrate myself on serving them. If I could persuade myself that I could find Him in a Himalayan cave, I would proceed there immediately. But I know that I cannot find Him apart from humanity. (H, 29-8-1936, p. 226)

My God is myriad-formed and, while sometimes I see Him in the spinning-wheel, at other times I see Him in communal unity; then again in the removal of untouchability and that is how I establish communion with Him according as the spirit moves me. (H, 8-5-1937, p. 99)

Charkha a Means

He who spins before the poor, inviting them to do likewise, serves God as no one else does. 'He who gives me even a trifle as a fruit or a flower or even a leaf in the spirit of bhakti is my servant', says the Lord in the Bhagvad Gita.

And He hath His footstool where live the humble, the lowliest and the lost. Spinning, therefore, for such is the greatest prayer, the greatest worship, the greatest sacrifice. (YI, 24-9-1925, pp. 331-2)

The world is weary of the after-effects of the War. Even as the Charkha is India's comforter today, it may be the world's tomorrow, because it stands, not for the greatest good of the greatest number, but for the greatest good of all. (YI, 10-2-1927, pp. 43-44)

I stand by what is implied in the phrase, 'Unto This Last'. That book marked the turning in my life. We must do even unto this last as we would have the world do by us. All must have equal opportunity. Given the opportunity, every human being has the same possibility for spiritual growth. That is what the spinning wheelsymbolizes. (H, 17-11-1946, p. 404)

Self-purification

Identification with everything that lives is impossible without self-purification; without self-purification the observance of the law of ahimsa must remain an empty dream;

God can never be realized by one who is not pure of heart. Self-purification, therefore, must mean purification in all the walks of life. And purification being highly infectious, purification of oneself necessarily leads to the purification of one's surroundings.

But the path of purification is hard and steep. To attain to perfect purity one has to become absolutely passion-free in thought, speech and action; to rise above the opposing currents of love and hatred, attachment and repulsion. I know that I have not in me as yet that triple purity, in spite of constant ceaseless striving for it. That is why the world's praise fails to move me, indeed, it very often stings me.

To conquer the subtle passions seems to me to be harder far than the physical conquest of the world by the force of arms.

...I have had experiences of the dormant passions lying hidden within me. The knowledge of them has made me feel humiliated, though not defeated. The experiences and experiments have sustained me and given me great joy. But I know that I have still before me a difficult path to traverse. I must reduce myself to zero. So long as a man does not of his own free will put himself last among his fellow-creatures, there is no salvation for him. Ahimsa is the farthest limit of humility. (A, p. 371)

Ends and Means

Means and ends are convertible terms in my philosophy of life. (YI, 26-12-1946, p. 424)

The means may be likened to a seed, the end to a tree; and there is just the same inviolable connection between the means and the end as there is between the seed and the tree. (HS, p. 71)

No Separation

They say, 'means are after all means'. I would say, 'means are after all everything'. As the means so the end.... There is no wall of separation between the means and the end. Indeed, the Creator has given us control (and that, too, very limited) over means, none over the end. Realization of the goal is in exact proportion to that of the means. This is a proposition that admits of no exception. (YI, 17-7-1924, p. 236-7)

Providence has its appointed hour for everything. We cannot command results; we can only strive. And so far as I am concerned, it is enough satisfaction for me to know that I have striven my utmost to discharge the duty that rested on me. (H, 6-5-1939, p. 112)

Rights and Duties

The true source of rights is duty. If we all discharge our duties, rights will not be far to seek. If leaving duties unperformed we run after rights, they will escape us like a will-o'-the-wisp. The more we pursue them, the farther will they fly. The same teaching has been embodied by Krishna in the immortal words: 'Action alone is thine. Leave thou the fruit severely alone.' Action is duty; fruit is the right. (YI, 8-1-1925, pp.15-16)

Rights accrue automatically to him who duly performs his duties. In fact, the right to perform one's duties is the only right that is worth living for the dying for. It covers all legitimate rights. All the rest is grab under one guise or another and contains in it seeds of himsa.

The capitalist and the zamindar talk of their rights, the labourer on the other hand of his, the prince of his divine right to rule, the ryot of his to resist it. If all simply insist on rights and no duties, there will be utter confusion and chaos. (H, 27-5-1939, p. 143)

If, instead of insisting on rights, everyone does his duty, there will immediately be the rule of order established among mankind....I venture to suggest that rights that do not flow directly from duty well performed are not worth having.

They will be usurpations, sooner discarded the better. A wretched parent who claims obedience from his children without first doing his duty by them excites nothing but contempt.

It is distortion of religious precepts for a dissolute husband to expect compliance in every respect from his dutiful wife. But the children who flout their parent who is ever ready to do his duty towards them would be considered ungrateful and would harm themselves more than their parent. The same can be said about husband and wife.

If you apply this simple and universal rule to employers and labourers, landlords and tenants, the princes and their subjects or the Hindus and the Muslims, you will find that the happiest relations can be established in all walks of life without creating disturbances in and dislocation of life and business which you see in India as in other parts of the world. What I call the law of Satyagraha is to be deduced from an appreciation of duties and the rights flowing therefore. (H, 6-7-1947, p. 217)

12

Gandhi and Dandi March

The march on foot undertaken by Gandhi and seventy-eight Congress volunteers was the most significant event in the history of the breach of salt law in our country. It was commenced in accordance with a fixed schedule to be carried on by them during the long journey ending at Dandi. Undoubtedly, it was a disciplined band of nonviolent satyagrahis who were to present a new model of Satyagraha which later on converted into a bigger movement at all-India level.

On 12 March 1930 at 6-10 A.M. Gandhi came out of his room, calm and composed, accompanied by Prabhashankar Patani, Mahadev Desai and Pyarelal, his secretary. He offered prayers, looked at his watch and exactly at 6.30 A.M. commenced his march with seventy-eight volunteers.

With his usual gentle smile, betokening his unifying faith in the justice of the cause he was pursuing and in the success of the great campaign he had embarked upon, he headed the procession with quick and unfaltering steps.

'Like the historic march of Ram Chandra to Lanka, the march of Dandi would be memorable' exclaimed Motilal Nehru in a message. P.C. Ray called it the 'exodus of Israelites under Moses?

Jawaharlal Nehru called Gandhi, '.... the pilgrim on his quest of truth, quiet, peaceful, determined and fearless who would continue that quiet pilgrimage regardless of consequences.'

The satyagrahis were to face a fatiguing journey through heat and dust of the Kheda villages. Thousands of men, women and children accompanied the marching column for a few miles and thousands lined the route and showered flowers, coins, currency notes and kum kum at the satyagrahis.

Following the commencement of his epic Dandi March, a tremendous wave of enthusiasm swept over the entire country. The historic day was celebrated all over India. Calcutta woke that morning amidst sounds of conch shells and shouts of 'Gandhiji ki Jai'. At a conference of the Congress leaders of Bengal a decision was taken to appoint immediately an ad hoc council to be called the Bengal Civil Disobedience Council, with the object of carrying out the programme outlined by Gandhiji. J. M. Sen Gupta appealed to all men and women of the province to enrol themselves as volunteers for the Civil Disobedience Movement. He said, 'Bengal is on trial. She had always been in the vanguard of the country's battle for freedom and cannot lag behind. Let us plunge head-long in the fight and regain the rights which are ours.'

In Bombay, a public meeting was held under the presidentship of K. F. Nariman. He exhorted the audience to get ready for the fight. The 'War Council' of the Bombay Provincial Congress Committee announced a Iit of 'iron-sides' to join the first detachment of volunteers from the town.

In Madras, at a public meeting at Tilak Ghat, prayers were offered for the success of Civil Disobedience campaign by the Madras District Congress Committee, Andhra Congress Committee, the Triplicate Congress Sabha and the political section of the Youth League. The meeting reiterated India's resolve to achieve Swaraj by nonviolent means under Gandhi's leadership by following his path.'

In Lahore, a band of Congress volunteers paraded the streets and raised shouts of 'Mahatma Gandhi Ki Jai'. In a mammoth meeting of the citizens of the town, held under the auspices of the City Congress Committee, Maulana Abdul Qadir, in opening the proceedings, said, 'The 12th of March would be a red letter day and it would figure in letters of gold in the future history of India'.

He hoped that the people of India, from that day onward would give practical demonstration of their determination to win freedom. He believed that as soon as the people of the Punjab would receive the news of Gandhi's arrest, they would suspend their business and work out the plan of the movement.

In Peshawar, the 'Satyagraha Day' was observed by taking out a procession and holding a public meeting. Resolutions reiterating the pledge of independence and wishing Godspeed to the soldiers of freedom and congratulating Vallabhbhai Patel on his imprisonment were unanimously passed. Besides, a large number of volunteers were enlisted for the Satyagraha.

Civil Disobedience Day was celebrated in Delhi in a meeting attended by about 10,000 persons, including a large number of ladies. Devdas Gandhi gave the detailed history of the salt tax and called it the most 'barbarous' tax which effected the poor classes, and pleaded for its abolition immediately. He also exhorted the people to observe complete but peaceful hartal if Mahatma Gandhi was arrested.

Allahabad, the nerve centre of U. P. politics, witnessed scenes of enthusiasm in connection with the celebration of the commencement of the Satyagraha campaign. Jawaharlal Nehru hoisted the national flag over the building occupied by the offices of the A.I.C.C., the City Congress Committee and the All-India Spinners' Association, U.P. branch. A large gathering participated in the ceremony. While addressing the audience, Nehru said that the pledge of Satyagraha laid stress on nonviolence which was the very basis of the Civil Disobedience campaign. He warned that only those who were convinced of the efficacy of that method either as a creed or as a policy in the present circumstances of the country, should take the pledge. He opined that nonviolence was not a convenient shelter either for cowards or for those who wanted to prepare for violence. He asked the non-believers in nonviolence to withdraw from the movement to give others a chance.

In Ahmedabad, a meeting of the Youth League was held in which a resolution was passed empowering the secretaries to enlist volunteers for Civil Disobedience Movement. About twenty-five names were enlisted on the spot including two secretaries and Miss Mridula Ambalal, daughter of a local mill-magnate.

The 'Dandi March Day' was observed in Nagpur by hoisting the national flag. A procession passed through the main bazaars of the town, and, thereafter, a public meeting was also held. Gandhi's letter to the Viceroy was read out and explained to the audience. An appeal for the enlistment of volunteers was also made. While exhorting the people to give the moment their whole-hearted support M. V. Abhyankar said, 'I shall perish in the struggle for Independence or live to enjoy freedom after its achievement?

Similar celebrations were held all over the country and considerable enthusiasm was aroused with people for participating in the Civil disobedience Movement. For the first time, a new spirit for Swaraj-full and complete-was found bubbling everywhere. The Viceroy informed the Secretary of State on 13 March 1930, 'Most of my thought at the moment is concentrated upon Gandhi. I wish I felt sure what the right way to deal with him is.'

The same day Gandhi and his satyagrahis reached a small village, Aslali, where they were received well by the villagers. Gandhi emphasised the importance of salt and criticised the salt tax levied by the government. He stated, 'The poor destitute villagers do not have the strength to get this tax repealed. We want to develop this strength. We should make a resolve that we shall prepare salt, eat it, sell if to the people and, while doing so, court imprisonment, if necessary. If, out of Gujarat's Population of 90 lakhs, we leave out women and children, and the remaining 30 lakhs et ready to violate the salt tax, the Government does not have enough accommodation in jails to house so many people.'

Next day, Gandhi, who was apprehensive of his arrest, informed Jawaharlal Nehru, 'The news given to me of my impending arrest was said to be absolutely authentic. But we have reached the second stage. We take the third tonight'

The second halt of the Dandi marchers was at Bareja, a village with a Population of 2,500. He emphasised the importance of Khadi, its production and use by the villagers.

'Khadi is the foundation of our freedom struggle.... I request you to renounce luxuries and buy Khadi from this heap before you.

'We have come forward to win our freedom from this tyrannical and oppressive Government. If we cannot put our own house in order in an organized manner, how shall we run the country's Government? I ask you, therefore, to learn order and organization.... This struggle against the Government on which we have embarked is not going to reach its conclusion with five, or twenty-five, or even millions of men getting killed. We have to look after other things also simultaneously.'

As Gandhi entered the Kheda district, memories-some sweet, some bitter-filled his mind. It was while working in this district that he became one with the lives of people. He had seen nearly all the villages of the district and had covered many of them on foot. He stated, 'I have come to Navagam in the middle of a battle... The Government found some pretext or other to arrest Vallabhbhai... Pressure was brought to hear on the Magistrate some how to serve a notice on Sardar and he was arrested. What could a poor Magistrate do where the entire atmosphere is vitiated?

When some headmen and matadars of Kheda district submitted their resignations as a protest against the oppressive policy of the government, Gandhi advised them, 'Remember that in the resignations, you have handed in I see God's hand. The Kheda District has made an auspicious beginning.'

At Vasana, where the villagers had gathered to accord reception to the marchers and listen to their leader, Gandhi explained that abolition of the salt-tax or remission of some taxes would not mean Swaraj for them. Winning of Swaraj was not going to be so easy as they might think. It was only a way to it and by following it they would reach the goal of freedom. He had a word of praise for the headmen of Navagam, Vavdi, Agam, Mahelaj and other villages who had tendered their resignations. 'Why should they stick to Headmanship for the mere five rupees a month that the government pays them? If the Collector summons a Headman, let him say, 'Give us back our Sardar. Grant us a remission in land revenue.'

At Nadiad, a town with a population of thirty-one thousand, Gandhi reminded the people, 'Bound by the chains of slavery, we are being crushed at present and we want to shake them off.' He wished all government servants to give up their jobs. A government job gave them the power to tyrannize over others. Finally, be asked them to enlist themselves as volunteers. And as soon as he got behind the bars or as soon as the All-India Congress Committee gave a call, they should come forward to offer themselves for being jailed. 'Then alone shall I believe that Nadiad has made its contribution to our struggle'.

In a letter to Jayaprakash Narayan which Gandhi wrote from Anand on 17 March, he explained, 'No where else have I observed such zeal for sacrifice as has been displayed by the Ashram women. At present the women are to a great extent managing the internal affairs of the Ashram. The chance of acquiring such experience will never be repeated. I would therefore advise you to send Prabhavati there. After my arrest the Ashram women too will court imprisonment. I think Prabhavati should join them. She is worthy in every respect.'

At Anand, an educational centre of Patidars, Gandhi demanded, 'In your hands lies the honour of the Patidars of Charotar. You are like salt in the sea of Patidars. If the salt loses its savour, wherewith shall it be salted ? Salt is more sapid than either sugar or juggery. The latter may even cause jaundice, whereas a pinch of salt adds flavour to the meal. If Anand gives up its savour if courage and such other virtues which have been attributed to the Patidars are not displayed in Anand at this juncture, where else can one see them?.'

The students' services to the national cause were also applauded. They were advised to suspend their studies for as long as this struggle continued. Formerly, Gandhi had asked his students to leave schools and to set up national schools.

But this time he asked them to leave schools and come out on the 'battle-field' and become 'mendicants' for the sake of the country. But he did not ask them to give up their studies for good, but only to give up book-learning so long as the struggle lasted. At Borsad, the reception of Gandhi and his satyagrahis was celebrated with the immediate announcement of the resignations of headmen, matadars and ravanias of twenty villages of the taluka. Over one hundred village officers of twenty-five villages submitted their resignations.

The government sources commented, 'Gandhi's attention is directed on two points *i.e.* resignations of patels and enrolling volunteers. Under his instructions local workers are trying to get more resignations under the threat of social boycott.

They were warmly received by the village folk. They were keen to listen to Gandhi's discourse· He explained to them, 'Our patience has been severely tried. We must free ourselves from the yoke of this Government and we are prepared to undergo any hardships that we may have to suffer in order to secure Swaraj, it is our duty as well as our right to secure Swaraj.

'Today we are defying the salt law. Tomorrow we shall have to consign other laws to the wastepaper basket. Doing so we shall practise such severe noncooperation that finally it will not be possible for the administration to be carried on at all. Let the Government then, to carry on its rule, use guns against us, send us to prison, hang us. But how many can be given such punishment? Try and calculate how much time it will take a lakh of Britishers to hang thirty crores of persons.'

Gandhi once again exhorted the students to leave their institutions and join the struggle for independence. He desired that all students studying in the local high school and who were above the age of fifteen, and all teachers too, should enrol themselves. He pleaded that wherever revolutions had taken place, that is, in Japan, China, Egypt, Ireland and in England, students and teachers had played a prominent role. In Europe, war broke out on 4 August 1914, and when Gandhi reached England on the 6th of the same month, he found that students had left colleges and marched out with arms. Gandhi further explained that his prostrating himself on the ground for the sake of removing the hardships of crores of people was of no avail. He had spared no efforts in drafting appeals.

He became a revolutionary when politeness and persuasion proved infructious. He indeed found peace in describing himself as a revolutionary and appealed that in a revolution of that nature which was calm, peaceful and truthful, people should get themselves enrolled regardless of the religious faith to which they belonged. He was confident that if they enlisted themselves with sincerity and if they could keep up their courage, the salt tax would have been abolished, this administration would have come to an end and all the hardships enumerated in the letter to the Viceroy as well as those which had not been enumerated would have to cease.

On 19 March, the party of satyagrahis reached Ras Taluka where Sardar Patel was arrested and sentenced to prison and in which he had carried on such a vigorous struggle in 1924 that the Government had finally to admit its 'error and mete out justice that should not have required a struggle. It is as if Sardar was sentenced to prison as a reward for having served you'.

During the short stay of Gandhi, some of the headmen and matadars had handed in their resignations. But Gandhi expressed unhappiness on the small number of resignations at Ras. In fact, the headman, talati and revania were the representatives of the government in the villages and it was through these persons that the latter carried on its administration. A village which was afraid of a handful of men and continued to act in a manner contrary to its own wishes, neither enhanced the prestige of the headman, the talati or the revania nor that of the villagers themselves. Sardar Patel had been making great effort to end this indignity.

Gandhi praised the services rendered by Sardar Patel. He also apprised the villagers of his mission. He explained 'Sardar neither made speeches nor came here to foment trouble. Neither the Magistrate nor you had acted any sort of trouble. The task for which Sardar had approached you was not a secret to anyone. A satyagrahi has no secrets....... What secret can a satyagrahi like Sardar have?' He had come there to clear the way for Gandhi and he had not come there to convey the message regarding salt. Gandhi was at a loss to know about the offence committed by Sardar Patel and wondered that a man of his stature should have been awarded a sentence of three months' jail and labelled it a matter of shame to the

Sardar and to the government. Gandhi wished that a person like Sardar Patel should be sentenced to a term of seven years' imprisonment or be exiled. 'It would not befit the Government to sentence me to three months' imprisonment. Exile for life or hanging would be a punishment fit for a person like me. I am guility of sedition. It is my dharma to commit sedition against the Government. I am teaching this dharma to the people. A regime under which tyranny is being perpetrated, under which the rich and the poor are made to pay the same amount of tax on an item like salt under which exorbitant sums are being spent on watchmen, the police and the army under which the highest executive receives a salary which is five thousand times the income of the cultivator, under which an annual revenue of 25 crores of rupees is derived from narcotics and liquor, under which foreign cloth of the value of Rs. 60 cores is imported every year, and under which crores of persons continue to remain unemployed, it is one's dharma to rise against and destroy such a regime, to pray that fire may consume its policies.

Meanwhile, the A.I.C.C. held a meeting on the banks of the Sabarmati on 20 March. Besides the president Jawaharlal Nehru, it was attended by other prominent leaders like Maulana Azad, Sarojini Naidu, P. D. Tandon, Abbas Tyabji, Darbar Gopaldas, J. B. Kripalani, N.C. Kalelkar, Kasturba Gandhi, Ansuyabehn and Mrs. Ambalal.

Many members excused themselves from attendance on the plea that they were busy with preparations for Civil Disobedience Movement, in their own areas.

The leaders met under a sense of 'heavy' responsibility and the result was foregone conclusion.

By its principal resolution, the A.I.C.C. confirmed the Working Committee's resolution authorising Gandhi to launch Civil Disobedience Movement. It laid down the conditions under which the various provinces should start Satyagraha on a mass scale.

The Provincial Congress Committees were given wide discretion about the manner, the form and the place of Civil Disobedience. It was open to them, to prepare their provinces for any form of Satyagraha, best suited to them. But it was clearly laid down that the salt Satyagraha should be undertaken in every province when it was possible. Other forms of Satyagraha might be prepared for, but should be reserved for the second stage of the campaign.

In case Gandhi was arrested, the Provincial Congress Committees should immediately determine to start Civil Disobedience, and if he was not arrested, they should await instructions which he might issue on reaching his destination. He would give the necessary signal and the Provincial Congress Committees would be informed immediately through the A.I.C.C. Office. The Government of India felt much concern over the resolution of Congress. The Home Member suggested, 'it is essential that we should able to give timely warning owing to local Governments'.

He also suggested that the correspondence of the members of the Working Committee; the correspondence of the head office of the Congress and of all provincial Congress offices and provincial Congress Presidents and of any particular individual whose correspondence in local government concerned might regard as likely to yield 'specially important' information, should be censured.

It was barely ten days ago that Gandhi had begun his historic march and the actual campaign was yet to be started. The whole country was already in a state of forewent for a parallel to which one might recollect the 'hottest days' of the Noncooperation Movement of 1920-22. People in the provinces were planning to start the movement, and in some cases preliminary steps had already been initiated. In Bengal, for instance, which had for the moment, lost both its outstanding leaders, a 'War Council' had been formed. In the United Provinces, the Provincial Congress Committee had started a Satyagraha committee consisting of prominent leaders, including the President of the Congress himself. Judging from the signs, the whole country appeared in the throes of an agitation of unprecedented magnitude.

The Civil Disobedience plans of Gandhi and the Congress leaders.

As the march proceeded, so the pressure of publicity and social boycott was built up and resignations began to occur in large numbers. By 22 March, approximate number of resignations were four from Ahmedabad district: twenty-seven from Kaita (of whom sixteen were from Borsad taluka) seventeen from Broach, and two from Surat. But Surat soon became the most affected district by 5 April. One hundred and forty headmen had resigned and ten clays later, the figure had risen to two hundred and twenty seven.

Gandhi warned them, 'It will be regarded as cowardice to hand in one's resignation and then to withdraw it. There is no compulsion to resign. It is advisable to give up the post of Headman, looking upon it as something base, dirty and filthy.'

The speech delivered by Gandhi at Broach on 26 March dealt with the communal question.

He explained that he had never dreamt that he could win Swaraj merely through his effort or assisted only by the Hindus. He sought the assistance of Muslims, Parsis, Christians, Sikhs, Jews and all other Indians. He needed the assistance even of Englishmen. 'But I know too that all this combined assistance is worthless if I have not one other assistance, that is, from God. All is vain without His help. And if he is With this struggle, no other' help is necessary.

In a letter to Jawaharlal Nehru on 31 March Gandhi expressed his optimism about he forthcoming movement. 'Things seem to be shaping very well indeed in Gujarat... I feel you are right in attention to the salt tax for the time being. What more we can or should do. Unless you hear from me to the contrary, please take 6th April as the date for simultaneous beginning.'

At Jambusar, Kamaladevi Chattopadhyaya arrived to see Gandhi to remove the general impression that had gone abroad that as he had not included women in his first batch of volunteers, they might not be taken up at all. Gandhiji told her, 'If impatient mothers will be a little patient they will find ample scope for their zeal and sacrifice in this national struggle for freedom'.

She asked Gandhi what women with children should do. He said that he neither desired nor expected women to neglect their children. They might have to wait and bide their time, and thus be of use in some ways. Those women, however, who could make some satisfactory arrangements to have the children well looked after, should join the struggle.

At Surat where Gandhi and the satyagrahis reached on I April, they received a big welcome. He called the salt tax as beastly, inhuman and a Satanic Law. 'I have not heard of such justice anywhere in the world where it prevails... To bow to an empire which dispenses such justice is not dharma but adharma. A man who prays to God every morning at dawn cannot, must not, pray for the good of such an empire. On the contrary while praying or saying the namaaz he should ask God to encompass the destruction of such a Satanic empire, such an inhuman government. To do so is dharma.'

In a message to the nation in the issue of Young India dated 3 April 1930, Gandhi exhorted the people 'Remember 5th April', and scart mass Civil Disobedience regarding the salt laws. He advised them to observe nonviolence in the fullest sense of the term. This was to be the spontaneous action. The workers were required to merely guide the masses in initial stages. Later, the masses would regulate the movement themselves.

The congress volunteers would render aid wherever needed. They, however, would be expected to be in the forefront. They were advised not to take sides in any communal quarrel. Wherever, there was a violent eruption, volunteers were expected to die in the attempt to quell violence. Those who were to be engaged in Civil Disobedience were occupy themselves and induce others to be engaged in some national service, such as Khadi work, liquor and opium picketing, foreign-cloth shops, village sanitation, assisting the families of civil resistance prisoners in a variety of ways.

Gandhi also expected that if there was a real response about civil resistance regarding the salt tax, people should by proper organisation secure boycott of foreign cloth through Khadi and secure total prohibition. This would mean a saving of 91 crores per year, and supplementary work for the millions of unemployed. 'If we secure these things, we cannot be far from independence. And not one of these things is beyond our capacity.

Thus at each village, where the party stopped, Gandhi spoke briefly, telling the villagers that a great ordeal was at hand. He filled his political appeal with exhortation relevant to village life, such as Khadi, cow-protection, cleanliness and untouchability. His appeal was not for money but for change of attitudes: he called on village officials to resign their posts which buttressed the exploitive regime. As he journeyed, he continued to give press interviews and to write to Navajivan and Young India, spreading his massage of Swaraj and giving instructions for the conduct of the campaign during the days ahead.

Out of twenty-five days, which the journey took, the party of satyagrahis had walked for twenty-two days, excluding three days of Gandhi's silence. On his way, Gandhi passed by forty villages and towns and everywhere he addressed the audience. The whole countryside was awake to the call of the Mahatma.

At least fifty thousand persons heard his stirring message to the nation: his speeches were generally impassioned and always brave and there was a tone of pathos which had gone home to the hearts of the listeners. Despite all the fatigue and other hardships of the journey, he never allowed himself any comfort that was denied to the last man of his 'army'.

The satyagrahis reached Dandi on 5 April. Sarojini Naidu had already arrived there to welcome them. When interviewed by special correspondent of The Bombay Chronicle, Gandhi said, ' Government, perhaps, deserves congratulations for their policy of non-interference which is not exactly in keeping with their proved capacity for provoking popular sentiment.'

Next day he was to break the salt tax law. If the Civil Disobedience Movement become widespread in the country and the government tolerated it, the salt law, Gandhi declared, might be taken as abolished. He indeed had no doubt in his mind that the salt tax stood abolished the very moment that the decision to break that salt laws was reached.

'If they arrest me or my companions tomorrow, I shall not be surprised. I shall certainly not be pained. It would be absurd to be pained if we get something that we have invited on ourselves.'

Gandhi advised the people to make salt freely in every home, as our ancestors used to, and sell it from place to place, and they should continue doing so wherever possible till the government yielded, so much so that the salt in government stocks would become superfluous. 'If the awakening of the people in the country is true and real, the salt law is as good as abolished'.

Gandhi highlighted the importance of Dandi and praised the efforts of the people of the taluka. He explained,' Dandi was chosen not by a man but by God. How otherwise could we have chosen for the battlefield of Satyagraha such an out-of-the-way place-a place where no food grains are to be had, where there is scarcity of water, where thousands can assemble only with difficulty, walking ten miles from the railway station, and where if you are travelling on foot, you have to negotiate creeks full of slush and mud? The truth is that in this struggle we have to put up with suffering. You have made the road from Navsari to Dandi famous throughout the world by arranging for free drinking-water at frequent intervals all along it... Dandi should be a sacred ground for us, where we should utter no untruth, commit so sin. Everyone coming here should come with this devout feeling in his heart.'

'If you have not yet gone out to remove salt, let the whole village get together and go. Hold the salt in your fist and think that you are carrying in your hand salt worth Rs. 6 Crores. Every year the Government has been taking away from us Rs. 6 Crores through its monopoly of salt.'

Gandhi and his volunteers broke the salt laws at 8-30 A.M. on 6 April 1930 by taking a lump of natural salt which was deposited in a small pit. Hundreds of persons witnessed this scene. Sarojini Naidu stood by Gandhiji's side, and, as the symbolic gesture was made, she cried, 'Hail Deliverer'.

Gandhi, while picking up a lump of salt in his hand, said, 'With this, I am shaking the foundation of the British Empire.' Not a single policeman or excise officer was present there. While talking to the representative of the free press, Gandhi said, 'Now that the technical or ceremonial breach of the Salt Law has been committed it is open to any one who would take the risk of prosecution' under the Salt Law to manufacture salt wherever he wishes and wherever it is convenient. My advice is that the workers should everywhere manufacture salt to make use of it and to instruct the villagers to do so.'

'Thus the war against the salt tax should be continued during the national week. Those who are not engaged in this sacred work should devote themselves to a vigorous propaganda for the boycott of foreign cloth and the use of Khadar. They should also endeavour to manufacture as much Khadar as possible.'

After Gandhi had addressed the meeting on 6 April about two tolas of salt which was taken by him in the morning and also cleaned by him, was auctioned for Rs. 525/-to Seth Ranchhod Shodhan, a mill-owner of Ahmedabad.

Gandhi's march on foot, form village to village through Gujarat which was his home and where his influence was greatest, aroused considerable interest and excitement. It has in fact appealed to the imagination of multitudes of people who were emotionally swayed by the dramatic turn of events. Throughout the march, Gandhiji went on preaching his cult of truth and nonviolence to the multitudes that gathered from far and near and he did not hesitate to impose the strictest discipline on the satyagrahis that flocked to his banner. The salt became the symbol of India's will to freedom. The same day the salt laws were broken throughout India at least by five million people at over 5,000 meetings. The entire countryside became acutely conscious of the struggle for Swaraj which was intensifying. The Dandi march received worldwide publicity. Soon the Civil Disobedience Movement spread simultaneously in western, northern, central, eastern and southern regions of India.

13

Gandhi: A Unique Practical Economist

Mahatma Gandhi had multifaceted personality. His aim in the life was to achieve enlightenment by serving his nation and man kind. He was born in India and so he was of the opinion that it was his first duty to serve India. He did it through his thoughts, creative activities, different movements, organizations, and his own lifestyle. His creative activities can be classified in 18 forms which cover mainly political, economical, social, educational, religious as well as medical fields. Out of 18 forms of his activities were related to economic wellbeing of society. He was clear that economic self sufficiency for an individual and for a nation is unavoidable. This led him to think about and study upon various economic problems of the country and device action plans for solving them. This was the root of his economic thinking. His work or discussions or writing therefore, were not educational fancy but were the requirement of time. He knew that the major part of human life is busy in economic activities. In that case economic activities can never be without ETHICS and NONVIOLENCE. Thus he absorbed ethics and nonviolence in economics.

He created a strong background for his economic thought. He studied the history of British India written by R. C. Dutt. He collected information about Indian Economy before British rule and the causes of the decline of Indian Economy during the British rule. He travelled all over India nearly for a year after his return form South Africa in 1915 to understand thoroughly about the Indian condition. He also got understanding regarding the prevailing different economic systems of the world. He studied Wealth of Nations written by the father of western economics Adam Smith to know about conventional economics. He read Das Capital written by Karl Marx to understand socialist thinking. He examined all these ideas in the context of India and Ethics.

With this strong background he had his own unique way of thinking about economics, economy, economic aims, and economic development process. He examined the usefulness and practicability of his economic thoughts by practicing them in the country. After getting favourable results he advocated them.bsp;

He had his original explanation about important concepts and terminologies of economics. He explained that economy did not mean the people of a country having the right to develop with the unlimited use of all the living and nonliving resources available in the country. Economy meant the total living of a country who have got the right to survive with coexistence. That is the cause he was the first man to care for ecology.

He rejected the idea of 'economic man'. He accepted the average man with all his characteristics. He said that an average man lives a satisfied life with his resources. 'Unlimited demand', 'Dissatisfied man ' and 'Limited resources' are wrong concepts. At the same time he explained about the required need. A man should have food worth 3000 calories every day, 15 meters cloth per year, a house of 100 sq. yards and educational and medical facilities. To satisfy such real need the resources are sufficient. God has given enough to satisfy the need not the greed.

Gandhi was aware of the effects of advertisements which misguided and attracted the people for useless and even harmful things in the life. In the context of such advertisements and created demands, the resources are felt limited.

His economic aims were different from conventional economics. His aims were sarvodaya, full employment, use of country's own resources, preservation of ecology, justice in income distribution and opportunities. Every body should be given the right to earn according to his capacity using just means. The rich should serve the society after satisfying his needs. Life is not meant for enjoyment only, but it is meant to help others.

For him the means are as important as the aims. The means must be nonviolent, ethical, and truthful in all economic spheres. He provided the new economic system with those means. He advocated trusteeship, decentralization of economic activities, labour intensive technology, and first priority to rural India. He explained that capitalism and mechanization would lead to unemployment, poverty, and inequality. Communism would not survive as it was inhuman. We have seen the collapse of communism and also observed unemployment, inequality of income and instability of common man even in rich a capitalist society.

He advocated to develop the rural economies with the development of agriculture and village industries. This way full employment for 80% of Indian population can be achieved. Even in the world economy nearly 70 % of the worlds population is rural population. Their development can be made easy by the development of rural economies. There should be small scale and cottage industries in these areas. That will create just distribution of income without special efforts.

The government must give full support regarding finance, technology, and market to village industries. The people of the country must give first priority in purchasing their rural productions. He advocated for Khadi and all other village industries and worked hard till his end. He even left the congress to concentrate fully in this activity since 1934.

He advocated SWADESHI and advised boycott of foreign goods, foreign companies, and foreign capital to maximum possible extent. This was not politically motivated. Not to punish the foreign countries but for the economic betterment of our country.

If we look into history, George Washington advised his countrymen to throw away European goods in the sea for self development. U. K. had passed laws prohibiting all types of Indian clothes during the time of their industrial revolution. Japan had resolved to consume her rough and inferior rice instead of foreign superior rice. These examples prove the importance of Swadeshi attitude even if the home made product is inferior for the sake of economic independence.

He was not an extremist. He was a practical thinker. He accepted the foreign economic relation for unavoidable useful things which could not be produced in the country. He also accepted some basic industry on large scale like mines, cement, electricity etc. He also encouraged big industrialists and big farmers with the expectation that they will develop the attitude of trusteeship. He warned them, that if they fail to accept trusteeship they will have to face bloody revolution. He also explained, with a real experience, about ideal labour union activities.

The agricultural activities should be done with the help of live stock and bio-fertilizers. He explained in detail how to produce organic fertilizer without any extra cost and minimum labour. He described the number of benefits which can be achieved from the use of livestock and cooperative farming. Today biotechnological revolution, popularity of organic fertilizer, and awareness against harmfulness of chemicals used in agriculture prove the worth of Gandhi's thinking.

He was against the prevailing methods of education as they had the importance of information only, were hardly practical, giving less importance to nationality, and ethical living in life. He suggested work oriented, skill oriented and nationality oriented basic education. He said that there should be a sufficiently big group of translators to translate important, useful knowledge of the world in Indian languages. He advised the development of research and science for helping the country and population at large and not to help a few rich. He also declared a prize for every such useful research.

He suggested that for nearly 50 years India would have to adopt his economic ideas to get economic independence and progress with minimum obstacles.

In this way Gandhi had his original vision in economics. He propagated a novel way of thinking in science of economics. He integrated economic aims and activities with morality and nonviolence. He integrated our successful past experiences with the recent development process. He made the use of labour force and live stocks and rural economy for the nation's smooth progress. He was the first thinker from the east who analyzed and rejected mechanization, capitalism and communism. He was the man who took the advantage of science and machine for the benefit of population at large.

He was the first man in the world who provided a practical alternative economic system against the prevailing economic system. The village based economy of China and Israel, the small scale industry base economy of Japan are nearer to Gandhian ideas in some aspects.

The literature survey of Gandhian economic ideas gives similar conclusions. 258 thinkers, who have reviewed his economic ideas, have been taken into consideration. Among them, London group of Professionals and The Club of Rome are considered as individual thinkers. Even the opinion of 53 noble prize winners is also considered in this literature survey. 96% of these thinkers admire his economic thoughts. They consider his ideas practical, useful and relevant in the present world.

A growth model for economic development is shown on the basis of Gandhi economic thoughts. This model is applicable to developing economies and India. His ideas are helpful for backward and developing economies in the world. His ideas are also useful for solving problems in capitalist economies. This proves Gandhi as a unique and practical economist of the world......

Relevance of M.K. Gandhi's Ideal of Self-Sufficient Village Economy in the 21st Century

Economic Development of a country depends on the proper utilization of resources (both human and non-human). India, at the time of her independence, had an economy with a low level of economic and technological development, low per capital income, slow pace of development of economic and social institutions and outdated methods of production techniques. Our objective then was to attain and accelerate the economic development of the country. At the time while India started formulating planning strategies in 1951-52 there was debate on India's development problems. The debate centred around the Gandhian approach and the Nehruvian approach. Nehru adopted modernizing approach of the planning *i.e.* socialist framework of economic policy. He also viewed planning as a way of avoiding the unnecessary rigorous industrial transition. He believed that this way would affect the people living in the rural areas. He also learned lesson from Gandhi and accordingly initiated policy which centred around the rural masses.

Gandhian approach has always said about the voluntary wants, the need for self-sufficient village communities and the issues relating to better balance between man and nature. Gandhi wanted to have an ideal society of his own imagination and his economic ideas are a part and parcel of his philosophical and sociological ideas. He was interested in the growth of human beings and more significantly the growth of the deprived and underprivileged group of people. He was, in fact, the supporter of the maximization of social welfare and he had a belief that the growth of an economy is relied on the development of the totality of human personality. According to him, an increase in personal income is an indication of the growth of national income. But the opposite may not be true *i.e.* the growth of national income may not always benefit every man in society.

GANDHIAN VIEW OF SELF-SUFFICIENT VILLAGE ECONOMY

Gandhi holds the view of the maximization of social welfare and for this he gives prime importance to the welfare of the individuals by reducing inequalities in income and wealth. According to Gandhi every person should be provided with bare minimum necessaries *i.e.* food, shelter, and clothing. Concentration of wealth to a few groups of people certainly will shatter the dream of a society which will be socialist in nature. Gandhi is in favour of the self-sufficient village economy where the villages will be the independent economic units. In agriculture that techniques will be adopted, which will not deplete the soil and pollute the environment. For this farmers should use eco-friendly production technique by using lesser and lesser amount of fertilizers, insecticides and pesticides. He prefers well irrigation instead of large hydroelectric projects since this will lead to exploitation. As regards the ownership of land holding, Gandhi is against the zamindari system and ownership of land should go to the actual tillers of the soil. He also viewed that there should be communal ownership of land for balanced cultivation and the surplus land, if any must be distributed to the rest of the village communities.

India lives in villages. Naturally the development of the country depends on the development of villages. All the goods and services necessary for the village members should be grown within the village. In a word, every village should be a self-contained republic. If every village distributes its surplus produce to the poor villagers then there will not be the problem of poverty and starvation in the rural areas. Only this can help eradicating poverty and thus people can be happy and self-reliant. Agricultural sector alone cannot solve the problem of rural poverty and unemployment. That's why Gandhi gives stress on the growth of the rural industries like Khadi, handlooms, sericulture and handicrafts. He opines that large-scale industries make people lazy and help concentration of wealth in the hands of few. On the contrary, rural industries are based on family labour and required less amount of capital. Raw materials are also collected from local markets and the goods thus produced are sold in the local markets. Therefore there is no problem of production and market. Large scale production creates conflicts between labour and capital. Here capital takes upper hand over labour. Such conflicts may not occur in the case of rural industries. Rural industries are the symbols of unity and equality. In India large-scale industries have been concentrated in a few big cities like Mumbai, Kolkata, Ahmedabad, Jamshedpur etc. Rural areas are without big industries. Concentration of these industries in few cities has led to a number of problems. The major problem is the problem of overpopulation in the industrialized areas. With this there arises pollution in the air and water. In addition, large-scale industries promoted monopolistic trends and unequal distribution of income. Rural industries, on the other hand, help decentralization of economic activities and a large proportion of income generated in these industries gets distributed among the workers and among a very large number of people. Gandhi is not in favour of large-scale industries in the sense that these industries are not related to a vast population living in rural areas. Thus industrialization, according to Gandhi, does not help the growth of the personality; contrarily it helps only the material progress of a few. Our handicrafts were destroyed by the use of machinery by the English rulers. Machinery, being capital-intensive, displace labour and naturally augments employment and underemployment. Machinery creates a Pareto optimum situation in the sense that it improves the economic conditions of a few at the cost of many unfortunate rural people leaving them unemployed and exploited. Therefore it is a situation of two-person zero sum game. But what is disappointing is that it reduces welfare of a large section of rural population.

Relevance of Gandhi's Economic Ideas

For attaining smooth development of the economy, it is imperative to develop all the regions of the country simultaneously. The overall progress of the entire economy depends on the balanced development of all the regions. In India there exists a huge regional disparity. In relative terms some states are advanced economically and some other states are backward. Even within a state some districts are more backward than the rest. In West Bengal, for example, the northern part of the state popularly known as 'North Bengal' comprising six districts are relatively backward than the 'South Bengal' districts in terms of productivity in agriculture, industry, educational development, health facilities, etc. Even within the South Bengal region of West Bengal state there are some districts like Purulia, Bankura etc. which are underdeveloped if we compare them with some districts like Burdwan, and Hughly. In this context Gandhian economics, is relevant which supports the attainment of self-sufficiency level of industrialisation or uniform economic pattern for each region. The Gandhian economics is of the view that every man should increase his personal income and standard of living by exploiting the existing natural and human resources fully eco-friendly.,

In line with Gandhi's dream of expanding village industries, industrial policy resolutions of 1948, 1956 and 1977 have offered a special favour for the development of small scale and village industries. The village and small-scale industries have been playing an important role in Indian economy in terms of employment generation and poverty alleviation. This is due to fact that these industries are labour-intensive and capital saving. The total employment created by these industries, for example were 3970000 in 1973-74. This rose to 12980000 in 1991-92. According to Economic Survey, 2000-2001 the estimated employment of the cottage and small-scale sector again rose to 17850000. The growth rate of this sector during 1991-92 to 19992000 was around 4 per cent. This sector's contribution towards exports during the same period in value term has increased from Rs. 9,100 crore to Rs.36,470 crores. This shows a growth rate of over 300 per cent. In the post-reform period Khadi and village industries play an important part in providing employment opportunities to disadvantaged group of people. These industries have spread in about 250000 villages out of total 581000 villages of India in 1997-98. In order to be more competitive in the world market the Khadi and Village Industries Commission has introduced Khadi denim jeans and Sarvodaya brand. These are eco-friendly and biodegradable natural products and have high demand in the world market. Mechanization in agriculture has increased productivity but at the same time reduced employment opportunity. This very fact has been supported among others by S. Valla of JNU. Naturally stress should be provided on the creation of rural employment opportunity in the non-farm, sector.

The Gandhian view of self-sufficient village economy is also relevant in the context of reducing poverty and unemployment in rural India. In 1972-73, 54.1 per cent people lived below the poverty line in rural India. This slightly decreased to 51.2 per cent in 1977-78. In 1983-84 it again fell down to 45.7 per cent. In 1993-94 this rate again came down to 37.3 per cent. In 1999-2000 it was roughly 30 per cent. The data presented here about poverty in rural India have been gathered from various issues of Economic Survey and Planning Commission. Although the ratio of poverty has been declining, roughly one-third of the rural people still live in abject poverty. In order to improve the conditions of the rural poor it is necessary to expand rural industries further at a rapid rate. At the same time it is essential to review seriously the rural anti-poverty programmes in the light of lapses noticed and in the context of formulating the tenth five year plan (2002-2007)

Conclusions

Gandhi is of the view that full employment of human resources is the basic need of a country. It is true that national income will increase if each and every persons (whether skilled or unskilled) is employed fully. This cannot be possible only with the development of large-scale industries because of their labour-saving nature. Agricultural sector too cannot solve the problem of unemployment or underemployment due to its seasonal nature. Therefore mechanization and large scale production cannot provide the solution to the problem of poverty and unemployment. Self-sufficient village economy is an alternative solution and in this context the role of institutions in the rural sector like the village Panchayat and rural multipurpose cooperative can play a vital role. We cite here an example of multipurpose cooperative society located at Sridharpur village of Burdwan district of West Bengal. The society is formed with the unlimited liability. It perform multipurpose activities like deposit mobilisation, credit supply, sale of inputs like fertiliser, HYV seeds, to the farmers, purchase of agricultural goods, cloth business! and ration shop. In addition to the above activities the society set up grain gola (grain warehouse) in 1951 The bye-laws of the society require members to purchase a share of the grain gola valuing three maund of paddy. The grain gola gives paddy loan up to six maunds per member in the off season. The grain gola helps the marginal and small farmers and landless labourers by providing paddy loans for consumption purposes at a reasonable rate of interest saving them from the hands of private hoarders who had been charging a very high rate of interest. The society has constructed a cold store in 1977 which gives preference to the members. After meeting the needs of the members the farmers of the locality are preferred. The society also gives loans to the people against their utensils pledged at a very low rate of interest.

This saves them from the clutches of the private money lender who had for a long time been charging an interest so higher that people could not repay loans and thus ultimately bound to sell their utensils to them at a much lower price. The society also provides irrigation facilities to the farmer members. For this twenty-one mini deep tube-wells were installed. This covers 80 percent land under irrigation throughout the year. This society has set an example in the sphere of performing society welfare activities. The statutory bye-laws providing for welfare and charitable activities are given successful shape of results, as a result of harmonious relation among members, the board of directors, and the members of the staff. All the welfare activities are so designed, identified and implemented that nobody is a loser and that everybody living in the villages emerges gainer. The society is able to create a benign atmosphere all around and members legitimately feel that it is their society upon which their development depends.

We therefore plead for Sridharpur type society which is free from political interference. This can fulfil Gandhi's dream of self-sufficient village economy.

TOWARDS UNDERSTANDING GANDHIAN ECONOMICS

Dean of Studies, Institute of Gandhian Studies, Wardha

The Most important task before a student of Gandhian economics has been to define in a distinctive way Gandhian object of economics which separates Gandhian economics from the mainstream economic tradition of Adam Smith. It is a fashion to say that Gandhi has not been a professional economist. Whatever Gandhi has written about economics has not been written in the language of economics. So the mainstream economics, known as professional economists, tend to ignore Gandhian contributions. But Gandhian economics, whether it is called by that name or by any other name, is gradually occupying the imagination of thinking people. We should analyse the crisis that is tormenting the mainstream economics, and then we can understand why Gandhian way offers a viable alternative. Economics as a discipline had a history of more than two hundred years. The appearance of Adam smith's book An Inquiry into the Nature and Causes of Wealth of Nations in 1776 is generally taken as the beginning of economics. Adam Smith defined the object of economics in the following words. He said, "The object of the political economy of every nation is to increase the riches and the power of that country". To Smithian economics wealth and power of a collective entity called nation or state is the most important. Nation's power increases with more and more production. That being the primary object of economics it ignored humankind completely. Production increases employment, employment increase income, income increases demand, demand increases and more productions. This is the chain of developmental logic. Basing on this logic there have been unchecked production. Production is not based on need. Demand is artificially created. Neither production nor demand is based on spontaneity. That is why production has seldom rationality. Gradually a pessismism has grown about the future of production-centric economy. There are a number of valid reasons for this. Firstly, growth rate is significantly coming down globally. The affluence of Western Europe and the United States has been decreasing. Secondly, growth means reduction of poverty. Today worldwide employment is falling and unemployment is increasing. So the misery of labourer is on the increase. Thirdly, inequality has been alarmingly increasing. It has been found that the top 1 percent gets 90 percent of total income gain in the USA and Europe. This trend is found prevalent in all the developing economics. Fourthly, wages have been falling. It was found that level of education has increased but the wage level has been falling. As the economic crisis deepens labour becomes flexible and labour market is becoming deregulated. Labour has further become dispensable due to technological innovation. Now technology is used almost blindly. Lastly, more important point is that with indiscriminate production the problem of scarcity of input in the form of raw material is increasing. Industrial Revolution began with abundance of mineral resources. They are being now exhausted. The resource-rich countries are fast becoming resource-poor.

During the latter part of the twentieth century global economy has been experiencing a new phenomenon. It is the phenomenon of unification and competitive globalizations of economy. This is a development which took place in the last two decades of twentieth century. Before that the majority of countries were following controlled economy. Following the model of soviet economy and so called welfare economy almost all countries ere practicing protectionism in different degrees. As a result capital and technology remained confined to a few developed countries. Initially the developed countries prevented them form exporting to less-developed counties of Asia and Africa. Today the developed countries are ready to transfer both capital and technology to the less-developed countries. This is a new phenomenon which has brought a new character to world economy.

Another development is the globalization. Globalization means easy entry of any country to another country to trade and to build industry, to invest and to have access to raw materials. This is a neo-colonial device by the developed countries to maintain their full control over the world market. Production needs expanding market. Rapidly investment opportunity is shrinking. By abolishing tariff barriers one can make the whole world open for investment.

The demand for globalization and liberalization came not from less-developed countries but from developed countries. All kinds of pressure tactics have been adopted by the developed countries to compel the less-developed countries to accept the globalization, liberalization and privatization. The industrial countries try to convince all other countries that globalization is the compulsive necessity for all. Their logic is that low growth economy gets capital and technology from the developed countries to build their economy on high growth rate and the developed countries get markets for their products. They try to conceal the fact that whole control of economy goes to the developed countries.

The ultimate goal of globalization is to sell more production. People today demand more goods, not because their real need have increased but because their psychological prosperity to consume has been increased through mass media. When we examine production analytically, we find that increasing production leads to waste of resources, both natural and mineral.

The waste does not appear as waste because it comes in the form of industrial and consumer goods.

Commodity fetishism of technocratic society has created a superstitious psychology and erroneous notion regarding progress and development. It can be said that few people and few nations has become rich. But the world has definitely become poor. Apparently the world seems to be affluent. Wealth of a nation, as the summation of goods produced in the boundary of that nation, apparently shows the sign of progress. Whereas taking the total stock of global categories of global resources have perceptively decreased. Industrialization has made earth poor in respect or natural resources, fossil fuel, mineral resources, greenery, maritime resources, sanitation health and ecology.

Production has created its own problems. These is no organic relation between production and needs. Production does not grow out of needs. In industrial society production has its own dynamism. The dynamism arises out of scale of production. The large-scale establishment is the logical development of technology. Economics of scale become a myth if considered from human management. Technology has a totalitarian connotation which ushered in the role of technology. Giganticism is besieged with structural problems besides many more social and human problems.

The issue before the global economy today is the production verses employment. The important problem in the respect is the problem of constant conflict between production and employment. The goal before the industrial unit today is the maximization of employment. It is almost axiomatic that more production leads to more employment. But in the operative scale production is growing at a much faster rate leaving wide gap between the two. This has been possible due to increasing reliance on technology. Employment has become the first victim of technology. Unbridled production now marginally generated employment. Technology after a certain stag replaces employment. At the same time conceptually we cannot think production will ever go on increasing. Daniell Bell pointed out: "Any growth which is exponential must reach a point of absurdity". The crucial task is to find out criticality of production point at which technology does not replace employment.

Technology intoxicates the people. Technology and technocratic view of society had a sweeping influence on the life of the people. Hedonistic concept of technology was never questioned. All efforts have been made to ensure freeplay of private enterprise. Competitive market economy has started replacing social well-being. Protectionist measures are rejected in favour of free trade. Subsidies as methods or protection are discouraged. Losing concerns are allowed to die. Profit-making has achieved inviolable sanctity in industrial theology. Government interaction in support of the weaker sections of society is not favoured. Labour is treated in a cruel manner. Gradually collective bargaining is not allowed. Job security is totally denied. To declare lock-out in an industry is the prerogative of management. Management has no responsibility to consult the workers lay off at any time is permitted but the strike is not justified. Disinvestment has become a new religion of industry giving farewell to public sector.

Market economy believes in capturing market by ruthless elimination of rivals and conquering their income. Market economy quickly converts this wealth in furthering inequality. Through mutual funds people are forced to become involuntary investors in business. By accumulating small savings, business houses collect huge funds from investment. This wealth further generated inequality. Capitalism grew through the classical accumulation process. It is acquired through a gambling house called stock exchange. Money market is a corrupt economy made more corrupt by gambling effect of stock exchanges. Stock exchange having wide linkages all over the world through similar stock exchanges makes the money market a closed system. So the small investors are helpless in relation to corporate bodies.

The functionality of the competitive market economy is argued in terms of its cost-efficiency and service-efficiency. The claim is based on doubtful evidence. There are literatures which are purposefully made to prove that market economy is better in terms of efficiency. The methodology used for measuring efficiency has its shortcomings. It failed to take into consideration the imperfection of market. It is silent on market failure. Studies of some companies in different parts of the world are now available. In these studies some selective indicators for the assessment of efficiency are taken. The selective indicators have been labour productivity, total factor productivity, enterprise profits and growth in value-added per employee. The criteria are chosen almost arbitrarily. In these categories welfare criteria are shrewdly avoided. Private companies operate only in the fields where profits are high and risks are low.

When we talk of efficiency, we need to be clear what we mean by efficiency. Efficiency may mean efficiency for earning profits for business houses. In that sense efficiency does not bring any benefit to public. It does not bring efficiency at social level or ecosystem. Efficiency is a highly loaded word. Nuclear source of energy may be a highly efficient source of energy, is it efficient for environment? In the name of efficiency when there is huge lay-off, we cannot take it as efficiency.

All the same time, enormous problems are developing in the agricultural field in India. Indian agriculture is a combination of capitalist agriculture and peasant agriculture. Myron Weiner has defined them in the following way in his book. The Indian Paradox: "Capitalist agriculture is considered as production for market and for profit, without regard to whether wage labour is employed or how much mechanization there is, and peasant agriculture is a form of production which does not go to market for profit." Gradually competitive market economy has entered into Indian agriculture with the system of patent rights. Through the system of patent rights a speculative element has entered into our peasant economy. There is a threat that controlling position in agriculture will go out of peasants' hands. Marx did not exaggerate when he said that capitalist agriculture was not only a move towards robbing the labour but also robbing the soil, because both farm products and non-farm products will gradually come under the control of the speculative elements. There may be difference and distinction between ownership and control of assets. The farmers may own the assets but for all practical purpose they may not fully control the assets.

It is therefore no more axiomatic to hold that industrialization will bring prosperity, efficiency and progress in the society. On the other hand, there are enough indications that industrialization an indiscriminate production rapidly impoverish the world. The present world will gradually find an unusual severity of economic crisis which according to Schumpter, is caused by vanishing investment opportunity. Gradually all big thing started appearing ugly and the small looked beautiful. The shadow of smallness is haunting the world.

Here comes the importance of Gandhian economy. If we look at global economy analytically, it becomes difficult to say that the people are engaged in economic activities only to increase wealth of their nations. Wealth of a nation in economics is estimated in terms of the Gross National Products (GNP). By exploiting more and more natural resources GNP is increased. What is development? Is it more and more production only? Development should have some relation with human values and human qualities. It is said that human quality does not improve as long as poverty and misery remain. Then the question can be raised, in terms of human quality are the developed countries in any way better? Are the rich countries going towards good society or sane society? We are more concerned about decline of profit of business houses. We are less concerned about degradation of human quality. As if profit is development, human quality is not. To Schumacher "Development does not start with goods, it starts with people....." We have been able to create prosperous countries, but we have failed to create better and better human beings. Prosperous countries are in no way good societies. Both poverty and prosperity degrade.

That is why Gandhi advocated neither an affluent nor a poor society. Gandhian paradigm of development is based on this principle. This can be called an economy of Swaraj-an economy of self-reliance. Economic activities cannot be abstracted from human life. Long ago this was systematically argued by Sismondi. He said the real object of economics should be man. To give importance to wealth and to ignore the human being is to distort the goal. He propounded a theory in which he said that distribution must combine with production. Gandhi's design moved in that line. Gandhi also wanted to ensure distributive justice and wanted to see that production and distribution were to be simultaneous. Sismondi realized the danger of over-production. That was why he wanted to employ the state in curbing production. Gandhi was attracted by the concept of a simple society of Tolstoy and Ruskin.

The basic hypothesis of the Gandhian system is "Earth provides enough to satisfy every man's need but not for every man's greed". Global system makes common people completely helpless in the matter of production and distribution. Gandhi visualized that it can be solved through the choice of technic of small scale production and through the system of Swaraj. Swaraj is necessary for the liberation of weaker economics from the commanding position of developed countries. Weaker countries were vainly struggling to achieve the level of growth of developed countries. The growth rate of the developed countries is a historical accident. It is doubtful that any of the developing countries will attain that level. It is equally doubtful whether the developed countries can sustain that impressive growth rate. It is to be realised that colonial foundation of the liberal economy is gradually coming to an end. Economic leadership of the west is being eroded. Comparative performance of the countries are only marginally meaningful.

The dangerous game of competitive affluence should be abandoned. It is becoming compulsive for the survival of the economy. Productivity is still based on overcapacity, which creates the crisis of survival. The concept of Swaraj is not an idealistic design. There is need for new conceptual framework in which each country attains Swaraj. In Gandhian system every country stands on its own strength.

The components of Swaraj are based on two independent variables-psychology and ethics. Since resources are scarce, production cannot be increased indefinitely. Psychology of affluence is an irrational phenomenon. The basic principles of economic activity are based on needs and not on affluence. Affluence breeds inequality, as it is based on economic distortion. Greed grows out of desire to be affluent. Human desire can be expanded to unlimited scale. This is true. But human desire also can be reduced. This is also undeniable. The crucial role is played by psychology. Values which condition the mind can change human behaviour. The goal of Swaraj brings limits to human wants, and it also limits monetary gains. In the present economic system even after a very impressive turn over, no one says he can stop now, that he has enough. Enough is a word not to be found in the dictionary of economics.

To Gandhi economic activities are not excluded from other activities. Economy is a part of the way of life which is related to collective mind and collective values. Economic activities cannot be abstracted from human life. Gandhi wanted to ensure distributive justice and wanted to see that production and distribution were not separated. The danger of unchecked production has produced a number of complex problems rooted in economic, social and environmental life. Economics of Swaraj is related to total life.

If economic Swaraj is taken to be the goal it is necessary to determine the ingredients on which it is based. First Gandhi put adequate importance to traditional sector. Highest priority is given to agriculture and agro-centric industries. The balance between primary, secondary and tertiary sectors should be skillfully made on the basis of available human resources. Direction of development is also very important. Directionless development, in the present form, ends in crisis. Two, villages must get more importance than cities.

It is a dogma to say that by shifting population from traditional sector to industrial sector the problem of unemployment can be solved in the less developed countries. This idea is based on colossal ignorance. For example, India has about 627 thousand villages and only four thousand urban centers. It is absurd to believe that the swelling population of 627 thousand villages will be employed in four thousand cities. It is equally absurd to believe that by transferring population from village to cities everybody will get factory employment.

Gandhi advocated wide use of technology of being self-reliant. To make village self-reliant Gandhi said, "There would be no objection to villages using even the modern machines and tools that they can make and can afford to use." In fact he was in favour of giving technology to everyone. His plan was to take technology to the grass-roots level. In his scheme human beings control technology and technology does not control the human beings. His policy of increasing human skill in the furthest corner of the country was visualized by bringing qualitative changes in socio-economic field. The method was Basic Education. Gandhi wanted to develop the foundation technology in every part of the country through Basic Education.

The enormous complexity of productive apparatus of present industrial society fails to develop inner capacity to sustain moral problems. It wrongly emphasises ethical neutrality of productive method. Social and moral consequences of economic activities are unreasonably and arbitrarilyexcluded from welfare concept. Welfare cannot always be determined in quantifiable terms. It should be conceived in totality, in terms of integrity of individuals.

Gandhi's position should be understood in this perspective. In he past agrarian economy declined under the transformation. Structural transformation is hailed by them for it has liberated economy from the bondage of feudalism. But still there are more than two million villages in the world and the number of cities is only few thousand. Few thousand cities cannot give employment to the people of two million villages.

In this regard it is interesting to quote Marx to find how Gandhi and Marx came close to each other. In German Ideology which Marx wrote jointly with Engels and published in 1845-46, they mentioned that in communism "(It is) possible for me to do one thing today and another tomorrow, to haunt in the morning, fish in the afternoon, rear cattle in the evening, criticize after dinner, just as I have a mind, without ever becoming hunter, fisherman, shepherd or critic." Such a simple society is close to Gandhian village system where division of labour does not exist. Marx's communist society can come if the society becomes simple idyllic in nature. So again in the The

Critique of the Gotha Programme, Marx wrote: The enslaving subjugation of individuals to the division of labour, and thereby the antithesis between intellectual and physical labour have disappeared........ when the all round development of individuals has also increased their productive powers and the springs of cooperative wealth flow more abundantly.......

Marx like Gandhi believed in need-based consumption. He announced his maxim, "from each according to his abilities, to each according to his needs."

Performance of Gandhi's system can be tested by the application of seven criteria. The seven criteria are:

I) eradication of poverty and minimization of affluence.

II) Self-sufficiency of every unit in basic needs

III) Identification of human needs and their fulfilment

IV) agro-centric economy as the basis to create economy of permanence

V) Need-based production as far as possible through small-scale units

VI) check on distortions through basic education and skill formation, and

VII) curtailment of concentration of economic power

The value-judgement of Gandhian system is quite clear. Here the criteria of performance are different from mainstream criteria, In Gandhian criteria, what is produced is to be judged along with how it is produced. Its buoyancy depends upon restructuring the rural economy. Gandhi observed: "You cannot build nonviolence on a factory civilization, but it can be built on self-contained villages... You have, therefore, to be rural minded. You can be nonviolent, and to be rural-minded you have to have faith in the spinning-wheel."

Gandhi is one of the pioneers of interdisciplinary approach to economics. In his thought economics cannot be separated from health, and health cannot be separated from sanitation, and sanitation cannot be isolated from nutritious food, etc. In his thinking all these stand ins close relation with each other.

Those who call themselves pragmatic feel that there is an overtone of idealism is Gandhi. So, it is thought, that his system has a doubtful applicability. His hypothesis is never tested. There is a tendency to reject it without verification. The fact is the present system of economy is dominated by vested interests. Whether Gandhi's ideas will be accepted or rejected largely depends on availability of raw material. To call Gandhian economy an ideal system is to ignore what is real. Reality changes with the necessity of life. Without entering into a philosophical polemics, it can be said, reality is not always real. The system which cannot be sustained is not real. The permission of global competitive economy generates optimism of Gandhian economy.

Source: Essays on Gandhian Thought from Institute of Gandhian Studies, Wardha.

GANDHIAN ECONOMY AND THE WAY TO REALIZE IT

If there is anything that characterizes Gandhiji's life, it is his devotion to Truth and Nonviolence. Any economy that is associated with his name should, therefore, answer to these fundamental principles. At the present time, the world is steeped in violence and false propaganda, and it is Gandhiji alone who stands beckoning the world, to these eternal principles and to the economy based on them which will be permanent and will lead to the peace and happiness of mankind.

The Natural Economy

The natural economy calls for the satisfaction of the demands made by the primary needs of our body and by the requirements to keep it in good working condition. As long as we satisfy our needs in this way without infringing on the rights of others, there is no occasion for violence.

The Artificial Economy

The ordinarily understood economic organization of the West believes in a multiplicity of wants. It creates the supply, and then creates a demand for it, and thus strives to dispose of its production. It therefore means cultivating a great many artificial desires. Such an economic organization produces goods without reference to the demand. A shoe factory, for instance, will work to its full capacity irrespective of the market it is intended for as it is working in competition with other similar units, and when it has produced its full quota of goods, then it seeks to dispose of these goods elsewhere. Italy may be producing, we may say for the sake of illustration, a million pairs of shoes and if these cannot be disposed of within the country itself, then she has got to find markets outside. She sees in Abyssinia, where people go bare-footed, an opportunity to "civilize" them and fit them with up-to-date shoes, and thus create a market for their own goods. To control other people's lives in this manner, it requires political power; and to obtain such power, it is necessary to resort to violence.

In the same manner, Japan when she industrialized herself in the beginning of this century began to push her goods in various countries. But she found as days went on that it was not possible to control her markets satisfactorily without direct political power. That then is the reason for Japan desiring to control China. When we buy foreign goods-especially goods other than luxuries-it will call for violence at one stage or another. Japan also came to India and sold her flimsy articles at cheap prices and captured a big section of her market. Now, after nearly half a century, Japan feels the necessity of having direct control over all her markets.

Foreign Domination

Thus, buying of foreign goods is a definite invitation to or a bait for foreigners to occupy our country. Therefore we, who want to be left alone, should reduce the demand for foreign articles. We cannot, on the one hand, extend an invitation to these countries to come to us by demanding their goods, and on the other hand, try to drive them out with machine guns and atom bombs. Where the carcass is, there will the vultures be also.

The best way to get rid of the vultures is to bury the carcass, and this carcass is our foreign trade in necessities. Such foreign trade as we might have should always be in surpluses. When foreign trade is restricted to the surplus, it need not lead ultimately to violence, because both the parties to the transactions are exchanging goods which they do not need for themselves; and this exchange leads to mutual profit;

and where there is complete satisfaction on both sides there is no occasion for violence.

Untruth in Business

This creation of a demand to take up the existing supply is generally done by intensive propaganda in the form of advertisement advocating the use of such stock. Therefore, such advertisements often infringe the borders of Truth and lead to false advertisements and over-statements and propaganda being based on falsehoods is objectionable.

Development of Personality

Our life does not consist in the multitude of things we possess. Our life is something higher than material possessions, and our life is also to be looked at from the possibilities of development of our personality. The personality of an individual does not require for its development the satisfaction of a multiplicity of wants. In fact, the simpler the life the more conducive it is for exercising the higher faculties. The phrase "to plan for the future of our country" commonly used by people to denote the betterment of the life of the people, is often misleading. They also talk, constantly, of "raising the standard of living". In a country like ours, where people live on the margin of subsistence, any such raising of the standard of living must refer to the satisfaction of the primary needs, and not the acquisition of new habits. The term "high standard of living" is often made use of to connote a life led with a desire to satisfy multiplicity of wants, and it has no reference to the qualitative condition of life. It refers to the quantitative aspect of one's existence. Therefore, the more accurate way of describing this position would be to talk of a "complex life" and a "simple life" rather than a "high" and a "low" standard. Simply because a British Tommy requires a hundred and one things for his apparel, food, drinks, smokes, etc., it does not mean his standard of living is "high" as compared to the life of say a person like Gandhiji. We may say that Gandhiji is a "high" standard of living while referring to the quality of life he leads and a "simple" life referring to his material wants; while that of a British Tommy would be a "low" standard of life qualitatively and a "complex" standard quantitatively. Hence, what we want to give our people is a high standard of life which will be simple. A great many possessions of material wealth will choke human life with the cares and worries attached to them. With such possessions and encumbrances, man is not free to think his higher thoughts and to develop freely, and hence a complex standard is like shackles to a man. It cramps his higher self from free development.

The Purpose

What the Gandhian Economy aims at is to furnish all our people with their full requirement of food, clothing, hygiene, etc. These are our primary needs and it is not beyond our capacity to meet them if we will only concentrate our efforts in this direction. Over and above these, if we aspire for luxuries and indulgences, man's life becomes wasted in the effort to acquire such things. Therefore, if any planning is to be done for our country, it should be with definite reference to an emphasis on our subsistence, such as food grains, vegetables, fruits, growing of cotton, and obtaining building materials for simple dwellings.

Distribution of Wealth

This must be done in a form in which it will distribute wealth, and will work in a satisfactory manner. Our problem is to give employment to 400 millions of people in such a way that everyone would get his own primary needs satisfied. That means, our method of work has to be such which will distribute wealth in the process of producing wealth. Distribution and production if they do not go together or take place simultaneously, often lead to accumulation of wealth on the one side, and poverty and misery on the other.

The Method

In our country there is a dearth of capital; while there is an inexhaustible source of human labour. Material wealth can be produced in two ways: One is by using capital instruments of production with very little labour, and the other is a minimum of capital instruments with the maximum labour. In the conditions that prevail in our country, therefore, the latter method is more suitable. People have not the capital to obtain instruments of production standardized and centralized industries. But we have unlimited labour power waiting to be used. In America and England, the methods of production that they have evolved, have a direct reference to the means of production that were available to them. There the labour force was meager, while capital was in plenty; while the opposite is true of our country at present. Hence to apply the methods that will fit into the set of conditions which obtained in the West to our country now, where another set of conditions prevails, would be a folly.

Real Values

The wealth of our country cannot be measured by the number of millionaires the country possesses. The country's well being is dependent on the happiness of the largest number of people, which means on the capacity of the largest number to satisfy their needs. In our country, therefore, it is not the accumulation of wealth, but the distribution of wealth as evenly as possible, that is to be desired. Even without any production it is possible to increase wealth by merely adjusting the distribution of wealth. For instance, a rupee in the hands of a labourer may represent the means of satisfying his hunger and the wants of his family for a whole day; while the same amount in the hands of a rich man may represent the cost of a chhota-peg, a cigar or just a tip to a taxi-driver. Therefore, when we take a rupee from a poor man and pass it on to a rich man, we are reducing the human value of satisfaction that amount can give; whilst the reverse process where the value of a cigar is made to satisfy the hunger of a family for a whole day increases its human value. The satisfaction of human wants in this case has increased the value of the rupee. In the same manner, even our governmental expenses should be so planned that the taxes that are collected from the poor people should not be used to benefit the rich; but the wealth should flow from the rich to the poor. This, in itself, will enrich the national wealth of the country even though there may be no extra production.

Trade Cycles

When we take to centralized methods of production, we have to sink a great deal of capital in the instruments of production. This capital represents wealth restrained from freely circulating in the country. Just as we put a dam across a river to accumulate water in a reservoir, in the same way the current of wealth has to be restricted so that it may accumulate capital. In so far as capital is a result of restricted distribution, it is an evil in itself. Periodically we have economic depressions and booms. These are caused largely because of such restrictions in distribution. A mill-owner who produces Rs. 10,000 worth of goods would pay in the form of wages and salaries about Rs. 3,000. That is, in other words, he puts into circulation Rs. 3000 while the stock of goods available in the market is increased by Rs. 10,000 worth. Naturally, therefore, there is not sufficient purchasing power to enable the public to take up all the production. When this state of affairs becomes common, it leaves a residue of production from every mill which does not get into the hands of the consumers. When such unsold goods accumulate, we have a period of depression and to liquidate this depression it becomes necessary to have a war.

War as an Economic Factor

These periodical business cycles are relieved from time to time by wars between nations. Wars, therefore, have become a part and parcel of the Western economic organization based on centralized production. A producer should aim at setting in circulation as large a purchasing power as is required to absorb his production, if he desires his goods to be taken up by the consumers. This can only be done when production is mainly based on the cost of materials and the wages. But when a large proportion of the cost of production goes into interest on capital and replacement of heavy instruments of production, immediately it restricts the distribution of wealth. This is one of the main causes of the periodical upheavals in the form of global wars that we are becoming accustomed to.

From what has been said hitherto, it would be clear that, in our country at least, the methods of production ordinarily used in centralized industries and highly specialized instruments of production, will be out of place, and id resorted to, will lead to unrest and dissatisfaction. Hence, if we aim at obtaining peace and prosperity for the masses, we should eschew the use of such methods of production.

False Claims

It is wrong to argue that centralized industries are m ore likely to utilize our resources to the best advantage. Take, for instance, a centralized paper-making mill which uses bamboo pulp as raw material. To feed such a mill, you will have t get a forest of tender bamboos which can be cut down and brought to the mill regularly, to supply raw materials. We have to have this growth of bamboos regulated according to the needs of the mill. On the other hand, if paper is made by cottage process, the bamboo from the forest is not used directly as raw material. First of all, the bamboos may be used for making mats, baskets, roofing materials, etc. These will serve their purpose for some years during which time they will get rotten and when they become useless, this material will be reduced to pulp and made into paper. Which then is the more economic use of raw materials-the bamboo which is fed directly to the mill or by a process by which the bamboo serves to satisfy several other wants before it is reduced to pulp?

As regards to cheapness of production often attributed to large-scale industries, there is not much basis for such an argument. The cheapness is largely due to the legitimate expenses that should be borne by the mill-owners, being borne from other funds. It is on the same basis as the selling of stolen goods. A man who steals a gold watch worth Rs. 100 can sell it for Rs. 15 and yet make a profit of Rs. 15 on it; because he himself has not borne the cost of the watch. But a goldsmith who buys the gold and makes a necklace or some such ornaments out of it will have comparatively very little profit. That does not argue that stealing is a better method of acquiring wealth. Cotton that is grown in the backyard of a cottage by a half-starved old woman and woven into cloth by a village weaver may be worth a rupee per yard, while the mill-cloth from Manchester Mills may sell at 6 annas per yard. The owner of the mill may be leading a life of luxury in England. It naturally seems to be contradictory to commonsense that the cloth produced by our poor people out of their meager resources should be more expensive than the cloth produced by the mill-owner. Therefore, it puts us on our enquiry as to why the mill-cloth is cheap. Cotton that is needed for the mills is long-staple cotton. This long-staple cotton has been produced in India with great research and expenditure of money for this research, and such cost has not been borne by the mill-owner. They have been paid out of the taxes to maintain the so-called Agricultural Colleges. The cotton is transshipped by railways to the ports. These railways and ports have also been built at public cost. The actual freight that is charged does not compensate for the construction and maintenance of these means of transport. The freight rates themselves are fixed by the Government, not on a cost basis, but to make it cheaper to send out raw materials and to bring in manufactured goods from abroad. That being so, here also the cost of the Manchester Mill has been made less at the cost of the public expenditures. Towards all these, the mill-owner pays nothing comparatively. Then, is it a wonder that his cost is low? If he is made to pay the full cost that is incidental to the supply of his raw materials, it would not be possible for him to sell his cloth at all. From this point of view, Khadi can be said to be an honest product as it bears all its own expenditure, while in the case of mill-cloth only a part of its cost is represented in the price. Therefore, when we buy mill-cloth, we pay only a part of the cost, the balance is made up by expenditure out of public funds. Hence its apparent cheapness.

Social Inequalities

The poor people use little or nothing of this fine mill-cloth, while the expenditure for producing this has been partly paid out of the taxes paid by them. Comparatively, the richer man uses more cloth than the poor. Hence, their benefits from the public expenditure are much greater. As we have pointed out earlier, this mode of expenditure which enriches the rich man at the cost of the general public, which is the poorer section, leads to the lessening of national wealth; hence the mill production of cloth harms the economy of the country. It makes the rich richer and the poor poorer.

Imperialism

Apart from this cost of production, a centralized industry has to draw its raw materials from the four corners of the world. That means a centralized industry should be able to control politically those places from where it gets its raw materials.

That again leads us to the use of violence, to subject a simple people to political domination and make them merely raw material producers, securing to the more violent nations the right and privilege of manufacturing the finished goods. This is the basis of all imperialism. If we feel that this form of political organization does not lead eventually towards a betterment of the masses of the people, then it becomes necessary for us to oppose these methods of production even from the point of view of equity. In India when we buy cheap foreign goods the lower price that we pay is in a measure made up by the loss of our independence. So that when we say a thing is cheap, it means we pay less for it in cash and make up the balance by our political bondage. Is this not too big a price to pay for what may be considered a transient and a passing advantage, if advantage it be?

14

Gandhi's Views on Labour

BREAD LABOUR

Divine Law: God created man to work for his food, and said that those who ate without work were thieves. (YI, 13-10-1921, p. 325) . The great Nature has intended us to earn our bread in the sweat of our brow. Every one, therefore, who idles away a single minute becomes to that extent a burden upon his neighbours, and to do so is to commit a breach of the very first lesson of ahimsa. Ahimsa is nothing if not a well-balance, exquisite consideration for one's neighbour, and an idle man is wanting in that elementary consideration. (YI, 11-4-1929, p. 144-15)

The law, that to live man must work, first came home to me upon reading Tolstoy's writing on bread labour. But, even before that I had begun to pay homage to it after reading Ruskin's Unto This Last. The divine law, that man must earn his bread by labouring with his own hands, was first stressed by a Russian writer named T.M. Bondaref. Tolstoy advertised it and gave it wider publicity. In my view, the same principle has been set forth in the third chapter of the Gita where we are told that he who eats without offering sacrifice eats stolen food. Sacrifice here can only mean bread labour. (FYM, p. 35)

Rule of Reason: Reason too leads to an identical conclusion. How can a man who does not do body labour have the right to eat? 'In the sweat of thy brow salt thou eat thy bread', says the Bible. A millionaire cannot carry on for long, and will soon get tired of his life, if he rolls in bed all day long, and is even helped to his food. He, therefore, induces hunger by exercise and helps himself to the food he eats.

If every one, whether rich or poor, has thus to take exercise in some shape or form, why should it not assume the form of productive, *i.e.*, bread labour? No one asks the cultivator to take breathing exercise or to work his muscles. And more than nine-tenths of humanity lives by tilling the soil. How much happier, healthier and more peaceful would the world become if the remaining tenth followed the example of the overwhelming majority, at least to the extent of labouring enough for their food!

Social Revolution: There is a world-wide conflict between capital and labour, and the poor envy the rich. If all worked for their bread, distinctions of rank would be obliterated; the rich would still be there, but they would deem themselves only trustees of their property, and would use it mainly in the public interest. (ibid, pp. 35-36)

God never creates more than what is strictly needed for the moment, with the result that if any one appropriates more than he really needs, he reduces his neighbour to destitution. The starvation of people in several parts of the world is due to many of us seizing very much more than they need. We may utilize the gifts of nature just as we choose, but in her books the debits are always equal to the credits. There is no balance in either column. (AOA, pp.62-63)

Every man has an equal right to the necessaries of life even as birds and beasts have. And since every right carries with it a corresponding duty and the corresponding remedy for resisting any attack upon it, it is merely a matter of finding out the corresponding duties and remedies to vindicate the elementary fundamental equality. The corresponding duty is to labour with my limbs and the corresponding remedy is to non-co-operate with him who deprives me of the fruit of my labour. (YI, 26-3-1931, p. 49)

True Service: Intelligent bread labour is any day the highest form of social service. For what can be better than that a man should by his personal labour add to the useful wealth of the country? 'Being' is 'doing'. The adjective 'intelligent' has been prefixed to labour in order to show that labour to be social service must have that definite purpose behind it. Otherwise every labourer can be said to render social service. He does in a way, but what is meant here is something much more than that. A person who labours for the general good of all serves society and is worthy of his hire. Therefore, such bread labour is not different from social service. (H, 1-6-1935, p. 125)

Obedience to the law of bread labour will bring about a silent revolution in the structure of society. Men's triumph will consist in substituting the struggle for existence by the struggle for mutual service. The law of the brute will be replaced by the law of man. (H, 29-6-1935, p. 156)

If everybody lives by the sweat of his brow, the earth will become a paradise. The question of the use of special talents hardly needs separate consideration. If everyone labours physically for his bread, it follows that poets, doctors, lawyers, etc., will regard it their duty to use those talents gratis for the service of humanity. Their output will be all the better and richer for their selfless devotion to duty. (H, 2-3-1947, p. 47)

Field of Application: Bread labour is a veritable blessing to one who would observe non-violence, worship Truth and make the observance of brahmacharya a natural act. This labour can truly be related to agriculture alone. But at present at any rate everybody is not in a position to take to it. A person can therefore, spin or weave, or take up carpentry or smithery, instead of tilling the soil, always regarding agriculture, however, to be the ideal.

Every one must be his own scavenger. Evacuation is as necessary as eating; and the best thing would be for every one to dispose of his own waste. If this is impossible, each family should see to its own scavenging. I have felt for years that there must be something radically wrong where scavenging has been made the concern of a separate class in society. We have no historical record of the man who first assigned the lowest status to this essential sanitary service. Whoever he was, he by no means did us a good.

We should, from our very childhood, have the idea impressed upon our minds that we are all scavengers, and the easiest way of doing so is for every one who has realized this to commence bread labour as a scavenger. Scavenging, thus intelligently taken up, will help to a true appreciation of the equality of man. (FYM, pp. 36-37)

Voluntary Recognition: Return to the villages means a definite, voluntary recognition of the duty of bread labour and not it connotes. But says the critic, "Millions of India's children are today living in the villages and yet they are living a life of semi-starvation." This, alas, is but too true. Fortunately, we know that theirs is not voluntary obedience. They would perhaps shirk body labour if they could, and even rush to the nearest city if they could be accommodated in it. Compulsory obedience to a master is a state of slavery, willing obedience to one's father is the glory of sonship. Similarly, compulsory obedience to the law of bread labour breeds poverty, disease and discontent. It is a state of slavery. Willing obedience to it must bring contentment and health. And it is health which is real wealth, not pieces of silver and gold. (H, 29-6-1935, p. 156)

Division of Labour: I believe in the division of labour or work. But I do insist on equality of wages. The lawyer, the doctor or the teacher is entitled to no more than the bhangi. Then only will division of work uplift the nation or the earth. There is no other royal road to true civilization or happiness. (H, 23-3-1947, p. 78)

The economics of bread labour are the living way of life. It means that every man has to labour with his body for his food and clothing. If I can convince the people of the value and necessity of bread labour, there never will be any want of bread and cloth. I shall have no hesitation in saying to the people with confidence that they must starve and go naked if they will neither work on the land nor spin and weave. (H, 7-9-1947, p. 316)

I adhere to what I had said in 1925, *viz.*, that all adults above a certain age, male or female, who would contribute some body-labour to the State would be entitled to the vote. (H, 2-3-1947, p. 46)

Work as Worship: I cannot imagine anything nobler or more national than that for, say, one hour in the day, we should all do the labour that the poor must do, and thus identify ourselves with them and through them with all mankind. I cannot imagine better worship of God than that in His name

I should labour for the poor even as they do. (YI, 20-10-1921, p. 329). No work that is done in His name and dedicated to Him is small. All work when so done assumes equal merit. A scavenger who works in His service shares equal distinction with a king who uses his gifts in His name and as a mere trustee. (YI, 25-11-1926, p. 414)

Service is not possible unless it is rooted in love or ahimsa...True love is boundless like the ocean and, rising and swelling within one, spreads itself out and crossing all boundaries and frontiers, envelops the whole world. This service is again impossible without bread labour, otherwise described in the Gita as Yajna. It is only when a man or woman has done bodily labour for the sake of service that he or she has the right to life. (YI, 20-9-1928, p. 320)

Duty of Sacrifice: "Brahma created His people, with the duty of sacrifice laid upon them, and said: 'By this do you flourish. Let it be the fulfiller of all your desire.' He who eats without performing this sacrifice, eats stolen bread,"-thus says the Gita. "Earn thy bread by the sweat of thy brow," says the Bible. Sacrifices may be of many kinds. One of them may well be bread labour. If all laboured for their bread and no more, then there would be enough food and enough leisure for all. Then there would be no cry of overpopulation, no disease, and no such misery as we see around. Such labour will be the highest form of sacrifice. Men will no doubt do many other things, either through their bodies or through their minds, but all this will be no rich and no poor none high and none low, no touchable and no untouchable

This may be an unattainable ideal. But we need not, therefore, cease to strive for it. Even if, without fulfilling the whole law of sacrifice, that is, the law of our being, we perform physical labour enough for our daily bread, we should go a long way towards the ideal. If we did so, our wants would be minimized, our food would be simple. We should then eat to live, not live to eat. Let anyone who doubts the accuracy of this proposition try to sweat for his bread, he will derive the greatest relish from the productions of his labour, improve his health and discover that many things he took were superfluities. (H, 29-6-1935, p. 156)

Gospel of Work: There can never be too much emphasis placed on work. I am simply repeating the gospel taught by the Gita, where the Lord says: 'If I did not remain ever at work sleeplessly, I should set a wrong example to mankind.'

...If I had the good fortune to be face to face with one like him [the Buddha], I should not hesitate to ask him why he did not teach the gospel of work, in preference to one of contemplation. I should do the same thing if I were to med...these saints (like Tukaram and Dhyandev, etc.). (H, 2-11-1935, p. 298)

God created man to eat his bread in the sweat of his brow, and I dread the prospect of our being able to produce all that we want, including our food-stuffs, out of a conjuror's hat. (H, 16-5-1936, p. 111)

We should be ashamed of resting, or having a square meal, so long as there is one able-bodied man or woman without work or food. (YI, 6-10-1921, p. 314)

I have indeed wept to see the stark poverty and unemployment in our country, but I must confess our own negligence and ignorance are largely responsible for it. We do not know the dignity of labour as such. Thus, a shoemaker will not do anything beyond making his shoes, he will think that all other labour is below his dignity. That wring notion must go.

There is enough employment in India for all who will work with their hands and feet honestly. God has given everyone the capacity to work and earn more than his daily bread, and whoever is ready to use that capacity is sure to find work. No labour is too mean for one who wants to earn an honest penny. The only thing is the readiness to use the hands and feet that God has given us. (H, 19-12-1936, p. 356)

...It is surely the duty of a Government to ensure bread labour for all unemployed men and women, no matter how many they are. (H, 11-1-1948, p. 507)

Intellectual Labour: Let me not be misunderstood. I do not discount the value of intellectual labour, but no amount of it is any compensation for bodily labour which every one of us is born to give for the common good of all. It may be, often is, infinitely superior to bodily labour, but it never is or can be a substitute for it, even as intellectual food, though far superior to the grains we eat, never can be a substitute for them. Indeed, without the products of the earth, those of the intellect would be an impossibility. (YI, 15-10-1925, pp. 355-6)

May not men earn their bread by intellectual labour? No. The needs of the body must be supplied by the body. "Render unto Caesar that which is Caesar's" perhaps applies here well. Mere mental, that is, intellectual labour is for the soul and is its own satisfaction. It should never demand payment. In the ideal state, doctors, lawyers and the like will work solely for the benefit of society, not for self. (H, 29-6-1935, p. 156)

Intellectual work is important and has an undoubted place in the scheme of life. But what I insist is the necessity of physical labour. No man, I claim, ought to be free from that obligation. It will serve to improve even the quality of his intellectual output. (H, 23-2-1947, p. 36)

A labourer cannot sit at the table and write, but a man who has worked at the table all his life can certainly take to physical labour. (H, 18-1-1948, p. 520)

LABOUR AND CAPITAL

Harmony of Relations: I have always said that my ideal is that capital and labour should supplement and help each other. They should be a great family living in unity and harmony, capital not only looking to the material welfare of the labourers, but their moral welfare also-capitalists being trustees for the welfare of the labouring classes under them. (YI, 20-8-1925, p. 285)

I do not fight shy of capital. I fight capitalism. The West teaches one to avoid concentration of capital, to avoid a racial war in another and deadlier form. Capital and labour need not be antagonistic to each other. (YI, 7-10-1926, p. 348)

Conversion of Capitalist: ....If I would recognize the fundamental equality, as I must, of the capitalist and the labourer, I must not aim at his destruction. I must strive for his conversion. My Non-cooperation with him will open his eyes to the wrong he may be doing....It can be easily demonstrated that destruction of the capitalist must mean in the end destruction of the worker, and as no human being is so bad as to be beyond redemption, no human being is so perfect as to warrant his destroying him whom he wrongly considers to be wholly evil. (YI, 26-3-1931, p. 49)

Exploitation of the poor can be extinguished not by effecting the destruction of a few millionaires, but by removing the ignorance of the poor and teaching them to non-co-operate with their exploiters. That will convert the exploiters also. I have even suggested that ultimately it will lead to both being equal partners. Capital as such is not evil; it is the wrong use that is evil. Capital in some form or other will always be needed. (H, 28-7-1940, p. 219)

Labour's Duties, Rights: It is my universal experience that, as a rule, labour discharges its obligations more effectively and more conscientiously than the master who has corresponding obligations towards the labourers. It, therefore, becomes necessary for labour to find out how far labour can impose its will on the masters.

If we find that we are not adequately paid or housed, how are we to receive enough wages, and good accommodation? Who is to determine the standard of comfort required by the labourers? The best way, no doubt, is that you labourers understand your won rights, understand the method of enforcing your rights and enforce them. But for that you required a little previous training... education. (SW, p. 1046)

But there is no right in the world that does not presuppose a duty. An owner never spoils his property. When you know that the mill is as much yours as of the mill-owners, you will never damage your property. You will never angrily destroy cloth or machinery with a view to squaring your quarrel with the mill-owners.

Fight, if you must, on the path of righteousness and God will be with you. There is no royal road, I repeat, to gaining your rights, except self-purification and suffering. (YI, 4-8-1927, p. 248)

Labour's Power: In my humble opinion, labour can always vindicate itself if labour is sufficiently united and self-sacrificing. No matter how oppressive the capitalists may be, I am convinced that those who are connected with labour and guide the labour movement have themselves no idea of the resources that labour can command and which capital can never command. If labour would only understand and recognize that capital is perfectly helpless without labour, labour will immediately come to its own.

We have unfortunately come under the hypnotic suggestion and the hypnotic influence of capital, so that we have come to believe that capital is all in all on this earth. But a moment's thought would show that labour has at its disposal capital which the capitalists will never possess. Ruskin taught in his age that labour had unrivalled opportunities.

But he spoke above our head. There is in English a very potent word, and you have it in French also, all the languages of the world have it--it is "No", and the secret that we have hit upon is that when capital wants labour to say "Yes", labour roars out "No", if it means "No". And immediately labour comes to recognize that it has got the choice before it of saying "Yes", when it wants to say "Yes", and "No", when it wants to say" No", labour is free of capital and capital has to woo labour.

And it would not matter in the slightest degree that capital has guns and even poison gas at its disposal. Capital would still be perfectly helpless if labour would assert its dignity by making good its "No". Then, labour does not need to retaliate, but labour stands defiant receiving the bullets and poison gas and still insists upon its" No".

The whole reason why labour so often fails is that, instead of sterilizing capital as I have suggested, labour, (I am speaking as a labourer myself) wants to seize that capital and become capitalist itself in the worst sense of the term. And the capitalist, therefore, who is properly entrenched and organized, finding among the labourers also candidates for the same office, makes use of a portion of these to suppress labour. If we really were not under this hypnotic spell, everyone of us, men and women, would recognize this rick-bottom truth without the slightest difficulty.

Having proved it for myself, through a series of experiments carried on in different departments of life, I am speaking to you with authority (you will pardon me for saying so) that, when I put this scheme before you, it was not as something superhuman but as something within the grasp of every labourer, man or woman. Again, you will see that what labour is called upon to do under this scheme of non-violence is nothing more than...the ordinary soldier who is armed from top to toe is called upon to do.

Whilst he undoubtedly seeks to inflict death and destruction upon his adversary, he always carries his own life in his pocket. I want labour, then, to copy the courage of the soldier without copying the brute in the soldier, namely, the ability to inflict death, and I suggest to you that a labourer who courts death and has the courage to die without even carrying arms, with no weapons of self-defense, shows a courage of a much higher degree than a man who is armed from top to toe. (YI, 14-1-1932, p. 17-18)

Conflict not Inevitable: I do not think there need be any clash between capital and labour. Each is dependent on the other. What is essential today is that the capitalist should not lord it over the labourer. In my opinion, the mill-hands are as much the proprietors of their mills as the shareholders, and when the mill-owners realize that the mill-hands are as much mill-owners as they, there will be no quarrel between them. (YI, 4-8-1927, p. 248)

The masses do not see in landlords and other profiteers their enemy. But the consciousness of the wrong done to them by these classes has to be created in them. I do not teach the masses to regard the capitalists as their enemies, but I teach them that they are their own enemies. (YI, 26-11-1931, p. 369)

There is a conflict of interest between capital and labour, but we have to resolve it by doing our own duty. Just as pure blood is proof against poisonous germs, so will labour, when it is pure, be proof against exploitation.

I never said that there should be cooperation between the exploiter and the exploited so long as exploitation and the will to exploit persists. Only I do not believe that the capitalists and landlords are exploiters by an inherent necessity or that there is a basic or irreconcilable antagonism between their interests and those of the masses.

The idea of class war does not appeal to me. In India a class war is not only not inevitable, it is avoidable if we have understood the message of non-violence. Those who talk about class war as being inevitable have not understood the implications of non-violence or have understood them only skin-deep. (ABP, 3-8-1934)

Constructive Use: Have I not said that, if they [labour] know their power and use it wisely and constructively, they will become the real rulers and the employers will be their trustees and friends in need and deed? This happy state of things will come only when they know that labour is more real capital than the capital in the shape of gold and silver which labour extracts from the bowels of the earth. (H, 28-9-1947, p. 350)

If every right flows from duty well performed, then it is unassailable. Thus, I have a right to my wage only when I have fully performed the duty undertaken by me. If I took the wage without doing my work, it becomes theft. I cannot associate myself with continuous insistence on rights without reference to the performance of duty on which the rights depend and from which they flow. (H, 30-11-1947, p. 448)

STRIKES: LEGITIMATE AND ILLEGITIMATE

Arbitration First: I know that strikes are an inherent right of the working men for the purpose of securing justice, but they must be considered a crime immediately the capitalists accept the principle of arbitration.(YI, 5-5-1920, p. 6)

Strikes and Politics: Strikes are the order of the day. They are a symptom of the existing unrest. All kinds of vague ideas are floating in the air. A vague hope inspires all, and great will be the disappointment if that vague hope does not take definite shape.

The labour world in the India, as elsewhere, is at the mercy of those who set up as advisers and guides. The latter are not always scrupulous, and not always wise even when they are scrupulous. The labourers are dissatisfied with their lot. They have every reason for dissatisfaction they are being taught, and justly, to regard themselves as being chiefly instrumental in enriching their employers. And so it requires little effort to make them lay down their tools. The political situation, too is beginning to affect the labourers of India. And there are not wanting labour leaders who consider that strikes may be engineered for political purpose.

In my opinion, it will be a most serious mistake to make use of labour strikes for such a purpose. I don't deny that such strikes can serve political ends. But they do not fall within the plan of non-violent Non-cooperation. It does not require much effort of the intellect to perceive that it is a most dangerous thing to make political use of labour until labourers understand the political condition of the country and are prepared to work for the common good. This is hardly to be expected of them all of a sudden and until they have bettered their own condition so as to enable them to keep body and soul together in a decent manner.

The greatest political contribution, therefore, that labourers can make is to improve their own condition, to become better informed, to insist on their rights, and even to demand proper use by their employers of the manufactures in which they have had such an important hand. The proper evolution, therefore, would be for the labourers to raise themselves to the status of part proprietors. Strikes, therefore, for the present should only take place for the direct betterment of the labourer's lot, and, when they have acquired the spirit of patriotism, for the regulation of prices of their manufactures.

Conditions for Success: The conditions of a successful strike are simple. And when they are fulfilled, a strike need never fail:

The cause of the strike must be just.

There should be practical unanimity among the strikers.

There should be no violence used against non-strikers.

Strikers should be able to maintain themselves during the strike period without falling back upon union funds and should, therefore, occupy themselves in some useful and productive temporary occupation.

A strike is no remedy when there is enough other labour to replace strikers. In that case, in the event of unjust treatment or inadequate wages or the like, resignation is the remedy.

Successful strikes have taken place even when all the above conditions have not been fulfilled, but that merely proves that the employers were weak and had a guilty conscience. We often make terrible mistakes by copying bad examples. The safest thing is not to copy examples of which we have rarely complete knowledge, but to follow the conditions which we know and recognize to be essential for success. (YI, 16-2-1921, pp. 52-53)

Political Strikes: Obviously, there should be no strike which is not justifiable on merits. No unjust strike should succeed. All public sympathy must be withheld from such strikes.

The public has no means of judging the merits of a strike unless it is backed by impartial persons enjoying public confidence. Interested men cannot judge the merits of their own case. Hence, there must be an arbitration accepted by the parties or a judicial adjudication.

As a rule, the matter does not come before the public when there is accepted arbitration or adjudication. Cases have, however, happened when haughty employers have ignored awards, or misguided employees, conscious of their power to assert themselves, have done likewise and have decided upon forcible extortion.

Strikes for economic betterment should never have a political end as an ulterior motive. Such a mixture never advances the political end and generally brings trouble upon strikers, even when they do not dislocate public life, as in the case of public utility services, such as the postal strike. The Government may suffer some inconvenience, but will not come to a standstill. Rich persons will put up expensive postal services, but the vast mass of the poor people will be deprived, during such a strike, of a convenience of primary importance to which they have become used for generations. Such strikes can only take place when every other legitimate means has been adopted and [has] failed.

Sympathetic strikes must be taboo until it is conclusively proved that the affected men have exhausted all the legitimate means at their disposal.

It follows from the foregoing that political strikes must be treated on their own merits and must never be mixed with or related to economic strikes. Political strikes have a definite place in non-violent action. They are never taken up haphazard. They must be open, never led by goondaism. They are calculated never to lead to violence. (H, 11-8-1946, p. 256)

Non-violent Strikes: A pacific strike must be limited to those who are labouring under the grievance to be redressed. Thus, if the match manufacturers, say, of Timbuctoo, who are quite satisfied with their lot, strike out of sympathy for its mill-hands who are getting starvation wages, the match manufacturer's strike would be a species of violence. They may and should help in a most effective manner by withdrawing their custom from the mill-owners of Timbuctoo without laying themselves open to the charge of violence.

But it is possible to conceive occasions when those who are not directly suffering may be under an obligation to cease work. Thus, if in the instance imagined, the masters in the match-factory combine with the mill-owners of Timbuctoo, it will clearly be the duty of the workers in the match-factory to make common cause with the mill-hands.

But I have suggested the addition purely by way of illustration. In the last resort, every case has to be judge on its own merits. Violence is a subtle force. It is not easy always to detect its presence though you may feel it all the same. (YI, 18-11-1926, 400)

A strike should be spontaneous and not manipulated. If it is organized without any compulsion, there would be no chance for goondaism and looting. Such a strike would be characterized by perfect cooperation amongst the strikers. It should be peaceful and there should be no show of force.

The strikers should take up some work either singly or in cooperation with each other, in order to earn their bread. The nature of such work should have been thought out beforehand. It goes without saying that in a peaceful, effective and firm strike of this character, there will be no room for rowdyism or looting. I have known of such strikes. I have not presented a Utopian picture. (H, 2-6-1946, p. 258)

In no case can I be party, irrespective of non-violence, to a universal strike and capture of power. (H, H, 28-7-1946, p. 237)

Sympathetic Strikes: Any premature precipitation of sympathetic strikes must...result in infinite harm to our cause. In the programme of non-violence, we must rigidly exclude the idea of gaining anything by embarrassing the Government. If our activity is pure and that of the Government is impure, the latter is embarrassed by our purity, if it does not itself become pure. Thus, a movement of purification benefits both parties, whereas a movement of mere destruction leaves the destroyer unpurified, and brings him down to the level of those whom he seeks to destroy.

Even our sympathetic strikes have to be strikes for self-purification, *i.e.*, Non-cooperation. And so, when we declare a strike to redress a wrong, we really cease to take part in the wrong, and thus leave the wrong-doer to his own resources, in other words, enable him to see the folly of continuing the wrong. Such a strike can only succeed when behind it is the fixed determination not to revert to service....

A strike may fail in spite of a just grievance and the ability of strikers to hold out indefinitely, if there are workers to replace them. A wise man, therefore, will not strike for increase of wages or other comforts if he feels that he can be easily replaced. But a philanthropic or patriotic man will strike in spite of supply being greater than the demand, when he feels for and wishes to associate himself with his neighbour's distress. Needless to say, there is no room in a civil strike of the nature described by me for violence in the shape of intimidation, incendiarism or otherwise. (YI, 22-9-1921, p. 298)

...What about the blacklegs, you may ask. Blacklegs unfortunately there will be. But I would urge you not to fight them, but to plead with them, to tell them that theirs is a narrow policy and that yours has the interest of the whole labour at heart. It is likely that they may not listen to you. In that case you will tolerate them, but not fight them. (H, 7-11-1936, p. 311)

The fundamentals reason for this spreading strike fever is

that life here, as elsewhere, is today uprooted from its basis, the basis of religion, and what an English writer has called 'cash nexus' has taken its place. And that is precarious bond. But even when the religious basis is there, there will be strikes, because is scarcely conceivable that religion will have become for all the basis for life. So, there will be attempts at exploitation, on the one hand, and strikes, on the other. But these strikes will then be of a purely non-violent character.

Such strikes never do harm to any one. It was such a strike perhaps that brought General Smuts to his knees. "If you had hurt an Englishman," said Jan Smuts, "I would have shot you, even deported your people. As it is, I have put you in prison and tried to subdue you and your people in every way. But how long can I go on like this when you do not retaliate?" And so he had to come to terms with a mere 'coolie' on behalf of 'coolies', as all Indians were then called in South Africa. (H, 22-9-1946, p. 321)

Bibliography

Arnold, David: *Gandhi, Harlow*, Longman, New York, 2001.

Bhattacharya, Bhabani: *Mahatma Gandhi*, Arnold Heinemann Publishers (India), New Delhi, 1977.

Bose, Anima: *Mahatma Gandhi: A Contemporary Perspective*, B.R. Pub. Corp., Delhi, 1977.

Clement, Catherine: *Gandhi: The Power Of Pacifism*, Harry N. Abrams, New York, 1996.

Dhanagre, D N: *Agrarian Movements and Gandhian Politics*, Agra University, Agra, 1975.

Edwardes, Michael: *The Myth of the Mahatma: Gandhi, the British and the Raj*, Constable, London, 1986.

Gandhi, M. K.: *For Workers Against Untouchability*, Navjivan Publishing House, Ahmedabad, 1954.

Gaur, V. P.: *Mahatma Gandhi: a Study of his Message of Non-Violence*, Sterling Publishers, New Delhi, 1977.

Ghurye, G. S.: *Caste and Class in India*, Popular Books, Bombay, 1950.

Green, Martin: *The Challenge of the Mahatmas*, Basic Books, New York, 1978.

Guha, Samar: *The Mahatma and the Netaji: Two men of Destiny of India*, Sterling Publishers, New Delhi, 1986.

Hunt, James D.: *Gandhi in London*, Promilla & Co., New Delhi, 1978.

Jordens, J. T. F.: *Gandhi's Religion: A Homespun Shawl*, St. Martin's Press; London, 1998.

Kasturi, Bhashyam: *Walking Alone: Gandhi and India's Partition*, Vision Books, New Delhi, 1999.

Kshirsagar, R. K.: *Dalit Movement in India and Its Leaders (1857-1956)*, MD Pub. Pvt. Ltd., New Delhi, 1994.

Lewis, Martin Deming: *Gandhi: Maker of Modern India?*, Heath, Boston, 1965.

Malik, Saroj: *Gandhian Satyagraha and Contemporary World, Rohtak*, Manthan Publications, Delhi, 1985.

Mehta, Ved: *Mahatma Gandhi and his Apostles*, Viking Press, New York, 1977.

Munshi, Kanaiyalal Maneklal: *Gandhi: the Master*, Rajkamal Publications, Delhi, 1948.

Nanda, B. R.: *Gandhi and His Critics*, Oxford UP, Delhi, 1985.

Nehru, Jawaharlal: *Nehru on Gandhi; a Selection, Arranged in the Order of Events*, J. Day Co., New York, 1948.

Pinto, Vivek: *Gandhi's Vision and Values: The Moral Quest for Change in Indian Agriculture*, Sage, New Delhi, 1998.

Prasad, Bimla: *Gandhi, Nehru & J.P.: Studies in Leadership*, Chankya Publications, Delhi, 1985.

Rao, K. L. Seshagiri: *Mahatma Gandhi and Comparative Religion*, Motilal Banarsidass, New Delhi, 1978.

Rothermund, Dietmar: *Mahatma Gandhi, an Essay in Political Biography*, Manohar Publications, New Delhi, 1991.

Sankhdher, M. M.: *Gandhi, Gandhism and the Partition of India*, Deep & Deep Publications, New Delhi, 1982.

Shirer, William L.: *Gandhi, a Memoir*, Simon and Schuster, New York, 1979.

Singh, Shankar Dayal: *Gandhi's First Step: Champaran Movement*, B.R. Pub. Corp., Delhi, 1994.

Swamy, K. R. N.: *Mughals, Maharajas, and the Mahatma*, HarperCollins Publishers India, New Delhi, 1997.

Uppal J. N.: *Gandhi, Ordained in South Africa*, Ministry of Information and Broadcasting, Govt. of India, New Delhi, 1995.

Wolfenstein, E. Victor: *The Revolutionary Personality: Lenin, Trotsky, Gandhi, Princeton*, Princeton University Press, N. J., 1967.

Index

❑❑❑